This book is dedicated to Elaine, Shomir and Marie. It is their support that made the trip possible.

Introduction

I have always enjoyed challenges to myself. This endeavor was possibly the most physically demanding activity that I have ever courted. The idea was to show the children of SPAVA that determination, courage, flexibility and persistence are necessary ingredients in life to succeed in any adventure. Acceptance of pain and undoubting faith are identical twins in the path of the journey of life and learning to handle agony and adversity propels us to our desired and perhaps to our predestined destiny. Anna was my companion through most of the journey and without her companionship I would have failed. This journey made my faith stronger than ever.

> How vainly men themselves amaze
> To win the palm, the oak, or bays;
> And their incessant labours see
> Crowned from some single herb, or tree,
> Whose short and narrow-verged shade
> Does prudently their toils upbraid;
> While all flowers and all trees do close
> To weave the garlands of repose!
> —Andrew Marvell, "Garden"

The story about the walk is true and the conversation is also true. However, within the stories the names of all characters have been changed and parts of the stories have been embellished to make sure that the reader did not make any connection with anyone living or dead. None of the stories are intended to diminish human dignity in any way but on the contrary the feelings of the author have been depicted the way some have interacted with him.

This is Gopalpur, India. It is in this Oberoi Hotel on the coast of the Bay of Bengal I ran into Tim. He and Ashoke Chopra were classmates. I am Phoebe. I loved both of them. One day when Tim and I were lying face down on a cot next to the ocean and an older man from Orissia was giving him a massage I had looked at him, not innocently. Many years have passed since then. But I returned here to sit by the ocean and reminisce of the days gone by. This is one of the books that I had read as I watched the splashing waves from my balcony.

A Glimpse into a Journey of a Lifetime

Most of the challenges in my life have been self-imposed and the walk across America was no different. During one summer, a couple of years back, an inner call urged me to walk to Portland, Oregon, from Louisville, Kentucky. This was going to be an event to bring awareness as well as a fund-raising effort for SPAVA (Society for the Prevention of Aggressiveness and Violence among Adolescents, www.spava.us). I decided to start from Louisville's Cox's Park, the week after Derby that is always held on the first Saturday of May. I hoped to finish the walk to Ft. Vancouver in about in eighty-seven days. I thought that Ft. Vancouver would be a more elegant place for gathering than downtown Portland.

My neurosurgical training had taught me persistence, flexibility and determination under trying circumstances to bring satisfactory outcome in my patients' lives. I have been eagerly waiting for an opportunity to demonstrate to the children of my elementary school class the role of perseverance to accomplish a goal that may be deemed difficult by them. In my seventh decade as I accept life with equanimity I thought that this would be an opportunity to show the children that I can handle adversity with discipline and aplomb. I did not want my age to be a barrier for participating in an extreme sport as long as I enjoyed the journey and I let my God decide the outcome.

I knew that Goethe finished *Faust* at eighty-one, Verdi composed *Othello* at eighty-four and Tennyson wrote "Crossing the Bar" at eighty-three. I said to myself that God had asked Abraham to move to a new land when he was seventy-five and promised him an offspring. Abraham believed, though a bit hesitant at first as exemplified by his escapade with Hagar. My task was minimal in comparison. I am not implying that my walk qualifies to compete with any of the above, although the joy that I felt could be compared with that of theirs. It could be similar to the joy one feels at the sight of a field of daisies swinging and gossiping with an island of goldenrods while a cardinal bird perches on a high sunflower in the field with its ears tilted as though trying to understand the alphabet of the conversation.

Professor Leonard Hayflick had discovered that healthy human cells can divide fifty times, which predicts a life span of 120 years. Most of us don't reach that age because the ends of the chromosomes (telomeres) get shorter as the cells divide and when the critical short size is reached the cells undergo apoptosis or death, as though the fuse becomes too small and the bomb explodes before we can run to safety. I do not know the status of my fuse or my "Hayflick limit." I thought that I better get going. It is only cancer cells that are immortal. I respect the fragility of my life.

I left Louisville in high spirits with a joyful heart and as I crossed the Second Street Bridge I knew that I was already on my journey to the West Coast. I marched along the country roads and the interstates singing songs from Ronnie Millsap and Steve Wonder but most of the times the lyric of the Beatles song, "With our love we can change the world." I walked through rain, scorching heat and strong wind and shared the land with antelopes, foxes, rabbits, eagles, prairie dogs and rattlesnakes in the spirit of "this land is made for you and me." Strangers brought me water and bought me lunches and shared their love with me. I thanked God every day and expressed my gratitude for the opportunity to love and to live. I remembered Ralph Waldo Emerson had said, "We force no doors in friendship, but like the Christ in Revelation, we stand reverently at the door without to knock—the glory of friendship is not the outstretched hand, nor the kindly smile—it is the spiritual inspiration that comes to one when he discovers that someone else believes in him and is willing to trust him. My friends have come unsought. The great God gave them to me."

Anna and I

"Anna, do you think King Lear had syphilis?"

"Why do you ask?"

"Well, I know that he didn't have the kind of syphilis that affects the blood vessels and the covering of the brain because then he would have probably died much earlier. I don't believe he had the kind that makes you walk with a wide-based gait and I don't know if he would have felt pain if I had squeezed his testicles or Achilles tendon."

"So what do you think he had?"

"Well, I am not sure. But I know that many have thought that he suffered from mania, senile dementia or brief episodes of severe psychosis or intermittent explosive behavior. I believe he was afflicted with general paralysis of insane. He was verbose, megalomaniac and he had no sensitivity for others' feelings and he was often abusive. Well, in Act 1, Scene 1 Lear says to Cordelia:

"'The barbarous Scythian
Or he that makes his generations messes
To gorge his appetite, shall to my bosom
Be as well neighbored, pitied and relieved,
As though sometime my daughter—'"

"What else you know?"

"Well, Lear tells Goneril,
"'Into her womb convey sterility,
Dry up in her the organs of increase,
And from her derogate body never to spring
A babe to honor her. If she must teem,
Create her child of spleen that it may live
And be a thwart disnatured torment to her.'

"He could not sleep. He rode out into the storm and from shelter in haste and then said:

11

"'Here is the place my Lord, Good my Lord, enter
The tyranny of the open night's is too rough
For nature to endure.'
"You know, Anna, those days people made fun of the mentally challenged and those afflicted with lack of mental stability often had to go out and beg. But Lear might have been insane yet he told Gloucester the meaning of life.
"'When we are born, we cry that we are come
To this great stage of fools—'"
Anna was walking in front of me. I tried not to trip her although I often felt like that. She was walking too close. It was a hot day with high humidity. We had just gone past Warrenton, Missouri. It was twenty-second of May and we were moving fast on the interstate going towards Kansas City. I could hear her asking me, "Do you know what is Lear Complex?"
A procession of semi-trucks whizzed past in succession. I didn't want to yell at Anna and so as soon as there was a lull in the traffic I said, "That is when a father discards his wife and marries his daughter.
"Lear becomes like a child and lashes out when he doesn't get his way with his youngest daughter, his favorite, Cordelia:
"'Haply, when I shall wed,
The lord whose hand must take my plight shall carry
Half my love with him, half my care and duty,
Sure I shall never marry like my sisters,
To love my father all.'
"Anna, you know that I am hoping that some young persons will read my book. I hope they don't find it offensive."
"No, they won't, because it is important for them to learn about incestuous behavior and report it to someone they can trust and hopefully to child protective services." I acquiesced to her suggestion.
I often stopped to drink water. The cars passed by me possibly at a speed of more than seventy-five miles an hour. Speed limit was sixty-five on some interstates. I was always about two feet inside the white line. I often laid down my walking stick for a few minutes and turned towards the oncoming traffic. Anna remained behind me. I did not want to talk about any derelict or people with injudicious behavior anymore. I know I was being judgmental but I was disturbed. I waved at the cars as they passed me and the passengers waved back. I noticed a service road and therefore decided to take the service road

at the next exit. I thought that it would be easier for the support van to follow. I looked at my watch and it was almost two in the afternoon. I had already walked twenty miles today. I turned around as I heard the honking from my support van. I got picked up for lunch.

Anna left me as soon as I got inside the car. Ms. G, the driver of the van, and I went to a Chinese restaurant to eat. This is the kind of restaurant I visited almost every day because my appetite had become rather large and here I could eat as much as I wanted for a fixed price. I took a long lunch break and started walking again at four in the afternoon. Anna walked to my side and then behind me till I called it a day and went to a motel at seven.

I was not tired but just thirsty. I had recited from Tagore's Sheser Kabita:

Blow gently over my garden wind of the southern sea
At the time my lover cometh and calleth me.

Anna listened to me all afternoon when I just sang or talked about my feet. "Just enjoy life and reach your goal through service," said Anna. I chewed the gum in my mouth faster at times and it sounded like chewing the cud. But there was no one but Anna who could hear that sound. And I knew that Anna wouldn't say anything.

In the motel I said loving words to my feet and cared for them. I have always cared for my feet because I believed that they will hold me up as long as I live and I also need them to stand long hours to operate. I told them how much I respected them and thanked them for accepting the pounding of the interstate in a kindly manner although they were swollen from the impact and the heat. The evenings were never too long because no sooner I ate dinner I was asleep. I knew that I had to be ready again by five in the morning the next day. I often dreamt of the next exit and the distance to the next rest area ahead where I would find some shade during the day. I often imagined that Anna would talk to me in a sweet voice. I knew that her being with me always made the distance shorter. I would walk faster in the mornings trying to catch up with her only to find that I could not keep up with her. She would tease me by putting her arm forward as I would try to touch her. Anna, I would like to lie next to you on the white sand beaches of Bora Bora. I wanted to touch you in the amethyst and turquoise waters in the bay next to those thatched huts. I would like to entice you to be intimate and then I would chase you along the reef bordering the beckoning green volcanic peaks. So I made myself happy thinking that I am at the Pirate's bar drinking the Tropical Itch while I read,

Une terrasse sur le logon
Un accueil chaleureux
Un transfert gratuity.

Anna always played hard to get!

It was the tenth of May when I left Louisville, Kentucky. My friends came to say good-bye and secretly some knew that I would never finish my journey. I learnt this much later from my barber when I went for a haircut after the trip later on during the year. I could not have known of the feelings of everyone of course.

I carried a sign that was attached to the top of my backpack. It said, "Walk for Kids" and that is what I was going to do. I was not walking for the cure of cancer, not for raising awareness for AIDS, not for supporting gender awareness issues, or to advertise for sexual orientation, and not even for preventing hemorrhoids, but just for the children. A friend of mine walked with me the first twenty-five miles. I was on my own after that.

John and I walked along SR 60, Indiana and time passed fast. John is a runner and so it was harder for him to walk but he didn't want to get me all tired out by enticing me to run. Instead he walked behind me and suppressed the urge to go ahead. We ate lunch at a KFC and he watched me put away large amounts of fried okras and fried liver. I washed them down with lots of refillable lemonade. I didn't want to lose any weight. I was afraid that I might get blown away by the speeding semis if I had lost any weight. Mostly I was afraid that if I were to get weaker I could potentially develop some infection or such.

We stopped that day just a little short of New Pekin. I had planned that the support van driver would bring me home every night to sleep for the first four days as I could walk only one hundred miles or so during that time. This was one way we would save some money. I thought that otherwise I would have to spend my limited resources paying for several more motels. I had planned to be driven to the same spot to start the next morning where I would stop the previous evening. Even by using this technique we ended up staying in seventy-two motels by the time I finished my trip. Whenever I could negotiate a cheaper rate we (support van driver and I) planned to stay more than one night at that place to save money. I did not have any sponsors because I did not walk for any cause that was popular at that time.

I passed through the city of New Pekin. I saw a sign that read: "New Pekin has been organizing consecutive 4th of July celebration than any other city in the nation." John and I saw couple of trains go by as we rested late in the afternoon. We drove home to sleep. I knew that John was not going to be with me the next day when I return to the spot where I got picked up that day. May in Louisville can be hot and this year was no exception. It was hot and muggy and I was on the road for about ten hours on the first day.

I remembered that September evening, on the field behind my house, next to the Washougal River when many of us were enjoying reading from one particular essay written by Charles Lamb. Several of us were partaking pieces of a pig while it roasted on the fire to complement what we were eating. I had organized a pig roast to introduce all the neighbors to one another. We watched the pig turn on the rotisserie inside a closed grill that I had rented for this occasion. We could see the pig through the opening on the side of the grill and the sound of the sizzle of the dripping fat made us salivate. We watched the pig get brown as it slowly huddled inside the chicken wire that enveloped it. I thought that this process would be less time-consuming than digging a pit and cooking it outside for twelve hours. It took us only five hours to cook almost a hundred-pound pig by this closed-grill method. None of us became excessively tired by waiting for the pig to cook and we still had plenty of time to drink beer and visit with one another.

It was then that my friend Glen had asked if I could walk from Louisville to Ft. Vancouver next summer to bring awareness for SPAVA. I had already consumed a few beers to make myself feel invincible. "Would you walk with me the last hundred miles?" I asked. He was equally inebriated and consented to join me at The Dalles. That was that.

I came back to Louisville and between my work and teaching schedule I started getting myself ready. I had never felt like Prometheus in life where I would be chained and lie like an impotent man while some eagle would come and eat my liver every day. I have always been a free soul and I have done just about anything I wanted to do. I didn't want to feel much like Icarus either because I knew that the hot weather I would experience on the way to Washington would possibly melt my feet if not my wings.

I read several books on the subject of long-distance walking. I read about the experiences of some others who had walked across America. I looked at different shoes and socks that I thought would be suited for such an extreme sport. I determined that there are no shoes that are designed for the kind of sport I was planning. So I concentrated on getting the proper socks that would comfort my feet. I walked in a local park daily so that I would develop calluses in my feet and toes. I assumed that this way I would hurt less during the long walk. But alas! I didn't realize that calluses wouldn't stay for ever and that my skin could revitalize faster than a rabbit can mate!

Because it rains a lot in Louisville during the spring months my wife bought me a membership at the YMCA. She thought this way I wouldn't miss too many days of walking practice when it rained. I started running on the treadmill to build my endurance. During this process all my calluses disappeared because my feet were not pounding on the concrete anymore. I felt disappointed because I knew that I would need those calluses to protect my feet during the long journey.

However, this process helped me to determine the amount of water I would need to drink and approximately the amount of calories I would need to eat to maintain my weight. I ran till I got cramps in my muscles and that way I knew when I would need to stop to prevent cramping during walking across America. Many persons have walked across America but no one had walked the way I was planning to do. By April I was running a hundred miles a week at six miles per hour at six-and-a-half-degree angle on the treadmill. I knew I had developed the endurance when I didn't get excessively tired even after running twenty miles. I didn't run anymore after the first week of April. I was afraid that if I were to get hurt I would not have had enough time to recuperate before the starting date, the Tuesday after Derby. I had decided that I would walk for WWW.SPAVA.US to demonstrate determination and perseverance to the children.

After I crossed the Second Street Bridge and entered Indiana I realized what lay ahead of me. I had decided to plan realistically every day so that I wouldn't be frustrated and disappointed with myself. I knew that I would probably not make it to New Pekin, Indiana, on the first day although it takes less than an hour to drive there.

It was the psychological preparation that helped me the most during my walk. However, it was organizing and planning the walk in my mind that had taken the most time. I had reached a stage in my mind when I could see the entire path unfold in front of me even when I would have my eyes closed. I felt the warmth of the concrete on my feet while I slept. I could see the innocent faces and the longing looks in the eyes of the Nebraska cows as they waited on the way to the slaughterhouse. I am not trying to make anyone feel bad about eating beef. I am not a vegetarian. I dreamed about seeing the wildflowers of Wyoming. I almost could smell the fragrance and see the antelopes running through the open fields of Idaho and Wyoming. I imagined watching the field mice sitting on their little behind and eating potatoes as I stood on the roadside of Highway 30 going towards Soda Springs. It is only then that I knew that I was ready for this adventure. I had studied the maps and had determined the best route for the season.

However, it was only after I could feel and see myself on the path and not worry about injuries or pain of any nature that I ventured out of my doors and augured my way to Portland not with the pride of walking across the country, "just because I can," but with abundant joy and happiness in my heart that buttered and greased my way as I toasted in the sun for almost eleven hours every day. Some people who are intelligent and wise often have fear and apprehension but I had no room for those feelings in my heart. I had already prepared myself psychologically to face the mental challenge of walking alone. I have drilled many holes in heads of different people and there have been times when the assistants have had to squirt water into the holes "in process" to prevent damage to surrounding tissues from the heat generated by the friction of the drill. In this case it is the encouragement of the children that was the sauce for me that lubricated the path, and made it possible for me to accomplish the task of this strenuous walk.

At the end of the second day I was about eight miles outside Mitchell, Indiana. I had gone past the sign for the Spring Mill Inn. I was reminiscent for a while. I remembered that day in June of 1969. I had spent two days, two wonderful days with a woman I loved. We were both young. It was not like Nabokov's "love of my loin." It was special. I recalled all the wonderful times that followed. It seemed I kept on walking faster with all the wonderful thoughts of buying groceries together, and raising the children. We had to work hard to make a living. I knew and acknowledged again that I could have never become a neurosurgeon unless I had the support I had at home. I was always tired but she always put a smile on my face when I went to work in the wee hours of the morning. Many times I had asked her, "Do you love me?" and she would fix the gramophone so we would hear Zero Mostel's *Fiddler on the*

Roof. We both went nuts. She started smoking and drinking, something she had never done before. She turned on the record player. I heard Genevieve singing, "Just love me." This was not because of someone like Sir Lancelot. Life changed. I punished myself by not realizing that I was incurring the greatest loss. I heard the words falling on me like a brick wall tumbling down on me, the very wall that had given me shade and support for my back when I was tired all those years. She had walked away so that my environment wouldn't be disturbed. I knew then just as I know even now that what I had heard that day is not true even today. I had consoled myself by understanding that I couldn't play "house" with someone who was unwilling to play with me.

I had stopped at Salem for lunch. About an hour before I would reach Salem I saw a red pickup truck on the road that had stopped facing the direction of my approach. As I got closer I saw a man standing next to the truck. "I saw you walking down the road so I turned around to give you what I have in my wallet." I told him to not give me the money but send a check to SPAVA. "No, the Lord told me to give it to you. You go and have lunch at Salem. I have eight dollars." He emptied his wallet. What is your name, I asked. Chapman, he replied. I gave him a hug with tears in my eyes. He turned his truck around and drove away. Several persons honked their horns as they passed me. Some rubber necked to read my sign as I moved along facing the traffic.

At times when a wide load passed me I had to scoot over to the grass lest my shoulder would be lost in the battle with the forceful mirror. I was always extra careful not to step in a hole. I was afraid that an ankle injury would destroy my ability to walk certainly for then if not forever. One time as I had stepped on the ankle-high grass by the side of the highway I had seen a striped reptile that made a rattling noise while it became stiffer than is expected in usual friendly intercourse. I had stepped back and had taken a picture with my phone camera. I believe the animal was happy to have been noticed and not trampled on by a stranger and felt confident enough to walk out of my way without lashing out with anger. This is what SPAVA teaches: It is harder to walk away from an imminent fight and not feel humiliated. I thought that people in Louisville area may not believe that there are rattlesnakes in Indiana but at least they can see the picture and make up their own minds. My friend, Mr. M said, "That was the only one over there." I did not have enough information to argue to the contrary.

A couple of people came out of their houses and waved at me and wished me well. "We saw you on TV yesterday. We figured you would be this far by today." It is about fifty miles from Louisville. I thanked them for noticing me. They offered me water which I accepted readily. I remained joyful and jubilant as I walked on the rolling hills. The sunshine bathed me all day. I was relieved from the heat by the shade of occasional trees that I encountered close to the road. In the evening I bathed my feet in warm Epsom salt and caressed my first three blisters of the trip. There were many crops of blisters subsequently. I treated all of them most kindly. I had brought a small surgical pack with me that had some needles to puncture the blisters and iodine to disinfect them.

It became clearer to me as I continued my journey that the enrichment of my soul didn't come from my ability to tolerate physical strain or from a sense of accomplishment. It was not about covering some distance on my feet and then gloating in self-adulation. It was not about me being able to place my feet up on a table and smoke a Cohiba because I was successful. But what I had at the end was the feeling of love, an envelope of a soothing balm that opened my pores and allowed a free passage of all the blackheads that were stuck to me filled with arrogance and self-aggrandizement. It was the love of the people that liberated me from my own delusion of grandeur.

I had met Ms. HR at a motel at Mound City, Missouri. She was cleaning my room and asked me what all this was about. She said, "I love the children. I hope they understand the value of learning to live together. We all have to live in America. It is here we make examples for everyone that we value life and liberty. It is here that Thomas Jefferson wrote our constitution. I will make a donation." I gave her a brochure and asked her to mail it to the office. A few days later SPAVA office received two dollars from her. I had already gone ahead a little over fifty miles but I called her and thanked her for her generosity. This, I thought, was giving! This reminded me of a story in *Times of India* where they reported that a woman beggar gave everything to the priest that she had saved by collecting in front of a temple in her whole lifetime! I continuously experienced these humbling gestures as I walked across America and that, I believe, helped my growth.

Anna remembers a lot of stuff and so she wanted to remind me from Luke 21: "Then He saw a certain needy widow drop two small coins of very little value there, and He said: I tell you truthfully, this widow although poor, dropped in more than they all did." This is my America!

The fair breeze blew, the white foam flew,
The furrow followed free
We were the first that ever burst
Into the silent sea.
—Coleridge, *Rime of the Ancient Mariner*

I remember talking to Anna about situations in life when I wanted to correct the wrongs that I had done in life. It was about repentance and forgiveness. I knew that a few of those that felt like outcasts in life had to do some daredevil things to escape from the misery of isolation and exclusion. I didn't belong in that group. But on many occasions in life I had been unkind and I asked for forgiveness. I had been mean to people who had loved me and I wished I had acted differently.

Sometimes it bothered me that I didn't live in India. I felt that maybe I was not truly patriotic. Maybe I didn't try hard enough to get a job after I finished my training. I could have been more like my father. He participated actively during the non-cooperation movement against the British by not wearing any clothes made in the British looms for two years. He had reminded me that Mahatma Gandhi had visited our home as did many of the leaders of India of the pre-partition era. He built a medical practice from nothing and helped the poor and the needy by seeing a large number of people for free for more than forty years in his office. I recalled that everyone had to take a number to see him in his office in the evenings, much like in an ice cream shop in this country. Maybe I had compromised and chose an easier life. There have been times in my life when I have felt that I might have grown older but didn't measure up to my dad. My dad was most generous in his ways of thinking and giving.

Whenever I told him as to how the British had exploited India I remember vividly my dad telling me, it is not that the British didn't do anything good for India but on the contrary, British helped develop a lot of schools. British were kind in many areas except when time came for power sharing and decision making by the people of India. It is all about economics. But never forget that the British people are blessed. In that little island of England God sprinkled a lot of intelligence among the people and gave those people opportunity to excel in many areas; however as has happened in the past with most rulers of colonies, greed and muscle power take over.

My father had told me about the caste oppression in India. The upper castes forced Harijans to dress appropriate to their status and that they couldn't be clean shaven or dress nice. In the middle of the nineteenth century the British governor of Madras tried to change this "dress code." He ruled that if Harijan women converted to Christianity they could cover their breasts and shoulders. Until then the rules set by higher castes did not permit them to do so. It led to a lot of conversion even during the mid twentieth century. But that has not helped the condition of these women even now in many areas.

Preparation, Anxiety and Perils

I had learnt about different worms and insects that could possibly bite me as I would be exposed to the elements over such a long period. It was a bit later during my walk it became clearer to me the need for better protection. I had worked in Africa and Central America and Brazil in the past where some of these insects are more prevalent. I read about *Tunga penetrans*, sand flea or chigoe to distinguish it from the red bug chigger so common in most of the States during the summer months. Chigoe is mostly found in Africa and tropical America. I was scared of *Dermatobia hominis*, Bot fly. I had seen a child in Africa once with an abscess in the brain inside which was a larva of a fly that had entered by puncturing the soft spot. Thank God my soft spot is pretty hard now. Certain flies like Chrysomyia lay eggs in the nose or openings near about that emit odor such as in sinusitis. These become maggots. I always drank enough fluids. I changed my shirts to avoid as much odor as possible. There are certain flies that are very clever e.g. *Janthinosoma lutzi*, that seizes a female mosquito and attaches its eggs to the stomach. So that when the mosquito bites, these eggs get inserted through the puncture of the mosquito and then a warble appears and the larva lives in it. After this I had stopped reading any more. But I do know that some crows carry their eggs into the nest of the pigeons and the pigeon not knowing hatches someone else's eggs. I had a clever chicken some time back. In the winter time I placed grain on the ground inside the fence close to my house when the ground was covered with snow. The sheep from the barn across the field would walk over to get the grain and the chicken that shared the barn often hitched a ride on the back of the sheep.

Human longevity has increased over the years and so have our abilities to participate in different sports. This type of extreme sport is usually contemplated by younger persons. Sir William Osler, the great professor of medicine, wrote in *Aequanimitas* about "two fixed ideas." He had said that one's best work is done by the age of forty, and that one should retire at the age of sixty. He subsequently modified his statement and said that "after the sixtieth year it would be best for the world and best for themselves if men rested from their labours." In 1906 Dr. Osler could not have known that these days many students do not finish their surgical residency before they are thirty-five years old and therefore our best work may not get done till we are way past sixty years old.

I had closed my neurosurgical practice when I was fifty-three years old so that I could be an elementary school teacher. During my training at the Ohio State University, Dr. William Hunt always demonstrated persistence and perseverance. He always taught adaptability and flexibility to match the circumstances during many brain operations. He taught us to always be prepared for the unexpected during operations and if nothing unusual happened then we were happy anyway. Somehow a lot had rubbed off on me and adventure has been my passion since childhood. Try to see the blood vessels under the brain before you actually see it, he often said. He wanted us to be prepared as we journeyed into someone else's brain. Those of us who were his students were grateful and we learned to visualize the brain with our eyes closed while planning the prospective operation in our mind.

Ulysses had an admirable spirit of adventure and he didn't care how much time he had for living. I remember reading Tennyson's writing "Drink life to the lees." You can find Ulysses in Dante's *Inferno*, in the eighth circle of hell when Dante has Ulysses explain that his love of adventure has made him neglectful to his family:

> Not fondness for my son, nor any claim
> Of reverence for my father, nor love I owed
> Penelope, to please her, could overcome
> My longing for experience of the world.
> —*The Inferno of Dante: A New Verse Translation* (Pinsky R)

That has not been my case. However, the spirit of adventure has driven me from one end of the earth to other. I remember that summer at Nepal very well. Phoebe and I worked for two months and then we took off for three weeks to walk in the mountains. We had a marvelous time loving and traveling together as we walked on planks and crossed streams. It is not an accepted behavior to have any public display of affection in Nepal and therefore we didn't hold hands while walking all the time but when I did, I always made it look like a protective gesture since we often walked on uneven grounds. I do not believe that I have ever been in so much love. Therefore, at Thorong La Pass, almost 18,000 feet high, we got married in front of God and our guide as the snow and the wind played the music of nature. The mountains and the clouds formed a canopy as we united as a couple. We practically ran down the mountain, at least 4,000 feet, as husband and wife in joyful jubilation. We celebrated our marital bliss by eating boiled eggs and Snickers bar while sitting on a meadow in a protected valley. There was no one to play Tabla or Shehnai but nature announced our wedding with a thunderous avalanche across the valley. We felt the blessing in our veins as we watched the cloud of snow above us dissipating into another cumulus that followed others and floated away. This cloud possibly had a different assignment. I had learnt from my grandfather as a child that even clouds had tasks to perform. Later that evening at Muktinath I had to care for my feet. There was massive bleeding under the toenails during the rapid descent. There was no possibility of trying any of the techniques of Vatsayana's famous *Kama-Sutra* in this condition of painful feet. Moreover, it was cold and I didn't feel clean. However, I was looking for opportunities of amorous nature. I clicked my temples to turn the pages from my memory bank.

Well! How about trying something from *Ars Amatoria*, the book that might have gotten Ovid into trouble? In this book of *Lover's Art* Ovid described for men and women some practical advice as to the methods of winning a lover. Sometime around A.D. 8, I believe Emperor Augustus banished Ovid to Tomis where he died after living in isolation for ten years. The evening passed and I felt content with Kingfisher beer in my blood and my bride on my side. I knew what God had said in Deuteronomy 24:5, "In case a man takes a new wife—he must make his wife whom he has taken rejoice."

Prior to undertaking the journey across America I had formed a committee to find volunteer drivers who would drive the support van. One of my friends is afraid to fly but he wanted to be one of the drivers. It was decided that the person who was afraid to fly would drive the first part because in six days I would be able to walk only about hundred and twenty-five miles and he would drive back with the support van and let the next person drive over and meet me on the road. The committee found nine volunteer drivers and tentative plans were made as to where the different drivers would need to be flown to meet me on the road. Ms. G. had volunteered to drive forty days. Mr. W wished to drive for a week. He is my minister. He hoped that I would not be in Nebraska when it would be his turn. He wanted to visit Idaho. Ms. D wanted to drive for eight days. She is my friend that I have known for almost forty years. Ms. B wanted to drive for a week and she wanted to be in Oregon. Mr. C wanted to be in the last part. I knew that the airplane tickets for so many persons flying in and out of different cities would be expensive. Therefore I didn't want to make any mistakes as to who would fly where and when because changing the tickets after they were purchased would have been even more expensive. Commander S and Master Chief M said that they could drive only on certain days and that too only for five days in the beginning of the trip. So I decided that I would make plans for airplane tickets for everyone after about forty days and by then I thought that I would pretty much know where I would be on the road or at least in what state and close to which large city.

At least the first eleven days I knew my plans for certain. We made plans that Mr. M, my friend of many years, would be driving the first part and the commander and master chief would take the second part. Master Chief had a mobile home and I knew that by using that to sleep during part of the journey we would save on the motel expenses as well. Everyone was happy with that plan vocally but under the breath I could hear mumbling because of the uncertainty. I explained that I did not know as to how fast I could walk and where I would be after eleven days exactly but I had hoped to be on the outskirts of St. Louis. I decided to ask for everyone's support so that I could complete this undertaking with their help. This is one of our SPAVA teachings: collaborate and collect positive vibrations from others to succeed. Phoebe volunteered to be on call in case someone backed out. Ms. S designed the web page. She owns a sign company. She and her husband made all the signs for my backpack as well. Phoebe also volunteered to be the coordinator for my messages and for organizing and purchasing airplane tickets for everyone. Ms. S and Mr. D made the signs for my car.

It must have been on the fifth or the sixth day that I had already walked past Shoals, Loogootee and Washington. The walk to Shoals was beautiful indeed. It was bit of a climb but I walked under the canopy of oaks and maple.

The fence line was punctuated with dogwoods and redbuds. I recognized several trees that were at a distance. The persimmon trees always have been one of my favorite trees. But I knew that the fruits were not ready yet. I know that persimmon cannot be eaten until the first frost. Those who do not know that can try it but don't forget that the cheeks will be sucked in and lips will get puckered.

The sky suddenly changed and with thundering noise it announced the drenching rain that soon followed. I walked through the storm except for short periods of rest to get respite from the wind. The trees were taller than I was so I assumed erroneously that I shouldn't worry about getting hit by lightning. However, I watched closely for lightning and listened for thunder. After each thunder I moved away from the trees a bit in case it got hit by lightning I didn't want to be near it. However, the wet shoes had prepared the ground for me to develop large blisters as the day got closer to the evening. By the time I got picked up by my support van my backpack probably weighed more than sixty pounds being full of water. My driver said, "It was not raining where I was!" Before coming to the motel that night I stopped at Wal-Mart and purchased some rain gear and spray for my shoes to make them waterproof.

This was our first night out. Until then we had been driving to the walk site in the morning after spending the night at home. But now we decided not to waste the early morning hours in the car because that was the best time to walk. We were far enough that it was taking longer to drive to the spot in the morning where I got picked up the night before. My routine was set now. I was on the road walking by seven in the morning and I walked till six in the evening almost every day. Although I walked till a bit later into the evenings on some days as I reached further west I was always careful not to test the patience of my volunteers who had been sitting in the hot cars all day waiting for me to reach somewhere.

I had walked seven days now and at the end of the day I had reached Olney, Illinois, on SR 50. I had gone through Vincennes and crossed the Wabash River. The early morning hours were cool and after midday it was getting close to ninety-two to ninety-five degrees. I had a Sprint cell phone but my support van driver did not have a phone. I talked to my friends and my wife every day to let everyone know about my global position. My wife had driven three hours that night and then introduced herself in the front desk saying, "I am for room number 23." Later on she realized that might not have sounded right. Later on the receptionist had informed her, "It will be two dollars extra." She told me that before she left when I laughed and retorted, "Usually the guy has to pay."

Her sweet smile, strong determination and joyful caressing always excite me. I like to please her and I find myself often taking on a challenge like her.

I continued from Salem to Olney and then on to Carlyle along SR 50. At Salem Mr. D had joined me for the day and walked twenty-five miles and then drove back to Louisville to work the next day. I called the next day to check with his wife to make sure he was well. He was an attorney and I didn't want him to be in a bad mood with his clients owing to having painful feet! A newspaper man from Salem met us and wrote a story about SPAVA in the Salem paper. The day with Mr. D went fast. The weather was perfect, eighty-five degrees with little humidity.

We walked fast and returned to the Wal-Mart parking lot at the end of the day for Mr. D to pick up his car and drive home. He just didn't want me to be alone and wanted to do his part. I didn't know then but a year from the day my friend passed on while being on a treadmill. He and I had grown to be good friends over the years. He had been a deacon of his church. He exemplified Christian brotherhood in all his actions and loved his friends like his own brother. He also had invited me to many UK football games. He was a great UK fan. He knew that I was a Cardinal fan. We always went to the Oaks race (the fillies' race on the day before the Derby) together. He had helped me in many different legal situations. I did not understand then, when we had spent the afternoon together, that though we accept the fragility of life how much of a loss it is to suddenly lose a friend.

The road had split many large fields that were covered with yellow flowers that I had determined erroneously to be mustard plants. One gentleman corrected us during lunch and told us they were weeds, goldenrods. We saw many oil and gas rigs whose body parts went up and down like teeter-totters.

I was not allowed to walk on the interstate in Kentucky, Indiana, Illinois and Nebraska. However, SR 50 took me to the outskirts of St. Louis cutting through Illinois in a diagonal fashion. I had planned a drive around St. Louis and therefore Master Chief and Commander S drove me to Warrenton, Missouri, on their last day. I had originally planned going up SR 61 but then I changed my mind and walked along I-70 towards Kansas City. As long as they were with me we did not have to stay at motels. Master Chief had parked his large fifth wheel in the military bases at the FAM Camp. We stayed at Scott Air Force base the first night of their driving. We had a couple of walkie-talkies that functioned only from yelling distance so we chose not to use them.

Every night we drank whiskey and that made us feel good. Early in the mornings Master Chief cooked me eggs and Spam and then we ate lunch on the road. During the breaks the commander took my backpack from my shoulders and offered me water. He is an ex-Navy SEAL. He is my friend and fellow Rotarian. He had made me a list of all the Rotary clubs that I could visit along the way and were situated close to the path I had planned. His job in the Navy was probably one of the most dangerous. He was a deep sea diver and detonated or activated bombs as was the case under the circumstances. As my friend he also taught in some of the high school classes the SPAVA curriculum. He talked to the children about the value of discipline and how to work under trying circumstances without complaining. During the Vietnam War he handled many dangerous missions and even now he is a consultant for the armed services. I loved the way he helped me with all this kindness and his humility. I felt happy that he is my friend. In the evenings he cooked nice meals that I devoured rapidly owing to my ravenous appetite.

We had stopped for lunch at Breeze, Illinois, at P.J.'S Diner. It is a fun place decorated with a big wooden statue of Elvis and his guitar placed in the middle of the restaurant. It is there that I had met Kristi and Billy, two young women who found my hat attractive. So I told them all about my walk and the reason my hat was clipped to my shirt was to prevent it from flying to Timbuktu when a semi went past me. It was actually a sailor's hat that I had saved from my sailing days.

They were so excited to learn about the walk that they asked the owner to buy our lunch and they even offered to have their picture taken with us standing beside Elvis! It was a proud moment for me because I never had a picture taken with two women and Elvis. It seems to me that whenever a woman admires something about me I feel charmed.

On the last evening with this crew we celebrated at Red Lobster. I think we drank enough whiskey such that if fish could swim in alcohol they would have swum out of our stomach. Master Chief ate a lot of sliders and I know that they melted before they hit the stomach floor. I had taken a full day off and half of another day off by now owing to the blisters. It appeared that by the time I reached the end of my journey I ended up taking two full days and four half days off to rest and recuperate.

Every time I finished walking through one of the states I tore up the map. Somehow that made me feel closer to the finish line and I told myself that I had less to accomplish after that. One day as I was walking in my happy positive mood along the highway I heard a loud horn coming from a truck that was moving at a high speed towards me. It came closer and closer and the driver kept on blowing his horn. I thought he was trying to greet me and so I waved at him with excitement and a big smile on my face. But I had to jump onto the grass on the side of the road as he passed me fast because if I hadn't done that his mirror would have taken me down. As he passed by me I noticed that he flagged only his middle finger towards me as he glided past me with his wide trailer attached behind his cab. The cab would have dragged me down the road and my backpack would have been the only remains left behind if I hadn't exhibited the quick reflex. I shared the story with Master Chief and he in his kindness said, "Well, I think he was possibly an amputee and he didn't have any other finger left on him!" But I thought otherwise. Since then I learnt to recognize the sounding of horns as a warning gesture and not a greeting one.

Every day I needed to cleanse my mind of all negative thoughts. I prayed and always felt excited as though I had a puff of goli (it is a mixture of hash and tobacco that is smoked from a chillum). The drug has a soporific effect and is often smoked for celebration. I recall being in a Rolling Stones concert once. The man sitting next to me was rather friendly and joyful and whenever he smiled it became apparent that his dentist had not been able to keep up with the losses that he had managed to incur on account of poor oral hygiene. Moreover, he exuded halitosis of pure Ganja possibly of Afghan origin. I am boasting. I am really not a hash connoisseur. However it became apparent that when the musician was demonstrating his love of the serpent my neighbor was almost hugging me while being lifted by high-class goli. I moved away so that I did not have to be a part of his amorous imagination as he attained a state of liberation.

The Road Continues

The wind often blew hot air towards my face. But the clouds above me moved ever so gently almost unaffected by the rush that I felt on my face. It was only later on as I walked through Nebraska I noticed whirling winds at a distance that carried the dust balls across the large fields towards the train track. The willful gusts of wind drove the giant corkscrews forward at times flaring up on one side and then blazing away from me to show off the new "top" thrown from the sky.

I was reconciling in my mind with some of my neighbors who by their behavior had demonstrated discontent towards me. I lived at Washougal, a small town outside Vancouver, Washington, for a while because I liked fishing. I lived by the Washougal River. The bank of the river was 414 feet from my back door. I knew the distance exactly. I had bought several extension cords to attach to my electric bush whacker to be able to reach the last blackberry bush on the adjoining river bank. I had cleared a narrow path to the river. The river flooded every January or February depending on the amount of snow on Mount Hood and water came almost within ten feet from our house. The houses were located at a higher level and there were rules laid down by FEMA for the seven houses that were backing up to the river.

No one was supposed to build any permanent structures or flood walls that would impede the flow of high water during the flood. That was the rule FEMA had laid down. I planted different trees to add color in the adjacent field and that was considered to be OK by FEMA. However, I soon began to see that as more houses were being built in the other parts of the neighborhood people living along the field, my neighbors, started building flood walls, shacks for storage, barriers to prevent people to get to the river and little bridges across the dyke next to the houses. The dyke was designed by the Corps of Engineers to allow the water to flow back to the river much like going through a detour in case of emergencies. I talked to the City Hall and someone from there told me that this was a small town and no one enforces rules unless someone complains. I talked to the people in FEMA's office in Tacoma and they wrote letters and visited and measured different distances and threatened but the enforcer did nothing. I knew that the insurance does not cover the total cost of a house in case of a flood. I was afraid of the unpredictability of flooding so my wife sold the house while I was walking to the west.

My neighbors tried to make it difficult for us to sell and pasted nasty notes on our door and promised to sabotage the sale but I told my wife that "my heart was pure and intentions were honorable." Well, I might not have been like King Arthur but the house got sold in less than two weeks. A gentleman offered full price in two hours after the For Sale sign was up. I have learnt recently (two years after we left) that nothing has been done to enforce the rules and the flood water had been much higher this year than the previous years. As a matter of fact, one of the neighbors was able to pick up two steelheads from the grass behind the house owing to the fact that the large fishes could not swim fast as the floodwater had passed through the obstructed slow-flowing dyke.

I am slow to learn about the behavior of some people. Anna wanted to know more about my experiences. But I told her that it would be her turn after this. I lived at Marshfield, Wisconsin, at one time. A beautiful farm town with two hundred doctors that worked in a famous clinic. One summer my wife told me that I needed to paint the siding of my house. I lived on a farm with several animals. I obtained several estimates and then decided to finish the job myself. The house had cedar siding. So I rented a sprayer and bought the stain and in one afternoon I sprayed my house. I had not covered the windows. Although my house was stained in a matter of four hours it took us four days to clean and scrape the windows.

It was one evening after that when my wife and I had gone to a local tavern for an evening out. We did this quite often. There was not much to do in a small town and so folks went to taverns. We had a nice meal and shot a bit of pool and played with some darts. Unfortunately, when we came out to go home I found that all four of my tires were clipped. My wife felt that one of the fellows who had given us an estimate might have felt slighted when we didn't hire him and this was his expression of frustration. When I was younger my father explained Kismet and Maya to me. I believe in both of those concepts. To say that Kismet cannot be changed sounds rather more like a fatalistic approach but it is not much different from predestination. Life is truly a Maya or an illusion in which we live. If we believe in science then we know that we are

not even particles in motion anymore. We are energy in oscillation. So when such mishaps face me it will be a lie to say that I do not get angry. However, it is clear in my mind that I have grown from these experiences. When I called AAA to pick up the car from the parking lot of the tavern the man was so nice that he dropped us off at our home although it was out of his way.

Missouri

I liked the fact that my cell phone would work now. The phone did not work for last five days as I walked through Illinois. Ms. G had a Nextel phone and that worked too. I walked westward in the blistering sun with untiring energy. I had become much stronger by the time I had passed St. Louis. I was not lonely. Anna was my companion all day. I was happy and reflective. My face was dark. My neck was like the color of burnt sugar on top of crème bouclé. My arms were like dark toast and only the skin under my watch reminded me of my true complexion. I was able to walk thirty miles the day Ms. G had joined me. At the end of the day I was not tired but I was ready for a shot of whiskey. Ms. G drank the military special vodka that I got her and we were both "out" before we knew it. By now we had figured out that she could meet me every three hours in the morning when it was a bit cooler but it had to be every two hours in the afternoon for my breaks. We communicated during the walk since the telephones worked. That gave me some peace of mind.

The outfit that I was wearing in the beginning of the walk had to be modified as the days became longer. I no longer could walk with shorts owing to bad burns of my legs and behind my knees. Short-sleeve shirts were not suitable anymore because of the burns on my forearms. I had to switch to plus-45 sunscreens from 30-plus to get better protection and I applied moisture to my skin whenever I could. I wore Capri pants and cut a long-sleeve shirt below the fifth button and wore it above a SPAVA T-shirt. This way I had a pocket and I also got the benefit of protection from the sleeves without getting too hot. This also gave me the opportunity to show people the name of the organization for which I was walking because the name SPAVA written on my T-shirt became visible below the shirt that I had just cut off.

My face was dark. Today I thought I was like Sea Biscuit. As I continued walking on Interstate 70 my dark brown torso was covered with bright orange reflective silk. I had met with AAA officials at Louisville prior to my departure

33

and they had donated these to me so that I would be easily visible and hopefully other motorists would not hit me as I would walk along the shoulder of the expressway. I felt that my backpack was a jockey. I walked as fast as I could. The blinders made from aluminum foil attached to the rim of my sunglasses prevented the wind pregnant with dust from the highway from hurting my eyes. This way I didn't worry about my eyes when the trucks passed me at eighty miles an hour. I was confident that no Man of War was going to worry me now and that the stone bruises and blisters had been hardened by my indomitable spirit and focused determination. I felt strong and invincible. I was in the race to win.

After I had a chat with my support van driver we determined that it would be better if the driver came to meet me from behind because that would cause me to have less stress as I would not have to walk to a designated place to meet the van. There were times when I was exceedingly hot and fatigued and needed to sit down but I couldn't because I hadn't quite reached the van. This way I had the option of waving the van to stop or go past me in case the driver arrived earlier than my fatigue had time to set in. I had developed psychologically more power by this arrangement and I felt more secure by this plan.

I changed socks twice before lunch and once after lunch to keep my feet as dry as possible. We developed signals by which Ms. G would know when to stop or when to go ahead of me as she drove past me fast on the interstate. We were not allowed to slow down the flow of traffic according to the state police. We developed a technique of slowing down the van for a split second on the interstate without interfering with the traffic. I learnt to "read the debris" on the shoulders of the interstate such that she wouldn't hit a nail when she pulled over either to just stop for me or to wait longer in case I wasn't ready to take a break. On many occasions the exits were not where we needed to stop so we made our own areas of stopping. Ms. G already had notified the state police that I would be walking on the interstate for sixteen to seventeen days.

We had gone through many small towns. I believe Watson was the smallest so far. If I am not mistaken the sign on the road leading to the entrance to the city said Population 98!

I was telling Anna how I felt when I had visited the church of the Gesu in Rome. I could not imagine that an ordinary guy like me had the opportunity to stand in front of the altars housing the relics of Ignatius of Loyola and Francis Xavier. A sense of serenity and calm had descended on me and I wept in happiness. I recalled reading from John Padberg, SJ in the Partners (Jesuit magazine) that the bones of another saint, Peter Faber, were buried there as well. Subsequently Anna told me a lot about the Jesuits. We discussed Karamazov Brothers that day for a while till the sun became too bright and Anna continued walking ahead of me though slowly moving to my side. There is a lot about the Jesuits in this book. I believe Dostoevsky became a Christian after he was pardoned by the czar about thirty seconds before being executed by the firing squad. I was telling Anna about Mary and Martha who lived in Bethany with their brother Lazarus. Mary had sat at the feet of Jesus and Martha prepared the food. There are times in all our lives when we are one or the other. Anna chimed in and said, "But we have to take time out of our busy schedule to sit at the feet of God. There are many ways of serving. Sometimes by just waiting we serve God. Milton wrote, 'They also serve who stand and wait.' Sometimes we are too busy organizing and cleaning and cooking and forget the meaning of life."

I prayed every day for good weather. I thanked God for my strength and asked Him to make me stronger the following day than the day before. I made progress every day with blessings from everyone. I felt as though my God took five steps for every one of mine as the blistering sun tried to evaporate me. He often sent a westerly breeze at times to caress my chest as I walked late in the afternoon. I began to eat more and more every day and drank enough fluids to keep my urine clear because I didn't want my body to become overheated.

I believe in predestination and therefore I never worried about the possibility that I may not finish. I believe that once I undertake any task my God will help me finish it. I believe that otherwise He would have never allowed me to start the project at all. This is a little different than having the freedom to make choices and the fall. I believe that the choices we make are guided by God as well. I have often questioned that event where Eve ate the forbidden fruit. I believe that the story is for us only to accept our weaknesses and it has nothing to do with God not guiding us. It had to be predestination that provided Napoleon with a mother that could improve his self-esteem such that he could conquer the most powerful nations. Ovid was destined to be a great poet despite his father, who wanted him to be a lawyer, a career in oratory at that time. So I marched on towards the west without any worry or anxiety because

I knew my purpose and I knew that I would be stronger every day than the day before. "The utterances of your lips you should keep, and you must do just as you have vowed to Jehovah, your God as a voluntary offering that you spoke of with your mouth" (Deuteronomy 23:23).

I had named Anna. I needed a companion as I was walking. My shadow had been with me all along but it was after St. Louis that Anna was christened. She had joined me soon after I left St. Louis. Faust had Gretchen, Napoleon had Josephine, Poe had Annabel and I liked Anna Karenina.

So I had Anna.

For the moon never beams without bringing me dreams
Of the beautiful Annabel Lee.
—Edgar Allan Poe

It had been several days that I had walked on the service roads. It was easier for me and this way we met different people. What's SPAVA about? Sometimes a few people would ask. So I would tell them that we teach about the peacemakers and the struggles they had to go through to make peace. So why are you walking? We give thirty to sixty children money for post-secondary education if they participate in projects of brotherhood/sisterhood and promote peace in the schools or in the community.

Ms. G would drive over next to me even before her scheduled time and most times I would take her offer to sit down and drink water and eat couple of power bars.

I remembered the day when I walked on the side roads and reached Weston, Missouri. It is a little town with lots of stores that sell old items and I guess they called them antiques.

I am getting to be an antique myself. I would love for someone to buy me and place me in a dignified place in the house. Everyone then would comment on my beauty, wonder how valuable I was and how wonderfully I had weathered. Well, that is not to be. I have to cut the grass and cook the meals and pay the bills just like the most of the people. Anna said, "Be happy that you are alive." I agreed.

I called Ms. G on the cell phone. I had made a few turns and she would have gone straight as per my instruction and we would have lost each other for a few hours. This happened on similar occasions as I walked further when I had failed to communicate with my support staff. I will only walk on the roads where there is a yellow line through the middle as a divider, I had told her. I often didn't follow my own rules.

I stood on the curbside as Ms. G drove up. Anna and I were talking about love when Ms. G arrived. I thought we would pick up the discussion later. I ordered a large ham steak, mashed potatoes, green beans and lemonade. I usually avoided sweets in the afternoon because it made me sleepy.

I met Joanna from Oklahoma. She was sitting at the next table. She had been visiting her friend at Columbia. After she learnt about my walk she said, "I have lost my son at the Oklahoma bombing." She wept while she was talking. "Our country is bent on mentioning the names of the killers on TV," she continued. "They never mentioned the names of those that died or felt sad as much as the guy that blew everybody away. But that guy, the white supremacist fellow was shown a hundred times. I am really angry with him. I am not going to say his name to honor him. I miss my John too much. I am not sure punishing someone to die is the answer," she said. "He is free and gone. I have to live and suffer every day for what he has done to my family."

I wept feeling for the mother. I told her that my grandfather had told me that the world is full of cruel people. Can you imagine sending mother Mary to have a baby in the barn? Can you imagine what the rest of the world felt when they beat and crucified the innocent Son?

Our waitress came and gave us the bill and didn't smile. I went to the reception desk and met Ms. Coral. She smiled and said hello as I shook her hand. She deserved a SPAVA T-shirt! I wanted to bring awareness and promote SPAVA to the youth of America through love and friendship. We said good-bye to our neighbors and moved on.

I adjusted my long-sleeved bra and painted myself with sun blocker and took off. I instructed my driver to meet me after two hours. Anna and I walked along the pavement and noticed that the cast-iron water meter covers are made in India. I told Anna that I loved her just because she is Anna. That made her happy. "Hey Anna, do you like sex?" She blushed and said yes. "Did your mother ever tell you that once the man gets what he wants he won't say that he loves you anymore?"

She said yes and continued. "I have read from the Masters and Johnson study that twenty-five percent of men are impotent by the time they are sixty-five and fifty percent are impotent by the time they are seventy-five years old.

So I want to enjoy my man while he can." Anna was always very open with me about her feelings. She was behind me now and so I had to really listen carefully to what she was saying.

The noise of the cars often muffled her voice. "I don't have all those inhibitions that Kinsey wrote about in 1953. I think modern women are more forward and less fussy about things such as what the neighbors think."

"I really like you, Anna. I think virility is a state of mind on most occasions, anyway. However, George Bernard Shaw had asked, 'Is it not delightful to be in love? —It has happened to me twice. It does not last, because it does not belong to this earth; and when you clasp the idol it turns out to be a rag doll like yourself; for the immortal part must elude you if you grab at it'" ("To a Young Actress," 1924, George Bernard Shaw).

Anna said that passion demands physiological arousal and often unpleasant experiences are arousing to us. "Anna, how is it that some women find it more arousing when they participate in the activity of the forbidden fruit?"

"Oh, men do the same. This is where you have to learn control and consequences. Negative consequences are a form of punishment but when we make a decision in a positive manner that does not hurt feelings then the choice is productive. If we jump in water we all go under for a split second; it is not going under that is important but more importantly we should decide will it damage the water if we jump? Will I feel good after the jump is over? Or can I do something to the water for it to come and engulf me and adore me without me having to rip through it for excitement."

Anna continued, "Isn't it more fun to be desirable? Isn't that what we are trying to do anyway when we are excited about the forbidden fruit? We get excited when we think that someone else besides our mate thinks we are desirable." Anna said the best way to love is to make your mate feel wonderful. "Life has to be taken in more practical terms at times. That's fine. Be critical in a positive way. But end the conversation with a compliment. Many times it will be difficult. It will sound phony. Remember love is a feeling and not science so feel it, don't analyze it," said Anna.

"Can you hate and love someone at the same time?"

Anna said yes. If you want to read Somerset Maugham, *Of Human Bondage*, you will understand. "He remembered her insolence; sometimes he had felt inclined to box her ears; and suddenly, he knew not why, perhaps it was the thought of hitting her or the recollection of her tiny beautiful ears, he was seized by an up rush of emotion. He yearned for her. He thought of taking her in his arms, the thin, fragile body, and kissing her pale mouth: he wanted to pass his fingers down the slightly greenish cheeks. He wanted her."

The days passed fast. Although I walked for almost eleven hours every day I neither felt bored nor did I feel that I had to finish anything in a hurry. I had spent the night at Sweet Springs, Missouri. But I had not actually reached there on foot yet. I was five miles short and I had planned to make up the distance the next day. I had to do this many times during the journey because I could not reach the exit on the same day and so we had to backtrack a few times. I had decided to walk on the country roads and translate the miles to the expressway. I thought that this way I would meet more people and my walk would be more valuable. After all, the purpose of the walk was to bring awareness about SPAVA and spread friendship and love and walking the expressway was not meeting that goal.

I met a Ms. J at the Jump Stop Restaurant at Williamsburg, Missouri. Her son had a brain tumor and she talked about him with me after she learnt that I was a neurosurgeon.

I think I was able to refer her son to the proper doctor near Columbia. She had served me the biggest ham steak I have ever eaten for five dollars.

Gus and Andy had come along as I was getting ready to leave. They had put the asphalt down that was melting in the heat and was getting stuck to my shoes as I was walking. At first I thought that it was fresh black top but Gus corrected me, "I had laid that asphalt down, it ain't no black top." I conceded that I had made a mistake. I said that people often confuse the difference between concrete and cement too. Dr. Henry Petroski of Duke University had explained that Portland cement is made by heating a mixture of crushed limestone and clay until fused and then the substance is ground into a powder. When it is mixed with water it undergoes a chemical reaction and develops strength and rigidity against being compressed. Joseph Aspdin of England had patented the process of making cement in 1824 and named it after the isle of Portland whose limestone it resembled when it set dry. Mixing sand and water with the dry powder is the mortar that is used to lay bricks. But when coarse particles such as broken stone or gravel are mixed with it then it is called concrete and that is what is used to build sidewalks and needs to be reinforced when used in buildings because it cannot resist being pulled apart. I told them that Epsom salt was also found by a farmer in England in Epsom. I think by now Gus was overloaded with information. I moved on.

After walking along this country road on the way to Watson I sat down on the side of the road where I met Clay. He was waiting for his dad, Mark, to join him. They had taken the day off. It had rained a bit earlier. They were getting ready for haying tomorrow. They wanted to know all about the nonviolence program. So I told them all about it. Clay knew about Mahatma Gandhi. He is a student in tenth grade. I explained to him that although Gandhi introduced Satyagraha or civil disobedience against the apartheid regime in South Africa and the British sedition rules, it is not an all-pervasive solution or panacea for all situations. I believe civil disobedience can only work when the opponent is civilized and has some sensitivity. Gandhi sometimes approved violence. He had approved the action of the Indian army being sent to Kashmir in October 1947 to fight pillaging tribal invaders. Pyarelal, in his book *Mahatma Gandhi*, wrote, "His exhortations to the defenders to be wiped out to the last man in clearing Kashmir soil of the raiders rather than submit were even dubbed Churchillian."

The issue of when the use of violence is unavoidable and that nonviolent ways will be effective has not been subjected to critical debate. However, I believe we should try to solve most conflicts in a nonviolent way. Ahimsa is an active form of nonviolence. I am not sure nonviolence works while defending a situation of status quo of peaceful society which is under attack where the adversary is on the offensive to change the existing order to suit their philosophy which is different from the intelligentsia. Stalin, Mao Zedong and Hitler were trying to change the society with enormous violence. I realized that our discussion might have been getting too deep. So I ended the discussion with a saying from a great German philosopher, Soren Kierkegaard, "Life must be understood backwards, but lived forwards."

My support van arrived. We sat and enjoyed the beauty of a field of hay swaying in the breeze. I loved the freedom of being able to stop and hear the sound of the silence away from the interstate. We left to go and eat in a Chinese restaurant that my driver had spotted. This is where I met Gwen and Ken. They had a deer skin in their back seat.

I asked Ken if it belonged to the one I had seen in the back woods a few days back. They chuckled. They are both in advertising. I took this opportunity to promote SPAVA. They asked me questions about my birthplace. After I explained to them about this journey I told them that the walk was symbolic, much like the walks of Gandhi and King. I had heard someone saying that if we didn't advertise it was like working in the dark. I knew what I was doing but no one else did. They laughed.

Then I recited a poem written by Tagore as a tribute to King Faisal of Iraq:

The night has ended
Put out the light of the lamp
Of thine own narrow dark corner
Smudged with smoke,
The great morning which is for all?
Appears in the East.
Let its light reveal us to each other
Who walk on the same path
Of pilgrimage.

Anna was behind me. I knew it was time to go. We said good-bye to our new friends and we went in different directions with different forms of transportation. They were in a pickup truck. I, on the other hand, had to rely on my legs.

An ambulance went past me with its lights and sounds on. So I told Anna that I had treated a man once who was hit on the head with a frying pan. After the operation I talked to his wife regarding the details of the event that led up to the "nut cracking" episode. I had worked with her in the past in the operating room. "He drives me crazy," she said. I had to make a domestic violence report despite the fact that she was a colleague nurse of mine. I had forgotten the details. I believe she had to do some community work or such.

Anna asked me about Titania. I knew that Titania had sent her fairy subjects off to sing and to cure the ills of wild roses and to frighten the owls away. I didn't like that Oberon could appear unseen and squeeze pansy nectar upon her eyelids and cast a spell such that Titania would awaken to see "some vile things near." Lysander, on the other hand, had Hermia and I needed someone like her to be with me to sink in the grass and fall asleep.

It must have been at Olney that I met a man from Australia. He and his buddy were driving by and had stopped for lunch or such. "So you couldn't afford a car, mate?" The gentleman with an accent typical of from down under humored me. I laughed and asked him about all the camels they have in the Northern Territory. "The camels were brought from near your part of the world, you know?"

"I thought they were from Peshawar, Pakistan."

"Well, close enough. The camels hauled gold and other products to help the missionaries and ranchers."

"So are you here to sell camels?"

"Hardly! No, by early 1930 the internal combustion engine had put most of the cameleers out of business. Now we ship them to the Middle East."

"Hey does that movie, *Rabbit-Proof Fence*, have any truth in it?"

"Oh, yes, I am sorry to say. I am afraid poverty and prejudice has kept the aboriginal people from getting opportunities in life. During much of the twentieth century government officials separated aboriginal children from their families and often treated them pretty rough to get them 'civilized.' We can't do much about the past. But now we are doing more. So let's hope in the end we can feel good about making amends. So, how about you? Do people treat you with prejudice?"

"Many do but probably the American Indians are subjects of greater prejudice."

It was shortly after I had passed St. Louis that Anna was telling me about the Indian civilization. The state of Illinois had acquired land rights outside the arch of St. Louis in Collinsville to set up the Cahokia Mounds state historic site. Cahokia was a major city in mid-America with about twenty thousand residents between the tenth through the thirteenth centuries. Anna wanted me to know about this important Native American historic site. No one is sure why this city was abandoned around 1400 AD. I did not have to stop there this time but I told her that I would return to see the archeological discovery.

I needed a rubber guard for my walking stick. So I went to a Tru-valu store at Concordia. Bill, the owner, took a picture of me and I took a picture of him. My walking stick was almost half of an inch shorter than what it was when I left Louisville.

"How many days have you been on the road?"

"Twenty days," I said.

"I am proud to have met you," said Bill.

I said, "Likewise."

I had walked almost thirty-five miles today. My feet didn't hurt anymore. However, I had developed a swelling of my right knee. Well, Icy Hot took care of that. I wore a brace as well for a short period. After a few days I told myself that I was a strong man and shouldn't need the brace.

I told Anna a story about an attorney that I had met many years ago during my neurosurgical practice. I had examined one of her clients for a workman's compensation claim. During a deposition out of desperation for her client's fake workman's compensation claim she had asked me, "Aren't you from India? What do you know about pain? Don't people in India walk on nails?"

I was proud of my comeback. "I think your bra is too tight. It's squeezing your brain." The court reporter had asked the other attorney if she should be typing the disparaging remarks. After the deposition we both had laughed at our wisdom. The deposition had to be rescheduled because the remarks from both sides were considered rather less than palatable for the judge to read. Anyway, I told myself that since I was born in a country where people can walk on nails and hot coals surely I shouldn't worry about little patellar tendonitis from overuse.

I told Anna that I was excited because my minister had volunteered to drive the support van during a part of the journey. He had hoped that I would be past Nebraska by the time it would be his turn. He had never been to Idaho or Wyoming and he thought this would give him an opportunity to see the countryside. So I asked Anna if she could quote from the Bible to say where there is a weather report. Anna thought for a minute and then said, "OK, it is kind of a weather report, 'When you see a cloud rising in the western parts, at once you say, a storm is coming, and it turns out so. And when you see that a south wind is blowing, you say there will be a heat wave, and it occurs'" (Luke 12:54-55).

I was a bit apprehensive about spending eight to nine days with the minister so I wanted Anna to help me with the good book. Anna and I had spoken a lot about my grandfather.

My grandfather had given everything away to the poor and Anna told me then to remember, "Take heed and beware of covetousness: for man's life consisteth not in abundance of things which he possesseth" (Luke 12:15). It was only later that it became very clear to me after Mr. W, my minister, came to be with me that I had no reason to be apprehensive and we had so much fun together. After being cooped up in the van all day in the hot Wyoming sun he always went for a run while I did some primping to get rid of my odor of profuse sweat and doctored my feet. But the thing I liked most about him was that although he was a minister he didn't mind me drinking a little Jim Beam in the night and at times he gave me company to soothe his nerves as well!

The next day began after breakfast at a Waffle House. I met Cyndi, a young woman of about twenty years. She asked me many questions about SPAVA. I gave her a brochure and a T-shirt. I was excited and energized as usual and planned to walk faster than usual on that day. I greeted the passing cars with my waving hands. Most of them waved back. A few young girls tried not to make eye contact because I believe their mama had taught them such. I still said Namaste to them. It is a Hindi word that means I worship the God inside you.

Anna said that "Don't make eye contact with strangers" is what their mama had told them. So I said, "What else did your mama say?"

"I can't think of all of them now. But I can tell you that she said that if a guy holding your hand plays with your palm with his fingers on the first date don't go out with him anymore. He has only one thing in his mind."

Some of the people of course didn't wave back because they didn't want to condone the activity of what they assumed was a homeless man walking with a funny sign.

Ouch! A bug bit me on my ear lobe. I thought I was clever by plugging my ears. But this bug thought that he was cleverer than I was. Blown by the wind of the semis its miniscule body wanted respite into my ear hole. However, unable to find the warm opening into a wind-free zone it lashed out at me in a manner that gave me great pain and blistering that was to stay with me for almost two weeks. I realized that it needed SPAVA class to learn anger management skills.

I always worried when I saw the gator skins on the shoulders of the expressway. It is the slang for the torn rubber parts of blown-out tires that lay around on the shoulders. I hoped that no one would have a blowout close to me. This is one issue that I had to be careful about while walking on the shoulders of interstates. Many years ago I had to attend traffic school because I was driving too fast. I asked Anna if she wanted to know about this. I didn't want to be repetitive. At times I forgot what I had told her. I recall the policeman telling me that if someone had a blowout of the left tire at seventy miles an hour the car would swerve badly and there was a high possibility of death or disfigurement.

I had already found many nails, screws and diapers and beer bottles on the roadside. I had to be careful not to step on them. Around Exit 48 I remember seeing that someone had thrown a baby bed onto the side of the road where it said, "$500 Fine for Littering." I thought that the person who had discarded this item must have thought that it was OK to throw items up to $500 value or didn't read English. There were some places on the road as I found later during the walk that there were posted signs, "Next five miles maintained by Rotary." I thought it would be nice if we taught our children not to litter as a lesson plan in school. I didn't think we Rotarians were in the road-cleaning business although we believe in "Service above self."

I was really mad. The van had a flat tire because it had run over some sort of hard piece of steel much like a large hook that someone had pitched on the shoulder. I was going on and on. Anna intervened. "So you want to bitch and complain and use up your energy? You need to be alert," Anna scolded me. I remained quiet. She quoted, "'Be not wise in your own conceit. If it be possible, as much as lieth in you, live peaceably with all men. Dearly beloved, avenge not yourselves, but rather give place unto wrath: for it is written, vengeance is mine; I will repay saith the Lord'" (Romans 13:16-19). I thanked Anna. I told Anna that I needed to remember this a lot more often. I had lost the love of my life once because I didn't heed what the good book had said and my anger made me a loser at the end. Ms. G had to go and find a place to get the tire fixed. I just kept on walking till the day was over.

I was a bit shaken up today by an incident that almost killed me. Anna wasn't with me at that time. It was an overcast day and I was walking on the country road. I was walking facing the traffic as the road slowly meandered to the left and then right and then left again. The trees shaded the road giving me a break from the sun. I was happy and singing Jaydev's poetry about how God arrives in different forms to cleanse the earth when people are damaging His creation. Actually Jaydev wrote his poetry in Sanskrit after Ovid wrote in *Metamorphoses*:

Iamque erat in totas sparsurus fulmina terras,
Sed timuit, ne forte sacer tot ab ignibus aether

Jupiter had called a meeting of Gods in Mt. Olympus and announced his intention to destroy the race of Man and create new mortals. This is much like Nataraja, Lord Shiva who is eternally prepared for the dance of creation and destruction if the need arises.

I was moving fast. The only sound I could hear was that of my walking stick hitting the concrete with a rhythm of its own design. An occasional car passed me by giving me enough room to ponder and enjoy the freedom of a country walk. My sign wiggled and danced as the backpack hummed a monotonous chopping tone while it hugged me to avoid slipping off my back at every step. I saw the shimmering shadows of the leaves on the road that swayed and danced to welcome a new visitor where possibly no one new ever came through.

Suddenly, a pickup truck came out of nowhere at a dangerous speed and cut through the silence as it screeched and skidded about sixty feet leaving dark marks of burnt rubber just about ten feet in front of me. It woke me up and stopped me in a state of stunned paralysis with a sense of irritation I would have felt if someone would have scratched a piece of chalk on a blackboard while I was meditating. I take meditation seriously. He didn't stop but just moved on as though he had nothing to say to any of us, the trees, the shadows and me. This was a SPAVA opportunity to ask for forgiveness but he missed it.

Later on when I saw Anna I told her about it. Anna said that punishment does not provide freedom in the heart to those who are convicted of a negative act or an act of reprehension. There are some who feel that just because they have served their time for their crime therefore everything is okay. You cannot get freedom until you repent first. Repentance is necessary but the only way to be free is to be forgiven, said Anna.

Autolycus was a robber and had the power of metamorphosing himself as well as the goods he had stolen. There are many among us who think like that, said Anna. It is like the guy who drinks and lives in the delusion that no one knows about it. Life is not magic. It is real and God is watching us every day. Professor S. Jay Olshansky and his colleagues wrote an article about "Confronting the boundaries of human longevity" in *Scientific American* volume 86. They stated that modern theories of senescence are invariably the result of influence of natural selection and on the timing and quality of gene expression. They explained that selection is now viewed as a process by which the frequency of favorable variants of genes (alleles) increases in a population at the expense of inferior genes that produce illness or death. The changes in frequency are brought about by differences in survival and reproductive success of the individuals carrying the alleles. I am not an evolutionary biologist but I know that such an accident would have destroyed a favorable gene from the population!

I walked slowly after all this. Until now I was swinging like the balloon above the Oreck air purifier but now my balloon of joy was wet in the sweat of anxiety and pithed by the spike of anger that I felt towards the irresponsible driver. I walked next to a big fenced field where cows were waiting to be slaughtered. I sat outside the fence on the roadside smelling the malodorous cow plops to recover from my stress when a dog that was at first shy jumped on my lap and consoled me with his slobbering tongue till Ms. G came and picked me up. I was done for the day. I needed an Atta Boy today! Now!

I was sitting with my legs stretched out and as the dog was licking me I was reminiscing that even a few days back when I had just left for my trip I was not sure of my endurance. It was not even four hours that I had been on the road that my support driver had thought that it was too hot outside and so he had gone home to rest. But I knew he loved me. I guess I just didn't understand how sensitive I could be when I was on the road all alone. The fear and the anxiety of not knowing my capability and the possible humiliation that I might feel if I was not able to finish the journey that I had undertaken to promote the children of Kentucky often troubled me. Ms. G had a hard time finding me because I was lying down on the grass but I was found soon! I had fallen asleep listening to the monotony of the noise of the cars on the highway nearby.

Games We Played as We Walked to Iowa

Anna started telling me a story today as I marched slowly towards Hamburg. I never was in a hurry. I noticed a cluster of butterflies sitting around some yellow flowers on the roadside and as I approached them they flew in different directions.

"Do you know much about butterflies?"

Anna said, "A little. I want to tell you about some butterflies."

I said, "OK."

"There are hundreds of different types of butterflies in the world. There are certain types that live only in certain parts of the world."

I interrupted and said that the monarch flies thousands of miles to Mexico from North America. I said that I want to play questions and answers because otherwise I would have to listen quietly and I felt like I needed to talk a little while I was walking.

"OK."

"What are the people called who know a lot about butterflies?"

Anna—"Lepidopterologists."

Tim—"The process of change from an egg or ovum to larva (caterpillar) and then to chrysalis (pupa) and finally to imago (adult butterfly) is called?"

Anna—"Metamorphosis. It takes about three days to two weeks for the egg to become a caterpillar. The caterpillar is like a teenager and eats all the time. The female lays the eggs on leaves and sometimes they stick underneath the leaves so the birds and insects cannot see them. The caterpillars are fuzzy and hairy. In two to eight weeks each caterpillar becomes a pupa covered in a silk cocoon and at times hangs upside down."

Tim—"In three weeks to six months of hibernation the adult butterfly is formed. Imago sounds like amigo, a friend. A butterfly cannot be an enemy! The newborn pumps up (I showed Anna my biceps) which forces the fluids into its body and in half an hour or so the wings become fully developed." I don't have much of a muscular body but every so often I like to show my muscles to my wife also! It somehow makes me feel manlier.

Anna—"Does the butterfly have a tongue?"

Tim—"I don't know."

Anna—"OK. I will give you an anatomy lesson. Yes. It has a tongue under its head. The males recognize the females by the scent and color perception. Butterflies have good vision for movement."

I stood a watched a monarch lead the way.

Anna continued—"They can smell through their antennae, which are important for balance and direction."

Tim—"Do you know about lime butterfly?"

Anna—"You are interrupting."

Tim—"Sorry."

Anna—"They have a primitive heart. The blood of a butterfly is free flowing without any internal structure (like our arteries or veins) but enclosed in a framework of a substance called chitin. It is thin and similar to the spider web."

Tim—"Do they have lungs?"

Anna—"Butterflies do not have lungs that I know of. They absorb oxygen by diffusion.

"I will tell you a story about butterflies another time. I can go places where you can't. I heard this story while standing under a tree on a hot summer day. And there was a lime butterfly in it."

I shared a story that Aunt Alma had told me once. Now her sister and I were real close. They both had grown a bit in their years. However Ms. M was becoming a bit out of the way in her thinking at times and she had burnt her toes with hot water while cooking.

So I had asked Aunt Alma if her sister could stay with her for a while since they loved each other and both had spent quite a bit of time together in the past. They both were past seventy-five years of age. However, after listening to my request Aunt Alma told me in a very sweet fashion, "Now if I am telling you something and you say to me, 'You know, Aunt Alma, I think you might have told me this story in the past,' I stop and talk about something else. But you know when I am with Marie she sometimes tells me the same story even though I remind her that I had heard that story once or twice in the past."

This was a hard day for walking. Well, every day was tough after St. Louis. As I continued on Interstate 29 I lost my support van for a while as Ms. G went in the wrong direction outside St. Joseph. However, we talked on the phone and saw each other from a distance and laughed. I told Ms. G that I thought I had developed hedonistic homeostatic dysregulation syndrome. She wondered what that would be in my case and she didn't know any medical terms. She often wondered if I was acting strange from heat stroke or such. I certainly had an alteration of appetite and I knew that I had hypersexuality and I thought that although I did not participate in aimless wandering but I was certainly wandering at this time. Dr. Giovannoni had described this condition in some people with Parkinson's disease because they felt as though they had too much of a good thing. I was thirsty and I needed my van because I had finished all the water I was carrying in my pouch.

I had moved on to Interstate 29 from outside Kansas City moving north to Iowa. I knew that I would have to be at the heel of Iowa before I could enter into Nebraska. This way I could go towards Grand Island without going to Omaha. I saved almost ninety miles of walking by choosing this path. There was not much to be said about this road except that it was not so well maintained. The shoulders were cracked and looked like the teeth that had not visited the dentist for a long time. There was no evidence of flossing either. There were a lot of small weeds that were growing through the cracks between the black and gray asphalt. It seemed that the interstate got a little confusing near St. Joseph. Ms. G and I saw each other on two different interstates when we were supposed to have met for lunch. The maze of the interstate was certainly a bit confusing for an ordinary driver. Although Ms. G is no ordinary driver it seemed I was walking north and she waved at me from an interstate where she had already turned going eastward. However, by now she had developed courage to participate in some challenging traffic rules that may be in fine print. I saw her back up the van and turned it around to go the correct way on the interstate. She thought that there was only a small section that was one way. I started humming the lyrics of the song "From a Distance" as it is in the album *Some People's Lives*. I am no Bette Midler or Whitney Houston but there was no one to challenge me.

God is watching us. God is watching us.
God is watching us from a distance.

I was excited about getting to Iowa. I don't why but I was thinking of the days in the seventies when Maharishi Mahesh yogi had come to Iowa and started the movement of Transcendental Meditation. I remembered reading articles about the awkwardness people felt with the meditators who always needed some time off during the day to meditate. I think I need to meditate more to be focused.

I walked to the next exit and consumed an enormous amount of food. I myself was a bit surprised at my capacity. But I consoled myself by thinking of Michelangelo Antonioni's 1966 film called *Blow Up*. In this thriller the photographer enlarged a snapshot of two lovers in a park in a manner of magnification that it gave the illusion of a man and a gun. So I thought I was tired and my eyes at times didn't focus well!

We were getting ready to move on to the next spot where I would meet my van but Anna came along and said that she remembered a story about driving. She knew Ms. M. She was an octogenarian and she had wanted to get a driver's license after her husband had passed away. She had never driven any motorized vehicle in the past except her tractor in the field to haul brush and tree cuttings. Her neighbor, also an older widow and her companion, had driven her to the license renewal place. It was a small town and she had talked with Kenny two nights back about giving her the test. She had known Kenny from the day he was born and she had walked Kenny to his kindergarten class many times. Kenny was also good at saying, "Sweet sixteen and never been kissed, rubbish!" every Friday evening at the local bingo parlor. Ms. M took the driving test and explained to Kenny, who was sitting inside her car, that she normally doesn't stop at the stop signs unless someone else is approaching towards her. Then she turned around on a one-way street to show Kenny how she could come over to the post office and the grocery store in case there was too much traffic on the proper road. Anna said that Kenny gave her a license but told her not to drive to any other place except to the grocery and the post office. Ms. M always walked to the local library to look at the stocks page in the *Wall Street Journal* to check on her investment. I chuckled because I had instructed her to glance through the pages of this paper so that she would get a thrill of knowing as to how secure she had been financially.

Most of the Super 8 motels had given me a good deal because I was walking for the children. However, I realized that generosity is not considered a virtue at every place and certainly it was not for me at St. Joseph. So I walked through St. Joseph and went as far as I could that day and drove back to a town outside Kansas City where I could find cheaper accommodations. The next day I walked from where I got picked up the night before and walked to Iowa. I became eligible to tear up another map. I had finished walking through Kentucky, Indiana, Illinois and Missouri. I was pleased with myself. I thought that even if I had to quit now I had gone further than one of my friends had said that I would go. "You wouldn't be able to go past the Mississippi," Debbie had said. Now, when I had heard that it made me feel badly because I thought that she had no faith in my abilities and will.

I saw many flattened animals on this part of the road. Some were on the shoulders and some others were on the road. I didn't like to see flattened animals on the shoulders. It was not that their legs got crushed and so they crawled to the shoulders to die. It was the torso that was flattened. I walked with caution.

I removed the ear plugs from the left ear to remain alert at all times. At the end of my walk this act caused me to develop significant high-frequency hearing loss in my left ear from hearing loud cars go by every day for eleven hours each day.

I was hoping to see some live animals but I realized that most of the animals hunt at night. I thought it would be fun to see a wolverine or a mountain lion. I would even be happy to see a grizzly at a distance. Pretty long distance from me! Well, there are no such animals in these states anyway. It is not that I was walking through the streets of India.

I recalled the time I had walked north of Hardwar, on the way to Hem Kund. I saw chickens, pigs, donkeys, horses, cows, water buffaloes, camels and at one place even the mahout was walking an elephant. Of course, everyone has seen the monkey men with two or three monkeys dressed in costume jewelry and bells around the ankles performing tricks. What is interesting is that when an unsuspecting observer is enjoying the performance of the monkeys there are trained pickpockets who empty the pockets of the men leaving no opportunity to tip the monkeys for the thrill! There were no snake charmers who would show off the doped-up cobras as they would slither out of the wicker baskets parked on the highway just next to the bear-man walking his bear on the way to see the Taj Mahal.

Interstate 29 seemed neglected by the government although this road led to Omaha. There wasn't much to see on the way to Hamburg, Iowa, as I quickly cut into Nebraska through the heel of Iowa. The corn wasn't as high as I thought it should be at that time.

However Anna wanted to tell me about Pond Inlet at that time. We had no rules. Anna liked me for having multi-tasking ability. In 1921 settlement began in Pond Inlet but the Inuit were not allowed to live on the land in homes until 1962. Moreover they were not given credit for their accomplishments. "How is that?" I asked.

"Well, Pamipakoochoo was the Inuit man that guided the St. Roch through the North West Passage but was never mentioned by the British."

Hamburg to Lincoln City is not that far that I couldn't make in one day. It just took more than eleven hours. I moved from SR 2 to SR 34 and eventually I walked on SR 30 that eventually took me through Wyoming as I realized much later. At Lincoln City I was able to make a connection with my Rotary colleagues. One of them wanted to walk with me. He owned a radio station. In the spirit of Rotary he announced my walk on the radio. So the next day many people honked as they passed by me. Some even walked over to congratulate me or to just say hello.

I had to walk with my head bent forward because the wind had picked up. In the afternoons the wind was hot and fierce. It took almost twice the strength to walk, not just for the wind but also because the outside temperature was about eighty-eight degrees and humidity was ninety-seven percent. My feet began to hurt because I felt the extra pull on my sign. The bent posture against the wind began to take its toll on my back. So I stopped every hour and rested a few minutes to recuperate and talk to my back so that it wouldn't be such a puny part of my body. I had a new crop of blisters at the ball of my feet.

Anna was much taller in early mornings when I started. One day I told Anna that I can hear God talking to me much like he talked to Joshua. "Moses, my servant is dead, and now get up, cross this Jordan, you and all this people, into the land that I am giving to them, to the sons of Israel" (Joshua 1:2).

"You have an amazing amount of strength and you would not have it if God didn't give it to you."

I agreed. I had already walked twenty-eight miles today. My lower back was hurting from the hamstring spasm. I had predicted to Ms. G that there would be a Chinese restaurant next to our motel today and we wouldn't have to drive to any restaurant to eat. It turned out to be a good guess. Couple of shots of Jim Beam before and couple after dinner joined hands with Icy Hot massage to alleviate my pain in the hips. It was five o' clock in the morning when I woke up. My God had healed me. I placed iodine and Band Aids on the blisters after puncturing them so that I wouldn't be feeling as though I was walking on sand-filled chewing gum in the bottom of my feet where the skin felt like it had been cut by corals.

My Dream

I woke up feeling refreshed. I was ready to see Anna. I had a story to tell her that I learnt during the night. It was CJ's thirteenth birthday. There was a small birthday celebration in his homeroom in Ms. Robinson's class. His actual name was John Calvin but he liked to be called CJ. During his time to give a talk before blowing the candles he said he wanted to be a zoologist because he liked to learn about animals. "I also like to dissect, so I can see the inside." Hearing this some of his classmates grimaced, gross! Ms. Robinson made it a point that her students just couldn't make a wish but they actually had to say what they wanted to be when they grew up. I had dreamt about three butterflies who wanted to do something to change the world. One of them was a lime butterfly and it said, "I have a short life to live. I want to do all I can before I die."

I ate breakfast of two eggs, four pancakes, sausage, potatoes and coffee and orange juice. I hit the road all joyful and new. The sun was behind me, Anna in front of me and I felt that my God was on my right as I moved towards York from Grand Island. I walked over a bridge over a parking lot that housed a million trains. Well, almost! I hadn't realized until later that these trains would be going back and forth by the side of my path for the next five or six weeks.

The sky was clear and the barn swallows dove in front of me and flew almost hugging the grass ahead of me. I recalled the scene of seeing happiness among animals, the porcupine caribous at the Arctic National Wildlife Refuge. The birds were happy and graceful. I almost felt that they wanted to announce my arrival in a joyful glee to the corn by the wayside.

I almost ran down the road with my head sticking out of the neck hole of my wet undershirt covered by my specially clipped hat to my long-sleeved bra. My dark sunglasses protected my eyes from the blinding bright sun. The Capri pants clung to me like gloves worn on moist hands. They hugged my hips because the overhanging fat had melted by now. I had prepared shields of aluminum foil that hung from the frame of my glasses to protect my eyes from flying rock chips that had hit me earlier as trucks went by fast. I felt that my brown body was like a racehorse with my blinders on my eyes and orange and yellow cover on my back was the seat for the backpack jockey that was ready to win this race through the country.

The corn was swaying in happiness in keeping in tune with the perfect pitch of the sound of the wind as it announced its power through the open fields. I saw some white buildings that looked like outhouses for vagabond walkers. However, a farmer explained to me that those were part of some communication system. That explanation helped me owing to the fact that I had thought differently. If I had sat down in one of those buildings to get relieved and suddenly someone had started speaking to me I would not have known how to answer them. These buildings allegedly provided communication to the missile defense system. Tom said that he had done a bit of reading on the subject and was concerned about nuclear warfare. Ray said that he was concerned about cancer and nuclear fallout after different tests that have been performed, some openly but mostly covertly.

The first test explosion of a nuclear weapon, Trinity, was in New Mexico on July 16, 1945. In August of 1945 Hiroshima and Nagasaki were bombed. We have learned since then that there has been an increased risk of cancer of bone and thyroid gland in Japan and in some other islands in the South Pacific where nuclear tests have been carried out. There have been several nuclear tests that have been performed by the former Soviet Union, Britain, France, China, India and Pakistan. President Kennedy had signed a Limited Test Ban Treaty in 1963.

Radiation fallout has been of great concern for most of mankind. The fireball that is created by the nuclear explosion expands and then cools down and loses its buoyancy and then the radioactive materials are dispersed by the prevailing winds. The microscopic particles fall on the ground and then animals eat the grass and then we get radiation by drinking and eating meat. They both expressed concern since Nebraska is considered the breadbasket of America for their production of wheat and corn. I told them that I was very concerned about the environment and thus protested against oil drilling at ANWR (Arctic National Wildlife Refuge). Tom knew about the herd of porcupine caribous, a hundred and thirty thousand of them, that come to have babies in that land every year. Ray stated that he knew that the reindeer population in Lapland had received significant radiation subsequent to the Chernobyl accident.

I expressed my gratitude for their opinions but I had to move on. My feet hit the road hard. The shoes absorbed some shock but my hips took a lot of hits. I had walked about three miles in the wrong direction after I had left Grand Island.

Ms. G had realized that I was going south and came and picked me up so that I would go west. I soon entered an area where I found the explanation for the "joyful" state of the corn. The whole area smelled like a gigantic fart.

I wanted to get out of this odoriferous cavity of the corn field where the odor of the manure moved through the air as indigestion gas moves through the haustrations in our colon in fast peristalsis. It took me a little over four hours to get out of this area.

I passed through Hampton and then just outside the city went to a bar for lunch. Several men were enjoying the afternoon with some cold beer and we were a little late for lunch. "Go to Woody's barbecue south of the track at the pole barn. He will fix you up as you watch the tractor pull," one of the men said to me. We ate our sandwich as the tractor pull competition went on. A couple of men sat in Harvester tractors and made the path smooth after each competitor finished in front of a guy holding a flag. We left soon after we finished eating. I walked to York. We had dinner at a friend's house. Ms. Rose had fixed a spectacular five-course Italian dinner. I enjoyed the meal immensely. This was my first home-cooked meal in about thirty-two days.

I hadn't realized until later that my walking stick was most beneficial in protecting me against barking and attacking dogs. These animals just stopped short of attacking me after running breathless and barking across the fields or the farmer's yards as I walked along the country roads of Indiana and Illinois. There were times when I stopped and yelled back at them. I even made faces at times. However, despite the advantages it awarded me, the continuous use of the walking stick led me to develop a painful condition of my hand.

By the time I had reached Cheyenne I had developed a painful trigger finger of my right ring finger. So one evening I injected into the tendon sheath through my palm some Xylocaine and Kenalog that I had brought with me. I had never given myself an injection until now. I think the only time I had shots that were administered to me were the times when I needed to be vaccinated for certain international mission work. I wondered about those that practice giving themselves injections on a regular basis just to be high. They must have a lot of courage! In less than a week my hand was better.

There was only one time when I beat my stick on a fence just for entertainment. It was somewhere along the road through Nebraska. There were bunch of rats coming in and out of an old car around which had grown an enormous amount of tall grass. They quickly disappeared into their home. I recalled reading some research about the impact of rats on the Easter Islands which were possibly brought by the Polynesian colonists. I thought in my mind these rats haven't seen the rats at the Victoria train station at Mumbai, India.

If I am not mistaken one of those vermin of India could outweigh these by about five to six pounds. I recalled eating one of these when I was working in Arequipa, Peru. I was uncomfortable about biting into it as I looked at this flattened rodent served on a plate with gravy and mashed potato and red beans but they explained that it was a delicacy and it was not a rat anyway. It was a field guinea pig because it didn't have a tail!

The next day there was no sign of Anna early on. She slept on the clouds on such days. I always carried my stick but I today didn't need my sunglasses. The temperature was pleasant for the first time. Anna soon appeared. The humidity was so high that when I spoke to Anna the words were wet and heavy. There was no wind. I was wet. Anna scooted over a few times as I was talking.

I said I was sorry and then I just stopped talking because I felt embarrassed. My sweat glistened in the sun. My back was wet and my skin felt cold. My pants were wet too. After I had walked about thirteen miles we had lunch.

The straight road divided the corn fields from the train track which stayed on our left for a long time. The corn fields housed some irrigation equipment that stood on big treaded wheels and appeared like some weapons with spikes that were on call to attack any alien ships that had intended to invade the corn fields.

I, on the other hand, felt like Peter O'Toole in *Lawrence of Arabia* and covered my face with my T-shirt because I didn't have the chuddar of the Bedouins to protect my face from the scorching sun. I yelled SPAVA because Aquaba was not in my way. I didn't miss the camels as my feet were holding strong and I didn't look forward to damaging any other part of my body as would invariably happen if I were to be riding on the back of a camel. I remembered a short ride I had taken on the back of a camel at Jaisalmer, a desert in western India, and that had caused me to have blisters on my derriere.

In the afternoon the road didn't curve at all. It felt as though someone had held a ruler at the edge of a paper and had drawn a straight line. I walked along the white line facing traffic. The doldrums of the equator that the Ancient Mariner had faced after killing the albatross almost became real to me. Anna was fidgety. Suddenly Anna disappeared. Cold wind impregnated with the sweet smell of moisture started pushing me.

La vant avant le pluis! I donned my raingear that I had bought from Wal-Mart. Soon the rain and storm came and washed me clean and the black clouds floated over my head. I knew Ms. G would be here soon unless she was reading a love story. I was glad that I had sprayed my shoes with some chemicals to keep them from getting soggy.

I had my sunglasses specially made scratch proof (at least that is what I had thought) before I left Louisville. I thanked Ben Franklin for discovering bifocals. I don't know what I would have done otherwise. I recalled when I slept at Grand Island, Nebraska. We had lunch at Roth's restaurant on the way. Everyone wanted to know what all this walking was about. I left early with the sun behind me. The road had been up and down and very hard on my hips. So I took this opportunity to talk to the two men parked on the side of the road a bit and get my hips a little rest.

There was no sign of Anna for a while. Clouds had moved in. The straight road divided the train track from the corn fields in the north side. I passed more silos and cement factories. Sure enough torrential rain started. My sweaty glistening face got washed clean and I had learnt to keep my sunglasses on during the rain to protect my eyes from dirty water hitting them when the trucks passed by. Soon the rain stopped and scorching heat of the sun dried me. My feet were my friends that galloped whenever I wanted to and my shoes were dry because I had sprayed them with chemicals.

I felt like a child that could play in the wide open world with not a drop of fear in the heart but full of joy and excitement destined to march towards Cheyenne because "it was written" that I would be there by June 21st! I do not make my life burdensome with lists that I cannot complete. Instead I finish what is necessary and do not feel obligated or trapped in one obligation after another. I have learnt to say no when my plate is full and that way I can dance like a child with a joyful heart rather than being chained to my responsibilities that are unending.

I think Martin Luther King and Malcolm X both believed that if you haven't found something to live for, you are already dead. I told Anna that I live for the children. I am very concerned about not doing enough to improve the self-esteem and a positive self-image of the African American children. Self-esteem means to me to have a favorable opinion of oneself and it is not a delusional experience but a realistic one. I try to teach the children about freedom and joy and I practice it.

Learning self-discipline is one of the important aspects of growth. I believe that I must think of the things that I can do to help myself and not what the others can do for me or that I am entitled to something because my great-grandfather was a slave. It is important to learn about the struggle of the Black people, about five million or so, that were brought in slavery. I think blaming for past acts and hoping to get financial benefit and/or developing a sense of entitlement for mistakes of our fathers will only make the present generation old. I believe valuable time will be lost with a generation that can be taught to make a successful living and can be a beacon of hope for the next group of Americans.

Now it is more important to think that the past is gone. We cannot change it. Jesus was crucified. We cannot pluck the nails out. We should not blame the guys that made the nails. It was difficult then but now I have the opportunity to excel myself. I may have to try twice as hard but that is what is needed to be successful through hard work. I must not complain about those who have more than I have but I must try on my own to get what I need. Education among the African American children has not been as productive. Parenting has been an important issue and in this setting lack of a father figure in the family has been found to be an important issue. Many children learn aggressive behavior as a method of survival in the neighborhoods where they grow up. Telling them not to retaliate when someone hits them usually appears not in sync with the coping mechanism available to some of them.

After the rain cleared Anna and I talked a lot about personal life and how I could redeem myself from all the hurts I had caused to others in life. I had read a lot about Feldenkrais, named after the professor who introduced the concept of growth through self-realization. Moshe Feldenkrais had written quite a bit about "Trust yourself to work out what is right for you." My friends in America always get excited about these aphorisms but I consider some of this type of practice, often a form of humanism, without the help of God. I have never been able to do much without divine help. I of course knew a bunch of this stuff growing up in India and also from my reading. A large number of these concepts are available in Eastern philosophy.

Conscience is the most important aspect of our psyche that helps us towards retribution, said Anna. Anna knew that I was in that state of mind when a person is ready to be cleansed. So she asked me, "Tell me a poem that you might have read about it." So I recited,

    "'Since then, at an uncertain hour,
    That agony returns:
    And till my ghastly tale is told,
    This heart within me burns.
    He prayeth best, who loveth best
    All things both great and small,
    For the dear God who loveth us,
    He made and loveth all.'"
    (Coleridge, *Rime of the Ancient Mariner*)

Anna said that redemption and repentance are necessary ingredients for growth and she thought that my asking for forgiveness even silently would change my heart because positive energy would be transmitted towards me as quantum particles from those persons that I might have slighted. I accepted the explanation. I had read a bit about the principles of quantum mechanics (small particles of energy) as explained by Max Bohr and also Einstein's theory of general relativity and of space-time (big particles of energy).

In the cosmos whenever there is movement of matter, there are sounds that are not audible because space is almost a perfect vacuum and the vibrations of sound are called gravitational waves that are transmitted by movement or acceleration of big masses. I told Anna that light is emitted when small electrical charges accelerate and colors are possible because of different refraction of light through different media. I felt that Anna liked to hear me talk a bit about science now and then.

I was craving for some colors on the ground. Rhododendrons, azaleas, the delicate flowers of weigelas, or the scented buddleias that I call butterfly bushes. I wanted some jubilation for my eyes. What happened to the Philadelphus and the hydrangeas? I had planted most of these plants in my yard some time or other and I was missing them.

But I started secreting Ghrelin in my stomach and pleased myself by chewing on a power bar while I imagined making fresh orange soufflés as I stirred the egg whites and butter, and sugar in my mind. I added orange liqueur, lemon juice and heated the ramekins on the baking sheet. A big pickup truck went past me and some fluid from the road splashed against me. It broke my cooking spell.

"So why does a plant leaf change color?" I knew Anna was up to something. I said it had to something with chlorophyll. Anna said, "That may be, but it is because of the change in anthrocyanin, a pigment that is present in the wall of the cells. Until a few years back the anthrocyanin was not thought to be important. But now the botanists suggest that this pigment is responsible for the red colors in the leaves in the trees, e.g. red oak during the fall that are found in our part of the country and also even in the tropics are owing to different combinations of anthrocyanin, carotenoids and chlorophyll." In some conifers that I saw on the fields while walking, the old leaves have color because of this pigment, said Anna.

Dr. David Lee and Kevin Gould in *American Scientist* volume 90 said that Dr. Lucas of the University of Hong Kong has stated that the young red leaves in tropical forests are edible and are important in the diets of some primates. They have shown that chimpanzees and monkeys in Kibale forest in Uganda eat these leaves because of their high protein content. They have also shown that red to green shifts in leaf color are important cues that led to the evolution of three-color vision in certain primates (including humans), unique among all mammals. I asked Anna how she knows all this. She said that she can read while I am walking because she is never hot owing to the fact that she is always in the shade.

The trains moved continuously and almost all of them carried coal from Wyoming. Mining is big in Wyoming, much like in Kentucky and West Virginia. I passed more silos, corn fields and cement factories. Every seven and a half minutes a train went by. Ms. G got to know most of the engineers as she spent hours sitting on the roadside. The engineers tooted their engine horn as they passed by her. She felt like a child being noticed and enjoyed the flirt.

The sun peeked again and Anna appeared. The wind started pushing me hard. I had to walk into the wind at an angle away from the white line. I used my SPAVA sign as a jib while my feet were the keel that heeled while my cane tried to unzip the wind by poking in an area of its vulnerability. By the time I had reached Shelton I was ready to call it a day. I don't believe it's any duck soup to walk in Nebraska wind in late afternoon on hot concrete. Anna agreed. Anna said it's easy to get thrown in front of a truck when it passes by and squirts water on the face. It took all my strength and body weight to stand straight.

Go ahead and watch Peter Brosnan in *The Thomas Crown Affair* and you will see how his sailboat crumbled with the force of the wind. I ended the day with a prayer. Lord, I could never be like Job but give me the ability to trust and be your servant. Anna said God blessed Job and gave him all He thought Job needed. "He came to have fourteen thousand sheep and six thousand camels and a thousand spans of cattle and a thousand she-asses" (Job 42:12). I made a joke and said, "I am glad God is not going to give me all that because I could not fit all that in my condo."

I told Anna that I believe we have the most joy when we can do something for others. We as usual had a big discussion about religion. Anna said that when women get older they become more religious but men do not change. I agreed with her. My father had told me that a long time ago because some Sanskrit scholar had said such. But now Betsy Carter who is a contributing editor of *AARP* magazine said in the November 2004 issue that forty-nine percent women are "very religious" in their seventies whereas only twenty-eight percent of men consider themselves as such. She also stated that forty percent of Americans over forty-five say that the most satisfying religious or spiritual act is helping others.

Anna continued. "To have a peaceful mind or true spirituality it really doesn't matter what religion one belongs to or as to which God one considers for prayer. After all, peace does not belong to any one club nor is it owned by someone in particular. Whether you listen to Rajneesh or Maharishi or the Beatles or Grateful Dead or Billy Graham, peace is in the state of mind. This can be obtained by meditation or by praying but mostly by being quiet and allowing the mind to have room for thoughts of joyful unfolding of the soul and to feel the gentle touch of the Supreme on the petals of your life. We are born with a book that has leaves marked with our days on it. Every day we turn a leaf and the past one is gone and we again have an opportunity to write on the new leaf before it is turned. The way to write beautifully is to participate with Ananda (supreme joy) every day. It is only then the leaf will stand out as a peaceful and loving experience.

"Love is an energy that is felt but not seen. It is in the eye and it is in the smile."

I said to Anna that I agreed with that. I had operated on a lady at Louisville for a brain tumor some time in the past and she did very well for five years but then the tumor came back. I told her to go home and love everyone because her time was limited. I believe that we surgeons sometimes cannot cure certain illnesses but we can certainly make people miserable at times. She lived for about three months. But before she died in her house I sat by her side and held her hand during the night with her family gathered all around her. I still remember that she had looked at me more than once and smiled and had said "thank you."

"Anna, I carry that torch of love. I wept when she said something to me but we both knew that God was the master and she was in peace. There was Ananda in her heart that she passed on by saying good-bye to her family and her doctor. She died in dignity and not in some hospital, comatose with a fresh cut on her head. She had peace and all of us had peace because we loved her. We celebrated her life!

"Ben Franklin wrote in his Autobiography, 'He that is secure is not safe.' I have often thought about it and felt that I worked so hard to be secure, financially that is, yet I have not felt safe. I don't know what exactly Mr. Franklin meant by safety. I think he meant that the person who is secure possibly quits working and helping others and stops trying to make a difference. He possibly becomes a bum."

Anna didn't know what to say. She said, "Sometimes a person who is secure acts rich, looks rich and clean and may appear smug. That might engender anger in someone else and that might get him killed!"

It was a spectacular day as I walked towards Kearney. I went to the restroom at a Sinclair gas station and as I came out a man was waiting for me to learn about SPAVA. We chatted for a while and then he ran ahead of me and took some pictures as I passed him and then he told me that there would be an article in the *Kearney Hub*. I had met several other newspaper persons on the way already who had expressed interest in the program.

The crisp and gentle sunshine had excited me so much that I felt that a genie of energy was sitting on my shoulder that had clipped me much like the jockey does to a horse before the finish line. I kept moving faster to catch up with Anna only to see her move just as fast. Today by lunchtime I had walked sixteen miles.

I kept seeing a mirage at a distance on the black road that shimmered just like the reflection of sunlight that produces the image of water in desert sand. The grass on the side was tall and green and it was speckled with baby morning glory and wild roses. An occasional dandelion stood up like a rooster with a yellow ribbon. The aroma of the air was fresh and I sang several Beatle lyrics about love and changing the world.

I didn't have to wear my bra almost till eleven o'clock today. My socks were happy and dry and my feet danced with the butterfly that flew around me much like the pizzicato from an E string. I saw many butterflies that had died on the shoulders of the highway. Some were lying on top of the other as though they had died mating. I thought what a way to go!

Sunshine song of John Denver came to my mind. It always makes me feel free and wonderful. I sang like Johnny Cash or at least I thought I did. "You are my sunshine and you make me happy." I held a butterfly just as lightly as I could and I let it fly away. Escaping the tornado at Hastings had made me happy. I knew that I was walking through the tornado triangle that extended from upper Texas through Oklahoma, Kansas to North Platte, Nebraska, and I had to be constantly careful about wind shifts and mammatocumulus clouds. I liked the big name of the cloud.

I had memorized in medical school the symptoms that can develop after getting leptospiroicterohemorrhagica from rats and I also was proud when I was able to say cyclo-pentano-perhydro-phenanthrene ring of cholesterol. I still remember learning those names in medical school and how proud I felt to be able to pronounce those without taking a breath. I mostly liked the name of the muscle levator labii superioris alequae nasi, the little muscle attached to the upper lip and lateral part of our nose that moves when we whimper or breathe deep after running.

Ms. G knew about the clouds also because we had talked about it. If you look up and see the sky that has a copper beaten appearance, come and get me in a hurry, I had told her. Anna had taught me to locate highs and lows in the weather pattern. Highs generally bring fair weather and lows often bring cold or poor weather, said Anna. I stood with my back to the wind and turned about forty-five degrees to the right keeping my back to the wind. The high pressure center should be to my right and the low pressure to my left since I was in the northern hemisphere. This way I tried to determine how the wind was blowing and what to expect in the afternoon. I watched the dust devils as they whirled away in front of me and in the fields at distance. Anna said that as the hot air expanded over the heated places it rose and flew outward higher up. The pressure dropped in those pockets and the surrounding air rushed in with a swirling motion to form the whorls of wind warts. I experienced the heat on my feet and body as I walked past these areas of disturbance. I was always a little apprehensive in the late afternoons, particularly if the cloud patterns changed. I sometimes felt the wind move counterclockwise as I watched at a distance cumulonimbus clouds rise upwards. I always got out of the road fast on such occasions.

Anna was there for a while. I did not know how long she would stay. She started talking about the progress of medicine over the years. I told her that I loved the practice of medicine but I didn't like the stress that comes with a tough surgical field. Anna said, "Have you read about some of the illnesses that afflicted our presidents?" I answered in the affirmative. "Do you know about George Washington?" I didn't know what she was talking about. "Well, in 1799 the president became very sick. The best of the doctors took care of him. Those days as you know mercury was thought to cure almost everything, including syphilis."

"Did the president have that awful illness?"

"No," said Anna as though she was there. "Well, I wasn't there but I read about it. Wheat bran poultices were applied and his body was blistered to draw off demonic or putrefying liquids that needed to be drawn out from inside him. Then calomel—mercuric chloride—was applied. He was barely able to speak possibly from fever and weakness but it is believed that he had asked the doctors to bleed him. He was bled on four occasions in twenty-four hours and then he succumbed to the treatment or the illness, we don't know." Anna's voice was shaking. The wind had picked up a bit. I was almost in tears feeling the pain the president must have felt.

"We have come a long way since then, Anna." I was a child in 1952. I remember one late afternoon of July when I went with my grandfather to a courtyard. A man had a shoe in his mouth and he was jerking while lying on cement floor and his mouth was filled with slimy froth like that in an angry steer. A big red ring was drawn around him with Sindur (a mercuric paint). There was a man clad in dhoti that was tied to his back through his crotch in such manner that he could jump freely holding a broom in his hand. He ran around the debilitated shaking victim who was lying almost unconscious on the hot cement floor. The fellow with the broom was also chanting some sort of syllables that were neither Hindi nor Sanskrit. The temperature was probably one hundred degrees with very high humidity. There were of course many observers as is often the case in any event in India.

Everyone was excited, hot and sweaty and many were readily offering their suggestions regarding the management of this illness called Mirgi. My grandfather explained to me that many a patient had died from dehydration and exhaustion and suffered permanent brain damage from such local treatment of seizures. However, none bit their tongue because of the placement of the shoe.

In ancient times, many people in the community felt that supernatural forces caused "the Falling Sickness" (Owsei Temkin, Johns Hopkins University Press, 1971). In Mark 9:14-29, Matthew 17:15, Luke 9: 37-43, a man brings his child with epilepsy to the disciples but they are unable to cure him. When the disciples asked Jesus as to why they were unable to cure the boy Jesus replied that this kind of "spirit can come out by nothing, save by prayer." When Othello kills Desdemona in an act of jealousy and then kills himself in anguish when he learns that it was a plot laid by Iago and Cassio was not involved at all in seducing Desdemona, he wails, "I loved not wisely but too well" (Act V; 2). But Desdemona believed that Othello had seizures because she whispers while being strangled:

"And yet I fear you; for you're fatal then
When your eyes roll so…" (*Othello* Act V; 2; 37-38)

The Brothers Karamazov was written by Dostoyevsky in 1879 where he describes Fyodor Karamazov and his four sons. Dmitri, the oldest, and two middle sons by a different mother and Smerdyakov, an illegitimate son who works as a servant in the house and resents the privileges the other brothers enjoy. Smerdyakov is described as having seizures repeatedly through the years. Then he murders his father, faking a seizure and subsequent sleep to establish an alibi for himself. He gloats when Dmitri is accused of the murder when Dmitri says, "I may be a thief but not a scoundrel."

In *Silas Marner* the reclusive weaver had frequent seizures and he became motionless and staring. Because he was a devout Christian these episodes were thought to be divine visitations. In more recent times Dr. Michael Crichton after graduating from medical school has written several great books and TV scripts. *The Terminal Man* (New York, 1972) is a story about Harry Benson who is a computer expert and is paranoid and thinks that computers are going to take over the world. He develops psychomotor seizures after an accident and begins to kill people. The impression some people got after reading the book was that most psychomotor epileptics are violent people with character disorder and now it is known that is not the usual case.

Continuing Fun Through Nebraska

There were indeed a few experiences that would be of interest to the reader in case any of them choose to walk through this area. I had walked past Dix and that was almost thirty-three miles that day. We had stopped to eat lunch at Ma Barker's place. This was a little place and was just right for me because I wanted to get out of the wind. My van met me at the door. An older man greeted us after we had waited for about ten minutes at the reception area and that too only when a younger woman (I presumed his wife) yelled at him. He came over and told us that he had an order of thirty hamburgers and he wouldn't be able to serve us for about forty-five minutes. It is interesting to note that we were the only customers at that time. I didn't want to argue with him.

We walked across the road to the next shed that served great food and the place was packed. I had many loose thoughts that went fleeting with the wind. I talked to Anna about Jack Kerouac and then hummed the lyric of Willie Nelson's song "On the Road Again." I liked the fact that there was no one to critique my musical abilities. This was a day that belonged more to Nat King Cole, "fly right with the monkey on the back." I had walked to Elm's Creek. I planned to sleep at Lexington because there was no motel before that. I thought we would drive the twenty-four miles to the motel and then drive back here in the morning to start my walk. As the day went further Anna moved to the side. I had to talk a bit louder because I had lost a bit of hearing by now. The train track had moved away for a while beyond the south shore of the ocean of cornfields. I drank about four liters of fluids today before going to dinner. Some of the evenings were always most wonderful. I drank about a pint of whiskey and then gorged myself with an enormous amount of Chinese food and fell asleep.

There were a few days when after lunch I rested for an hour or so to avoid the incredible heat of the road. Anna knew that I usually read those days a bit.

I was always learning ways to avoid trouble on the road as well. I moved some stuff from the road wearing rubber gloves that I carried with me. I also used sterile gloves when I cleaned my blisters. "OK, so you want to play a game to see who knows more about latex?"

I said all right thinking that I might know more.

Anna—"Do you know that natural rubber latex allergy can be life threatening?"

Tim—"Yes. Dr. Halstead from Johns Hopkins introduced rubber latex gloves in surgery in 1890 because of his acquaintance with a nurse who was the daughter of the owner of Good Year rubber."

Anna—"I didn't know that. Tire dust, the black powder residue on the road or in the air contains NRL protein (natural rubber latex) components. These can sensitize a person at most inconvenient times! Allergic reactions to latex are caused only by NRL derived from rubber tree sap."

"OK, Anna, you tell me where does the sap come from?"

"Hmm… OK, from South America but now mostly from Malaysia. OK, Tim, since you teach school you should know this. Pencil erasers, mouse pads, hot water bottles and Band-Aids are normally non-allergenic but may spark a reaction at times."

I said, "We surgeons have to be careful of the powder that comes with many gloves. It can retain the protein and then it becomes airborne after donning the gloves and can precipitate asthma or dermatitis."

I always enjoyed these question/answer sessions with Anna. I always felt that these are the types of questions that require quick thinking. I had prepared for the oral examinations that I had taken in the past by using this method. I remembered asking my colleague, Dr. Tom Farmer, professor emeritus of neurology of the University of North Carolina, to give me a practice test before I had taken the neurological surgery board examination.

The horn honked. Ms. G had come early. She told me where she was going to be so I would know exactly how far to walk before the next water break. I had progressed to Kearney and then I walked towards Brady.

Ms. Minnie called. "Hey Dad, guess what? I want you to come and take care of me for a few days before I have the baby." I was flattered. I put more muscle into my walk. She had taught the other two children to sign before they had learnt to talk. Dr. Linda Acredolo, professor of psychology at the University of California-Davis, and Dr. Susan Goodwyn, professor of child development of California State University at Stanislaus, had co-authored a best-selling book, *Baby Signs*. "Dad, the baby sign language has reduced the frustration and thus my children don't have the tantrums," said Minnie. We talked about the weather in the Bay area.

I was surprised that the wind picked up by nine in the morning. It came from the east. I withstood lashes of wind that practically pushed me onto the oncoming traffic. It whinnied as it went between the cuffs of my hat and my ears. I kept walking with my knees partially flexed and hips steady and my body like a boat kept going forward on a steady keel. I felt a new blister as it was developing in my right heel and the left shoe felt a little tighter. I knew that this peculiar posture caused some swelling too.

I held my SPAVA sign high, much like the soldiers held the American flag in the movie *Patriot*, though it flittered and fluttered as the wind tried to tear it off my backpack.

This walkathon was for the kids and I didn't want that fact to be diminished by taking down the sign. I was angry at the wind and then I became depressed being afraid of the possibility that I might not be able to complete the journey if my feet hurt too much more.

I tried to change my thinking process. I tried to prepare my class lessons in regard to littering. I had already listed in my notebook mirrors, screws, nails, doorjambs, toilet paper, empty Kleenex boxes, cigarette packs, bikinis, condoms, beer bottles, personal bloody items and diapers filled with feces. I planned a discussion on respect for the environment.

At this moment I also felt a great need to be loved. I had felt like that in the past at times. What I mean is that in such situations I just like to be held and to hear someone tell me that I am wonderful and that everyone is proud of me. Anna wasn't there today. So I yelled hoping that she would hear. Do you know that almost 30,000 people committed suicide in the United States in the year 2000? Do you know that many children feel that they are unlovable? And for that matter many adults feel very similarly. I felt helpless, just as many children feel before they kill themselves. I felt that I would feel ashamed if I hadn't finished the task. Maybe everyone would be better off if I were dead and particularly if I couldn't live up to my promise.

I remembered that when I was about eighteen years old I had jumped off a pole that was almost two stories high and had broken my ankle. I had climbed the pole to show off in front of girls. After reaching the top I had realized that I would hurt my hands if I were to try to come down the same way I had gone up. I was always extra careful with my hands because I knew that someday

I was going to be a neurosurgeon. I had walked almost an hour on the broken ankle till I succumbed to the pain. Well! I think I fainted on the road.

It was little past two in the afternoon and I had sat down on the grass a bit as I did many times because I had no urgency and I liked to enjoy the scenery rather than just walk past everything and not even see them. A lizard was sitting on a piece of wood and it looked up at me. It had stopped raining and Anna had returned. The grass was a bit wet but I had a plastic raincoat in my pack and so I didn't care. So I was telling Anna about the Geiko commercial with the voice of some guy speaking English with a funny accent. "Do you know much about geckos, Tim?" I said that I have seen many in India on our walls. Grandpa had said that they ate the mosquitoes and other insects. I always admired their ability to walk on the vertical walls and the ceilings. Grandpa had said that they have special toes that have gripping power.

But now I know that one of the greatest gecko experts is actually Professor Kellar Autumn from Portland, Oregon. He wrote an article in *American Scientist*, volume 94, "How Gecko Toes Stick." He said that the pad of a gecko toe is crossed by ridges covered with hairlike stalks called setae, which branch into hundreds of tiny endings. He went on to say that gecko toes do not get dirty and it can attach to any surface except Teflon. Anna was amazed to know that there are 14,400 setae per square millimeter of its feet. The professor quoted many other scientists and said that gecko adhesion is certainly the result of "molecular interactions rather than mechanical interlocking."

Professor Autumn is trying to design boots that can be used to climb vertical walls. I guess we won't need Jackie Chan or James Bond anymore!

I had to shut my eyes each time as the cars and trucks squirted water on my face as they passed me going in opposite direction. My legs and my hips were inflamed from the repetitive syndrome of walking daily to such great distances. I could not take it anymore. I just lay down on the side of the road as I stared at the cows that stood in muddy corrals. The rain had gotten me wet. Ms. G passed me by because she couldn't see me on account of me being so close to the ground and pouring down rain. However, she returned soon knowing that I could not have walked as far as she had gone.

The wind had died after pushing me around for a while. The rain stopped again. After changing my clothes I limped to Cattlemen's Lounge and ate a huge lunch. I decided on another SPAVA lesson. I thought that it would be important to teach about the sadness that overcomes us when we feel that we are burdensome. I thought that we need to discuss with the children that there are almost 800,000 suicide attempts every year and SPAVA can help reduce that. A classmate of mine had killed himself after feeling jilted. He was a professor of psychiatry.

We had reached Gothenburg, our destination for the night. It was a little restaurant. The name slips my mind. "So you are the fellow walking with a sign that I had seen earlier?"

"Yes, that's me," I said softly. I stopped eating to talk to him.

"I overheard your conversation with this lady over here and it seemed to me you are some kind of a doctor or such."

I introduced Ms. G to him. "I am a neurosurgeon."

"So what has that got to do with the walk?" I told him that there was no connection. "I am not asking for a free opinion or such." I figured he was disturbed about some serious problem. "My grandson is six months old and he has kind of a long head you know. It is not real long or such but different from mine. The surgeons are planning to do an operation in a couple of days."

I reassured him and told him that sagittal craniostenosis is not uncommon and the operation will improve the shape of the head of the baby. There is a slight chance of developmental delay with single suture synostosis but he should talk to the doctor for proper follow-up and reassurance.

He was pleased. "Can I buy you a dessert?" I said yes. I knew he wanted to do something. I feel good when I can do something for someone else and I figured he did too.

People in Nebraska were friendly and they stopped and asked me about the walk. One person said, "Are you crazy? People die in this heat."

"No," I said, "I am just a neurosurgeon."

I thought that this was my opportunity to get to know the great state, Nebraska, the state of the financial guru, Warren Buffet, home of Arbor Day Foundation and the temporary home for the cows that qualify to be Omaha Steaks. So I talked to people and learned all they could tell me. I had stopped at Brady for the night before I took off for North Platte. I passed by a big junk yard where I saw many cars in different stages of decomposition. Rust was the predominant color that they had acquired. I didn't notice any maggots on the steel but there might have been a few rats. I was high spirited. Anna was tall in the morning. "Don't chew too much gum," she said. "You will get TMJ pain." I agreed.

The wind came from the northwest today. It was cold. I almost ran the last eight miles. I was excited like the horses that race at Churchill Downs during the fall season. I was clammy and my shirt was wet. I was sweaty but I felt good when I took my shirt off. I was becoming slightly narcissistic. I almost liked the sweet smell! "I am glad that you strengthened your lower abdominal muscles prior to starting your walk," said Anna. "Nobody can prepare to not have blisters in this type of an extreme sport." I agreed.

On the way to Paxton I met the owner of a hunting lodge. It seemed that he was a promoter of some sort. I moved on. I stood in the rain next to a pay phone and talked to Mr. Reed from the local radio station. My Sprint cell phone did not work through most of Nebraska.

I went to a barber shop at Chappelle. "What kind of clipper do they normally use on you?"

"Number 2 for the top and then number 1 for the sides. I also like my neck and the whitewalls done with a razor please. I have brought my own razor."

"It is not necessary. I have disposable razors." He had a tie and a suit on.

"How long you have been cutting hair?"

"Almost forty years. I was born just a few miles west of Chappelle. I have eight siblings. I served in the navy during the Korean War and after that I went to Omaha to go to the barber school. My name is Kirk. It is pronounced just like 'jerk' except with a K. It is a Czechoslovakian name."

"What do they grow over here?"

"This is all wheat country."

"Do you live on a wheat farm?"

"No, I can't afford it. I am not that rich. An average farm here is about ten to fifteen thousand acres."

"How much do I owe you?"

"Seven dollars." I liked that. I gave him a two-dollar tip and a SPAVA shirt. Just before I left I told him to see a Steve Martin movie called *The Jerk*. I told him that he would have a few laughs.

I started walking in the afternoon towards Ogallala. I had passed through Sutherland earlier. It is a small place with a restaurant at Maline's grocery. I had a long chat with Mr. Maline during eating. I met Ms. Vivian. A kindly woman she is. She served me the salad because she realized that I didn't want to get up to serve myself. My husband is a state trooper. He was posted at Ft. Knox for a while. We talked and asked each other questions about Dixie

Highway and the places where we both might have been in the past. I had told her that I had an office on Dixie Highway about twenty- five miles outside Louisville. She gave me a gift of a can of energy tea without sugar. "You will like this," she said. I certainly did. I bought two gallons of it on the way.

I walked a bit late into the afternoon. Suddenly strong wind came gushing towards me and almost ripped my clothes off. Later on I heard the weatherman on TV saying that the wind gusts might have been fifty miles an hour. I began to feel like a dressed chicken. "The only animal that is actually naked when addressed as dressed," said Anna. I had been to a chicken factory once. I saw how the chickens are placed in a centrifuge and whirled at the speed of a comet so that the feathers fly off leaving a clean dressed and limp chicken. I stopped before the latter happened.

I told Anna the story of a patient of mine. I had stopped in his room to see how he was feeling after heart surgery.

He said, "At 4 p.m. a nurse came and said, 'You are going to have a little blood test.' Shortly after that Tammy, a phlebotomist, came and took six tubes of blood. Before I could recover from my anemia an orderly came and said, 'I have to shave you a bit.'

"Well, shaving he did indeed, from my chin down to my toes after lathering me up. After he left I looked at myself in the mirror. I couldn't believe it. I looked like a turkey or more like a white whale with some flakes of egg whites on my skin, a bit of the shaving cream that he had missed when he had wiped me clean. Then in the evening the doctor came and said, 'John, it's going to hurt a little bit when you wake up.' Well, the doctor had a bigger tolerance for pain than I did. It didn't hurt him a even a little bit whereas I woke up with a tube in my throat and tubes and pipes hanging from every opening in my body and the nurse told me not to move too much but just let her know if I was hurting! I couldn't talk much on account of a tube in my nose and a sore throat."

I don't wear a piece so I didn't worry about the wind blowing it off. I was moving as fast as I could. The train track had returned to my left again after having gone to my right for a short time near North Platte. Anna had left. I was thinking of Don Giovanni refusing to repent in death bed and then the violin in full harmony. I looked up and saw Anna's legs dangling from the clouds. Think of William Tell and you will be energized and hold your son high in joy and love. Anna, I would like to go to sleep and feel the warmth of the light of the candles from the candlesticks that the Bishop gave to Jean Val Jean. Just about this time a truck whisked past me and filled my face with a spray of water that was far from the holy water I was dreaming about. I decided to call it a day.

The day began with Surya Pronam. I was joyful and happy. Anna was with me. The sun was mild and it shone through the clouds such that the rays projected like spikes of a comb and gently scratched my back. The consort wind was a mild breeze that caressed me. I felt loved. I was on Highway 30 West, passing by Lake McConaughy, at Ogallala on my way to Sidney. Anna and I played an animal game. Tim—alligator, Anna—beaver, T—cat, A—dog, and we went on till we could reach zebra.

I was like a racehorse. But I have never been given the opportunity to be tied up for providing special services that good thoroughbreds get to provide when the mares are brought to them. Don't give up. Abraham impregnated Sarah when he was more than a hundred years old. "Do you know why Abraham didn't know how to add?"

"No," I said.

"That's because God told him to multiply!"

I was beginning to develop Stendhal syndrome, which is a condition named after the nineteenth-century French novelist and is manifested by exhaustion, nausea and disorientation not unlike common shock. It resulted from the visitors being overwhelmed by Italy's beauty.

So I often sat down to enjoy the scenery. My goal was coming to fruition. It is much like Focus Zen, i.e. different goals can be reached by persistence and determination. I had long passed Kearney and through Brady I had moved towards North Platte. I had to walk a bit to get outside the town till I found a safe shoulder. Anna wasn't there most of the day. But for me it was a "superfragilistic" day. Soon after 9 a.m. the wind picked up. It came from the east.

I was whipped by the lashes of the wind that came in gusts practically throwing me forward every few minutes. It whinnied and screamed as it ran between the cuffs of my hat and my ears. I had to keep my knees partially flexed and hips steady while I imagined tacking my sailboat to keep going forward.

I developed a new blister in the right foot because of the constant changing dynamics of my feet. I noticed that sometimes there was more swelling of one foot and at other times the other. I passed by many cows that looked at me longingly. However, there was nothing I could do. They stood in the rain in muddy corrals. My ischial tuberosity, the bone under my butt, had become extremely sore because the hamstring muscles were exercised to their full potential for prolonged periods.

I limped into a restaurant lounge and Ms. G soon joined me for lunch. I told her that on the way I saw a guy in a pickup truck dump trash on the highway including tires and some chicken wire etc. I acted like I didn't see him. I was afraid that he would run me over if he thought that I had seen him. I had passed through a small place called Overton that was hit by a tornado about three hours after I had left. Today I had to change my shirt several times because I was often drenched in sweat from the extra work against the wind and I was feeling cold from the moisture.

I had a very difficult time on the way to Sidney. The temperature had gone up and humidity was almost ninety-seven percent. I was drenched in my sweat so much that I was getting cramps. I drank two Gatorades and then a Red Bull and stopped for lunch at Kitchen Kettle. On the way a couple of dogs started barking and almost attacked me. I pointed my walking stick and yelled "Down, boy." The dogs sat down and wagged their tails. I had learnt this trick with my cane from the Charleston Heston movie when he was Moses and had made snakes with his stick and subsequently he had split the Red Sea. I felt powerful, but maybe not as much as he had felt!

I knew that walking through Nebraska in summertime is risky because of the unpredictable storms. I was way past it now. I had to remember every day what Katherine Matheney had written in the Salesian Mission Inspirational Books about trusting God.

He won't forsake or turn away,
He will guide you safely home some day.

In my case I was hoping that I would be home in about ninety days.

The train whistled. It was getting late and I thought this would be the time to quit today. I ended the day with a recitation from the Bible, "In green pastures You let me graze; to safe waters You lead me" (Psalm 23:2).

I was talking about the fact that my cane often helped me when dogs chased me or were trying to bite me. It has been sometime past when I had trained my dog so well that it would walk side by side with me without a leash.

I have observed many times when people take their dogs for a walk it is actually the dog that is pulling them. I never liked that. I never liked it when I visited some people's house and their dog came and rubbed its body against my clothes. So I trained my dog such that he did he not do that but would kiss your cheeks if you extended your arms and invited the dog to show its affection. My Lassie placed both front legs on my forearms and reached to kiss me when I came home.

So I was thinking how a domestic animal is distinctly different from a tame individual of a wild species. A dog is a domestic animal and a wolf is not, even when it is brought up from birth by humans. A tame animal does not pass its tameness to its offspring: taming is not a genetic heritable change but in contrast domestication is genetic. I had a Malamute once. It never barked and was very well trained. But every spring it chased the baby sheep when they were born and ate them whole. Baby wool and all! That was his wolf trait. In the evening Blondie raised its head towards the sky and howled.

I knew that I had spent a night at Kimball in a motel. The people who helped me were less than courteous. She complained that her daughter is attending U. Penn and it costs forty-five thousand dollars per year and therefore she did not want to give me a discount when I had asked for one. "I don't care much for non-profit organization," she said with an East German accent I think. I did not argue. I ate at BJ's at Kimball. A young college student, Kyle, who was going to school at Hastings, served us. His smile was the best part of the dinner. He had served me an eighteen-ounce steak and had charged me only ten dollars! I gave him a SPAVA shirt on top of his tip. He was mighty pleased.

The road was straight and the air was full of bugs. The gnats tried to get inside my nose and the aroma of my face had attracted flies. They continuously sat on the rim of my hat and flew in front of my face. I was getting supremely aggravated. So I took my undershirt in my left hand and continuously swung it in front of my face as I marched forward. Anna was talking about horses and wanted to distract me. "Have you ever ridden horses on a beach?"

I told her that I have ridden horses on the beaches of Agadir. I cantered through the waves; fell in the ebullient and effervescent froth of the tired waves as they were crawling after having entered the beach with forceful thrusts. I have galloped on the brown sand, soaked in sunshine and rested in a Bedouin tent while licking on scoops of ice cream tinged with Campari and Galliano.

It was at Katmandu that I met this beautiful Arab girl. She had a tanni shyma (Sanskrit for a narrow waist) with limpid eyes that had a mesmerizing effect on me. I felt like I was sitting in a warm bath with half-shut eyes with arms and legs stretched out. I needed… well, I wanted her to seduce me. She walked in with water dripping from her hips that were built like that of a *yakshi* and her pink nipples were playing hide and seek through a partially wet choli as she moved around in a rhythmic raga. She pressed a button and the record player started playing an old Bengali song, "Ai Sundar Sarnali Sandhya Eki Bandhane Jarale go Bandhu" (In this beautiful golden evening my friend how have we gotten entangled). Her hips swayed in a slow gyrating motion that progressively went up in tempo. I suddenly became aware that my mouth was open. Well, it was only possible in Nepal that I was able to get an Israeli girl to share a room with an Arab woman.

"Come and visit me if you ever come to Lebanon," she said as I went to say good-bye to her. I have not been to Lebanon yet.

It was at Ogallala that I had met Ms. S. She was wonderful and kind. "I am always looking for a discount in life," I told her as I was checking in her motel, Comfort Inn.

"I will call Alex and see if he can do something to help you." She let me stay for free the next two nights. She said that Alex said that he couldn't walk with me but he wanted to help. Alex owned the place. I said I was grateful. Whenever I got such a discount I spent two or three nights in such places. I walked about fifty miles ahead of the place by the end of second day and although it was inconvenient to drive back to sleep I still saved money this way. I needed to do that since I didn't have any real sponsors.

"Hey, you want to hear a joke?" said Anna. I was eager to hear anything that would lighten my load. She said that she had heard it at Hawaii during a medical meeting. Mr. Clinton had invited Mr. Sharon to the White House for some sort of peace deal between Palestine and Israel. Mr. Sharon was curious about the three telephones in the president's office. Mr. Clinton explained that the red phone is dusty because we don't talk to the Russians anymore. The white phone is worn out because it is used to talk to the senators. The most expensive gold phone took fifty thousand dollars to install and it costs ten thousand dollars a minute for the long-distance call to God.

A few months later Mr. Bush visited Israel and saw three phones that Mr. Sharon had installed. Mr. Sharon explained that he had gotten the idea from the Americans. The red phone was not used anymore because Arafat had died. The white phone is worn out from using it to ask the Americans to quit bothering him and the gold phone is the least expensive. It cost twenty dollars to install and it is ten cents a minute for the call because the call to God is local!

Anna sometimes talked politics with me and at other times just whatever was in her mind. She started talking about Bill Clinton and Al Gore and we were discussing the speeches they gave to impress us prior to the election. I recall hearing, hopefully incorrectly, Al Gore saying something like he had something to do with the invention of the internet. Anna said Tim Berners-Lee of MIT envisioned the global information space where documents stored in computers everywhere could be interconnected and would be available to every ne.

"Anna, do people with different names than the majority get less respect even now?"

"Well, there is still quite a bit of prejudice," Anna said. "If someone's name is Latowan and he applies for a job with a guy named John it is possible that the latter would get the job and the boss man would find some excuse to make sure that his decision won't sound like a racial bias. For that matter all ethnic names get a seat in the back of the bus, I think. Faulkner wrote in *Light in August* after Armstid got into his wagon: 'He waked the mules. That is he put them into motion, since only a "negro" can tell when a mule is asleep or awake. His name is Christmas. Is he a foreigner? Did you hear of a white man named Christmas the foreman said? I never heard of nobody a-tall named it.' Well, thinking like that is changing. Look at the scene at Louisville. Folks treated the Japanese goods as cheap replicas. Now there are fancy sushi places and people are learning the culture rather than consider it inferior.

"I think that some of the Americans got it wrong for a while about people that came from different lands. Many people thought that just because America had won the Second World War therefore the people in it must be superior. That is far from the truth. America is like an orchard where almost all the trees have been grafted with varying genetic material, thus producing different fruits and flowers that are better and more productive than the original kind. And that is progress," said Anna.

"America is benefiting from the diverse genetic pool producing smarter people and they also live longer. Faulkner wrote 'My, My. A body does get around. Here we ain't been coming from Alabama but two months, and now it's already Tennessee.' I am myself a foreigner and have an ethnic name to boot." Anna was listening closely what I was going to say next.

I was getting closer to Wyoming every day. I thought I could be at Cheyenne in less than seven days. I could talk to Anna about everything. I had nothing else to do but talk Anna.

"Do you know anything about condoms?"

"No. I don't need them."

So, I wanted her to know about it. I had nothing else to do but talk. Anna said, "Tim, you have a habit of trying to educate even if someone does not ask you." I knew she wasn't angry.

"Julius Schmidt was a German immigrant who had become rich by designing condoms based on his knowledge of sausage casings. The strange thing about it is that he was paralyzed."

Anna said, "Everything is possible in America because the last three letters of American are I Can."

"Bravo! I didn't know that. I had bought some shares of a condom company in the mid eighties. I lost quite a bit of money because the folks that contracted HIV infection didn't buy as many condoms as the company had predicted according to the pre-marketing study."

"The invention of the pill revolutionized the American sex arena and gave tremendous freedom and of course as with any freedom when not used correctly harm overcomes," said Anna.

"The Victorian ethos of self-control and participation in self-abuse has never been too successful for the population at large. Condoms helped prevent some venereal disease, I believe."

Anna nodded. "I don't have the data from the time of the World War I," said Anna.

"There is a lot of discussion about passing out free condoms to the youth by some while others promote abstinence."

Anna said, "Our social statistics indicate that promoting abstinence is fine but availability of condoms to those that can't control themselves or their urges might reduce sexually transmitted diseases and also unwanted pregnancies."

I don't know how the topic of Mt. St. Helens came up but I believe because we were talking about condoms and explosions. But I was telling Anna that when the top blew up in 1980 the ash fell from the sky all the way to outskirts of Vancouver, Washington. There are many myths and rituals that are associated with volcanic eruption. Some people believe that volcanoes erupt for justice or vengeance.

I had been to Tanzania and Kenya in the past and I knew that the Masai tribe honors Oldonyo-Lengai and believe it is giver of good things. I had read that young mothers expressed their gratitude after an eruption by expressing their breast milk on the ground in the past. Hawaiians believe that the volcanic eruption is the menstruation of goddess Pele and the crack in the mountain is considered to be the huge vagina and the flow of the lava to the sea is the same path that the women took to cleanse themselves in the past. I have been to the big island of Hawaii to see the lava falling into the ocean!

It was time for lunch and "feet care" because I had developed gigantic blisters on the inner side of my big toes despite the use of mole skin. Yes, they were gigantic! The blisters extended from the inside of my feet to halfway to the bottom along the ball of my feet. I changed socks two or three times per day almost always. The shoe aficionados always say that ill-fitting shoes give rise to blisters. I agree with them on some occasions. The friction of the feet inside the shoes and the heat from the road cannot be controlled adequately to halt the devastating effect on the feet. I felt that I could have walked forever if blisters hadn't hampered my progress.

I sat in the van with my feet up on the dash for a while. After they were kind of dry I looked at my feet. I always felt worse after I saw the heaps of fluid-filled "gol goppas" (small puffed round Indian bread which are punctured with the thumb and filled with tamarind juice prior to eating) under my toes, along the entire bottom and now at my heel. The ones at the heel were most painful.

I sterilized my sewing needle with a lighter and then punctured every one of these fluid-filled malefactors and drained their disdainful sticky secretions. I was angry at them. But I was always respectful of their potential to do harm and thus wiped my wounds with iodine and Mercurochrome prior to covering them with my socks. Some of these blisters were underneath calluses that had formed over previous blisters and thus required a deeper puncture and a bit of gritting of my teeth as I squeezed them to get rid of the turgid tension. In such situations I always thought of the joy of drinking whiskey in the night and that somehow helped me to tolerate the present situation better.

Philosophy on the Road

Bhagavad-Gita says, "All sorrows are destroyed upon attainment of tranquility. The intellect of such a tranquil person becomes completely steady." I told Anna that I have a hard time following this because I often get angry and then if I can't do anything about it I get sad. Anna quoted from Buddha's saying. "Holding on to anger is like holding on to a hot coal with the intent of throwing it at someone else: you are the one who gets burnt." This is what we try to teach in our classes.

"Did you know that you were predestined to participate in this walk?"

"Yes," I said. But I have real problems when I hear strong views whether it is in Christian faith or in Islam. Hindus and Buddhists accept everyone although orthodox Hindus may not 'break bread' with folks of different religions. I once heard a Baptist preacher strongly criticize Hinduism because he thought people believe in Karma.

"He said this was a fatalistic statement and there was no recourse whereas in Christianity we go to heaven no matter what. Well, here is the issue. 'As you sow, so shall you reap' is the law of the Karma. The 'reaping,' I believe, is implied across several life spans and not necessarily during the time of 'sowing.' Buddhists believe in reincarnation as do the Hindus.

"I think some preachers clearly do not understand or do not preach from the pulpit the distinction between way of living and the way to Heaven. I cannot imagine that loving God would allow us all up there, the way we are most of the time on earth, with Him to sit on the same bench. I mean all those who are kind and generous with those who are mean and thieves and disrespectful. I do not claim to understand His ways but I know that there would be a chaos 'Up There' if we didn't change during the transit because otherwise the final place wouldn't be so attractive. Many are either sitting or not sitting besides thieves and criminals now. So what would be different? I do not know if I will have consciousness like on earth. If so what will make me feel so good to sit next to a thief in heaven if I don't sit next to him on earth now? I know I am not supposed to be judgmental. I know I am a sinner but I would have to be transformed in my thinking not to be judgmental because there is no grading in sin business. Because when Jesus said, 'Let any man who is without sin through the first stone,' no one did.

"The Bible clearly talks about our 'work' on earth, which is basically Karma, and 'free will' concept is from man's point of view because God already knows what we are going to do under all circumstances."

Anna said, "But here is the catch. If you are a believer God will make your free will to match with divine intentions and thus your Karma will be such that it will liberate you from perpetual births."

After Kimball I was on a roll. I could dream of Pine Bluff now. I knew that I could make it in a couple of days. I sucked on my water pipe often today and walked on a straight line. I practiced walking straight, like the Native Americans are known to be capable of doing, on the white line through the middle of the road. I realized that I could never be an iron worker, walking on the bars of fifty-first floors in open air carrying a pouch on my hip, building the Empire State Building or any building for that matter.

I could see for miles that no cars were coming. So I would walk towards the track and pee whenever I wanted. Thank God I am a man. I ate a banana and drank some more water. I was always in a happy mood because I ate a lot of protein and the walking released a ton of endorphins. I am a big believer of Dr. Robert Cloninger's research from Washington University of St. Louis. He said that individuals largely inherit their temperamental styles and characters. These traits are based on novelty seeking, reward dependence and persistence. The St. Louis scientists devised three character dimensions such as self-directedness, which is a measure of the goals and purposes in life. They also stated that character development includes cooperativeness associated with strong feelings of spirituality and connection with nature.

There was no one around me and so I thought I would run for a while. I picked up the tempo and praised the Lord for my feet and also for the love in my heart. I also thanked my mom who gave her life for me.

I ran just a little bit and thought in my mind that preparation for this walk was probably the most difficult task I had carried out already. The thought that I couldn't finish had never entered my mind. I just wanted to know in my mind when that time was going to come. I sometimes wished that life would be easy like when I am doing a load of laundry. As soon as the spin cycle would end I would know that in a short period my clothes would be ready and dry. Hardest thing for me always has been the uncertainty and lack of control. My lawyer once told me that. You don't have to control the money or anything after you are dead. Let it be someone else's decision. Let it go. This walk I thought would teach me self-control and conquer the spirit to let go. I wanted to have the power of not owning and not having, not possessing but just of letting go and yet loving. The processing of plans in life is typically iterative, and that is as life changes or different goals are identified, changes in one part prompt changes in another. I often am not aware of my impatience.

I was feeling stronger and my feet had become used to the fact that they had an assignment and they were obliged to fulfill it. I wanted to tell Anna about my grandfather because I always think of him whenever I am alone. Then I don't feel lonesome.

"Do you know why you feel that way?"

"What's that?"

"Like no one is around you?"

"I think part of it is because I am a surgeon and I have gotten used to the fact that everyone does something continuously to help me to do what needs to be done. I think it is not possible to have someone else in life who likes the similar things as I do all the time. But secretly in my mind I wish I had a person beside me with whom I could share all my weaknesses. I am tired of being tough. So I cry silently and don't even wipe my tears. I let them run to my lips and I taste the salt and cry some more. Sometimes I don't even know why I cry.

"Do you know that it is almost impossible to be a perfect fit with your spouse? It is impossible to be able to fulfill all the dreams of each other or meet all our partner's needs, intellectual, emotional and sexual. I think meeting the sexual need often fulfills the others for men. I am not sure that I fit tidily into the mold of a traditional husband and yet I have this spirit of expecting my partner to fit into the traditional mold in a traditional closed marriage. I am not like Procrustes of Eleusis who cut off bits and pieces till he fit in the perfect mold. But it seems that I need a better mold. I think there is a great weakness in myself. It is a sense of hidden jealousy. My ego will not allow it to be exposed even to myself at times by creating all sorts of barriers so I can deny it. Nena and George O'Neills suggest a few guidelines in their book on Open Marriage. (1) Each person is entitled to enjoy new companions and experiences outside the marriage (2) All of us need someone to share our deepest intimacies: someone whom we can trust and someone who returns the trust. My upbringing has made me a traditional husband with one great inadequacy that many traditional couples share.

"There is a romantic notion in my head that my partner should somehow guess what I think, feel and long for and should be eager to give it to me! Well! It has happened once but not going to happen again."

"So why don't you learn to communicate better?" said Anna.

I unbuttoned my shirt for some air to cool my skin. It was a blistering day with warm air that was trying to scald my eyes. I thought that Anna touched me and kissed me on my wet cheek. I sat on the side of the road on my mat. There was often a small road that connected Highway 30 to someone's property on the south or north side of the train track. I used these oases to place my back against the telephone poles and faced the track. The trains that went by were always carrying cargo such as coal in open containers or large metal containers that became the cargo for the semis. I assumed the coal came from Wyoming. I didn't want to expose myself in front of others and therefore I waited for the engineer sitting in the engine to pass first. They don't have cabooses anymore so I didn't have to worry or hurry.

"The belief that I have grown up with a traditional regard towards marriage has shaped me and has caused me discomfort at times. The idea that a 'good' marriage should be exclusive and permanent probably stifles a person's ability to enjoy freedom. The Book of Common Prayer extracts certain promises from couples that may be restraining. A famous psychologist, Albert Ellis, extolled the virtues of extramarital sex but I believe there are important issues on the negative side. So the best thing to do is to remember that yelling is not abnormal in a relationship. But follow it with love and hug. Drag your partner to bed and just hold and touch." I loved to hear this from Anna. "I think it is important to understand that if we fell in love once with someone it is possible to fall in love again. Talk!" said Anna. "Put your hand where you think she might like and put hers where you want! Remember, your partner might do things that you don't like much like your walk across the country has taken you away from your spouse and it is likely that she doesn't approve the loneliness that you have inflicted on her." Anna could be too truthful at times.

"I liked to be greeted at the door by a naked woman or maybe by someone wearing a pink baby doll outfit. I like belly dancing. I like to be served a drink while the woman makes out with me with her eyes!"

"Just say it," said Anna. "Do something for her too. Maybe make love for two hours!"

"I don't know about that."

"Well, maybe cook a dinner and serve it with a fancy presentation."

"What do you suggest?"

"Well," Anna continued. "Cook a pheasant. Just brown it slightly and serve it belly side up, legs separated by a crochet needle or Steinman pin on a white plate and border it with raspberry red juice in a heart-shaped drawing and then place boiled green peas laced with carrots cut like lattices next to the meat. Take the stone out of an avocado and place a small fortune cookie containing a solitary pearl necklace inside and then place the avocado on the left of the meat.

"Women always eat what is on the right first. Serve a glass of Chateau Mouton Rothschild and sing to her 'I love you.'" Anna was out of breath. I tried to hug her and thanked her. Anna was excited. "It is important for your partner to feel secure in your commitment and to the future of the relationship for love to gel. Love is an emotion evoked by chemistry and action between the two.

"Your actions are the ingredients that continuously generate this chemical reaction. Not everyone can make love for two hours. However, it has been found that in five hours a female Scottish Soay sheep copulated with seven rams for a total of 163 encounters. A male dung fly copulates with a female for a full forty minutes. Dr. Tim Birkhead of the University of Sheffield wrote that females of most species routinely copulate with several different males. It is also well known that female promiscuity triggers a war between the sexes and between the males. One of the greatest sexual encounters known to man is about the male red back spider. It somersaults into the mouth of the female within seconds after copulating and lets her eat him as a post-coital meal."

Anna was exhausted today. This was a difficult topic for her. The day ended. It was time for her to go. She had grown tall behind me.

Dr. David Buss, professor of psychology, wrote about the strategies of human mating after completing a study of 10,000 men and women in thirty-seven different countries over a period of six years in collaboration with fifty other scientists. They published part of their research in the *American*

Scientist, volume 82. It has been believed that people search for mates who resemble or have qualities of the opposite-sex parent, as might have been suggested by Freud and Jung. Some possibly marry mates that are complementary or similar to one's qualities or with mates one could make equitable exchanges of resources or unite resources to be stronger such as in the weddings of many cases of monarchy.

However, Drs. David Schmitt and David Buss proposed a framework for understanding the logic of human mating patterns from the standpoint of evolutionary theory and made predictions regarding the sexual behavior based on the desires of either casual sex or a long-term relationship. We are obviously the descendants of people who had mated successfully and the desire to mate is universal and that is evolutionary in origin.

Darwin had explained that although the bright plumage of the male peacock was a disadvantage from the point of view of being a subject of predation, it has been an advantage as an attractive sexual feature. Recent studies have suggested that human females are very competitive to access mates as are the same-sex competitions among males.

Darwin had suggested that preferential mate choice operated primarily through females who prefer particular males. Dr. Robert Trivers, in 1972 had proposed that relative parental investment of the sexes influences sexual selection. He said that specifically the gender that invests more in offspring is selected to be more discriminating in choosing a mate, whereas the gender that invests less in offspring is more competitive with members of the same sex for sexual access to the high-investing sex. Parental investment theory accounts in part for both the origin and the evolutionary retention of different sexual strategies in males and females. Parental investment theory predicts that women will be more choosy and selective about their mating partners. Women desire those men who are able and willing to provide resources to her and her children.

They also found that an average man was willing to have intercourse with a woman even after knowing her for only one week, whereas the average woman was highly unlikely to have intercourse after such a short interlude.

Men all over the world valued physical attractiveness more than women did in short- or long-term relationships. Men and women both considered high-quality genes that could be transferred in a long-term relationship along with qualities of parenting and commitment. Laura Betzig of the University of

Michigan studied the causes of marital dissolution in eighty-nine cultures from around the world. The most prevalent cause of divorce was sexual infidelity, a cause that was highly gender linked. A wife's infidelity was considerably more likely to result in a divorce than a husband's infidelity. Dr. Betzig also found that one of the strongest gender-linked causes of divorce was a woman's old age and the inability to produce children. A woman's old age was significantly more likely to result in divorce than a man's old age. They also demonstrated clearly by verbal and physiological tests that men would be more upset if their mate was having sexual intercourse with another man whereas women were more upset if their mate was more emotionally attached to another woman. They stated that American men are concerned more about the future fidelity of a mate than with her prior escapades.

I was telling Anna about odious characters that are displayed in many of the operas and paintings. There was one particular painting that I had seen in the past and I could not remember whether I had seen it at the Louvre or Prado. The painting was by Piero di Cosimo (1490). The title was *A Satyr Mourning Over a Nymph*. This was based on a story from Ovid about Procris and Cephalus. Procris had heard false reports of infidelity of her husband by the fact that Cephalus had spied on him. He had mistaken her for a wild animal and killed her with a spear. A satyr had come to mourn her death.

"So, your father told you all the right stuff, eh?"

I agreed. I said that all his ideas do not apply to second marriages except the concept of resources but everything else that he told me when I was twelve years old was born out by the research. I think the guys in India, particularly the Sanskrit knowing gurus had many great ideas. I was humming a song from Patsy Cline,

I love you honey,
I love your money.

The wind had picked up. A person had stopped to see if I needed any help. He offered to give me a ride. "You will get there much faster," said Jerry. He was going to Cheyenne.

I secretly admired my energy. I always believed that the Chakra at the umbilicus was pretty dynamic for me. And I believe all energy begins there anyway. The sound "OHM" actually should come from the umbilicus according to the teachings that are passed on to the young Brahmins. After the "Thread" ceremony, which is similar to the Barmitzfa, the young Sannyasin is whispered the Gayatri mantra by the priest. It must not be heard by the non-Brahmins "lest it loses its power." The priest reminds the young guru that the sound must arise from the umbilicus, the source of all energy. This is where you were attached to your mother. The priest makes sure that the mantra is memorized and then everybody rejoices at the birth of the new Brahmin.

The young Brahmin walks into the crowd that his father is feeding with a smile of excitement while sporting a bald head with a "Tiki," a shaft of hair left in the back which I believe, works as an antenna that can catch heavenly messages!

Although Brahma, Vishnu and Shiva are revered, it is the women (Durga, Kali, Akash Devi, Patal Devi and others) that can calm the unruly and cleanse the impurities of the mother Earth. In India it is not unusual to find women worshipping the mother ocean after she causes havoc and destruction in the form of Tsunami. The worship is sincere and with reverence. It is not about throwing a few hibiscus and Sindur on a rock.

Every fall Goddess Durga is worshipped all over India as a symbolic event of destruction of evil. The Chandipath is recited from early mornings for four days. This is a Sanskrit description of the powerful goddess who has been gifted by Shiva with the trident, Vishnu with the chakra and Indra has given her the thunderbolt. She embodies Shakti and rides a lion to hunt down the demon that had been bringing death and destruction to the gods and humans. Durga is the militant personification of Parvati, consort of Shiva. She kills the buffalo demon Mahisasura who had the ability to change his appearance and it needed a woman to abscond him because the gods were not able to find him.

Anna was thrilled with the story from India. According to the Hindu scriptures Durga personifies Mother Earth and stands for cosmic stability and through eternal Leela (game of delusion) sustains all creatures and provides food for everyone from her own body. "This is too much for me," said Anna. "You almost have to smoke Ganja to absorb all this," she continued. I agreed that a little hash helps in understanding these deep metaphysical thoughts.

According to the Puranas, Durga assumed ten forms to overpower Sumbha and Nishumbha, two demons who were the scourge of the world. As being ten-armed she destroyed their army, as being mounted on a lion she killed Sumbha (Mahisasura), as Kali she killed Raktabija and then being headless she killed

Nishumbha. Jaydev in his poetry described that God returned every so often in different forms to cleanse the earth of impurities and thus made the earth like heaven, clean and joyful. Durga returns in another form to receive the blessings of the gods. In Hindu religion Durga is Shakti, the purifying energy that is persistent, permanent, indestructible and adored by and created by unification of all gods. The folks who like Harrison Ford might enjoy seeing the scene where a guy pulls out someone's heart in the name of Kali!

How I Energized Myself

I had my backpack resting next to the telephone pole lying beside my walking stick. I had sat down by the side of the road as I often did for a power nap or rest so that I would not get tired. I opened my eyes and realized on many occasions that I felt energized by my power nap and that I could walk another twenty-eight miles if I had to at that time. But today no sooner had I stood up I heard the familiar horn of my support van. Ms. G had already found a motel and we were finished for the day. I always sat in the van for twenty minutes to unwind before going to a motel. However, today I was already rested.

I have been on the road for more than forty-five days by now. I have had no stress but only pain and that too is self-inflicted by the desire to participate in this extreme sport. Anna had asked me once as to how I dealt with stress. I think the best answer would have been to have said that I did not handle stress very well. I truly believe that if I had not retired when I actually did I would have died by now.

Drs. Glaser and Kiecolt-Glaser recently wrote a review article on stress-induced immune dysfunction and its implications on health. They indicated that hypothalamic-pituitary-adrenal axis is stimulated and also sympathetic-adrenal-medullary axis is jarred releasing glucocorticoids and epinephrine and nor-epinephrine. These hormones and the glandular connections to the nervous system have direct as well as indirect effects on the immune cells. Fourteen-hour days and the constant stress from worrying about lives of others had taken away my joy of living. I just did not know that there was a life out there where I could just sit and wonder why the bats always fly to the left when they come out of a cave. My cholesterol was almost three hundred and fat level in my blood was ten times normal despite the fact that I was participating in moderate exercise almost daily. I was suffering from continuous trauma to myself.

Professor Edna Foa of Pennsylvania had defined a traumatic experience as an event that either a person had experienced or had witnessed another

91

person experience. Either he or she or the witness is injured, or dying, or died, or in danger of dying from such an event. The person who is experiencing the event is "horrified, terrified, or feeling helpless," she had said.

Anna said that I had become numb. I cried because my soul welled over my numbness. I had become rude. I was abrupt. I constantly interrupted. I kicked the lawnmower if it didn't start with the first pull. I had developed post-traumatic stress disorder on account of continuous suffering from being part of manmade disasters such as accidents or misfortunes of serious life-threatening illness.

This walk has released me from the womb of the wounded. Now when I cry it is owing to my freedom. I cry because I love my fellow brothers and sisters and not because my soul is drenched in sorrowful misery. I even cry in joy sometimes. I cry in depression for my feelings for others when they suffer. I remembered a poem by Dorothea Barwick explaining that sometimes we may feel God has picked a full-blooming flower too soon,

" But God knows the perfect time to gather flowers from the ground."

I slept better now. I fell asleep soon after I drank the whiskey and woke up at five in the morning being completely rejuvenated. It is no wonder that I had a larger middle during my working days.

Studies have shown that sleep deprivation raises the level of ghrelin, a hormone produced by the stomach that made me eat large amounts of carbohydrates and at the same time it reduced the level of leptins in my blood which is supposed to stimulate my fat cells to burn.

Anna said, "Lack of sleep can have dire consequences." Anna continued, "Even the busiest of animals like dolphins and other cetaceans sleep with half a brain at a time floating on the surface with one eye open and alert while the other is asleep."

Anna said that women sleep about 636,000 hours in a lifetime whereas men sleep about 481,000 hours. Anna is good with numbers. I have read many publications by Dr. Thomas A. Wehr, one of the sleep experts from the National Institute of Mental Health. These days many people think that waking up from sleep and staying awake for a while in the middle of the night is abnormal and therefore there has been a recent increase in the sale of hypnotics. All sleep hypnotics work at least partly by enhancing gamma-amino-butyric acid transmission and it has not been proved that any one drug is superior to the other. However, those who have interrupted sleep get anxious and doctors don't like to argue and so if one drug doesn't work they try another. Sleep experts believe that the normal sleep behavior of the past has changed because of industrialization where artificial light extends the day. Wehr conjectures that our present sleep pattern, in which we fall asleep rapidly and expect to sleep uninterrupted for seven to eight hours, may be an artifact of chronic sleep deprivation and artificial light.

I know that most neurosurgeons are chronically sleep deprived and suffer from stress-related symptoms. I don't jump out of bed when the phone rings anymore because I don't have to rescue any more children that will arrive in ER with jart stuck to the head. And I do not have to spend twelve hours operating on patients with gunshot wounds of the head. Now I just have to get up to walk on the interstate! Now my genes that are up-regulated in waking and down-regulated in sleep do their work casually so I have peace knowing that my heat shock proteins and chaperones and energy molecules such as mitochondrial proteins have time to think because they don't have to cruise down the Watterson Expressway yelling for the Codman drill or the Crutchfeld tongs to operate on a blood clot or stabilize a broken neck.

I don't have to worry about lawsuits from doctor-targeting attorneys or workman's compensation related abuse of the system. I had seen a commercial on TV some time ago when an attorney had said that he would take a case of trauma and sue the presumed inflicting person even if someone felt traumatized by watching an accident. I wanted to think positively. I recalled reading the poem of some anonymous writer:

> For every hill I have had to climb
> For all the blood sweat and grime
> My heart sings but a grateful song
> These were things that made me strong.
> What are the reasons why dreams die stillborn?
> Vision without work is a dream
> Work without vision is drudgery
> Vision and work together
> Make the dream a reality.

Anna said that Eleanor Roosevelt had said that "the future belongs to those who believe in the beauty of their dreams." I didn't want to appear less informative. So I said that Kahlil Gibran had said "when you dream alone, it stays a dream, but when you dream with others, it can become a reality."

Now as I walked I stopped for a chipmunk and at times I even sat down just to watch the jack rabbits scurry through the bushes. The sunshine on my skin was brighter. My fat cells were sliding off the abdominal teeter-totter and I was high from my very own happy drug, pain killer endorphin.

Anna laughed and chimed in, "Your cholesterol is better too." Now I can feel when I listen to John Denver's song, "Sunshine on the water makes me happy, and sunshine on my eyes can make me cry and sunshine always makes me high."

I knew that there wouldn't be much of anything to see near Pine Bluff except more wheat fields. I was tired when I reached there in the evening. Suddenly Nebraska was coming to an end and I was getting ready to be on the interstate at Wyoming. The entrance was a little confusing for me but I arrived. The day went rather fast. Nothing unusual happened. Just more wheat fields on both sides of the road. The train track stayed on my left though at times it moved far away from me.

"So have you been working on the curriculum?"

I said yes. I had read part of the speech by David McCullough as it was printed in the *Imprimis*, a publication of Hillsdale College. I have had many professors and all of them have shaped my thinking, some directly and others indirectly. David McCullough is one of those who has influenced me indirectly. My admiration for him is not because he received the Pulitzer Prize or the National Book Award. He is a historian from the American perspective and his presentations are so sincere and so convincing that every time I have read his material I have just been totally taken by the depth and the challenge that he has presented to the reader. "Nothing happens in a vacuum," he wrote. There are consequences for every action "These all sound self-evident. But they are not self-evident—particularly to a young person trying to understand life." I liked this.

"This is true in every respect," said Anna.

I remembered an older doctor telling me a story once. It was his off day and he had asked his son to help him with the cleaning of the horse stalls. They both had pitchforks in their hands and were working hard to clean the manure piles and spreading straw on the ground. Then they checked the chicken coop and picked up the eggs and placed them in a basket. Then he told his nineteen-year-old son to clean the hog pen and wash the cement floor with the hose that was attached to a tap outside the barn. The young freshman retorted, "You know, Dad, I am going to take couple of years off and try to find myself." His father, the older doctor, didn't miss a beat. He quipped, "You know, Son, you have a pitchfork in your hand and you are standing on a pile of manure and you just found yourself." Now to some liberal-thinking person this might have sounded a little harsh. However, I feel that it is perfectly fine to go and find myself at my age with my nickel but when my daddy is footing the bill I have a responsibility to be self-sufficient and get on with my life so that I don't become a public charge and complain that the Indians are taking our jobs.

The curriculum that I teach in the SPAVA program is based on respect, honor and integrity. Anna said to teach the students about gratitude. I believe humility and paying respect to those that have gone before us and have made our life easier is one of the most important lessons that I have incorporated in the curriculum. I enjoyed reading about Margaret McFarland the way Mr. McCullough mentions it. I am a big believer in the expression of an energetic attitude during teaching.

Anna said that we can also pass positive energy from one to the other just by our handshake and smile. More than half of the children in this world don't get the opportunity to get an education the way we get in America. Many children don't get enough food for nourishment of the brain or the body so they can't learn. We have free lunches. We have food stamps and we have many nonprofit organizations and activists that try to help our society improve. Our society is not perfect. However, America is one country where everyone is striving to make a few things better today than they were yesterday. Yet many of our children in the schools eat too many potato chips and grow to be fat and many others watch TV till wee hours in the morning and fall asleep in the classrooms. So Ms. Abigail's writing to her husband, John Quincy that "How unpardonable would it have been in you to have turned out a blockhead" is admirable indeed. Knowledge may make some persons pompous but it is to be had and the opportunities are at times being wasted. So I am going to try to make history more interesting for the children and teach it with greater vigor to demonstrate the hardships our predecessors had to bear to bring us where we are today.

Wyoming

Anna and I often talked about topics that were not related. And today Anna disappeared. It was cloudy but I liked it. I reached Cheyenne. At six in the evening it was still bright. Ms. G had planned for me to take the next day off. I talked to a Rotary meeting at breakfast time. The fellow Rotarians as usual were most hospitable and informed me about some of the activities in which they have been involved and wanted to learn about my club at Louisville. They provided some financial support for my organization as well.

I spent the rest of the day with Ms. G and Ms. P, my two trusted support van drivers. We enjoyed looking at the train museum and learning about the support that Abe Lincoln had provided to develop the railroads in the West. The dedication and innovative spirit of the people in this part of the country is most admirable indeed. The development of the technology and the hard work of advancing through challenging snow and ice was to me another example of American ingenuity. Now we can see the trains go from the West to the East almost every seven minutes carrying coal. The evening ended early after eating a large meal in a restaurant that had a decorative cowboy boot parked in front much like we have decorative horses in Kentucky. I talked with the manager about the boots at different places in town. I learnt that the businesses get to keep them for a year as an award for donating money to the different civic causes in the community. Anna and I talked a bit about the mining of coal and what it does to the land. I believe more laws are being made to avoid strip mining and mountaintop removal because they destroy the land to recover the coal underneath.

> By him first
> Men also, and by his suggestion taught,
> Ransacked the center, and with impious hands
> Rifled the bowels of their mother Earth
> For treasures better hid.
> —Milton, *Paradise Lost*

In this part of the country we have a lot of warheads and underground facilities of research and nuclear capabilities. I met people later on who are driven to their place of work that is all located underground. Anna wanted to tell me about all the sunken nuclear warheads that she knows. I wanted to hear because I didn't know much about them.

"In 1963 during the Cold War, the US nuclear-powered submarine *Thresher* sank with 129 men and two nuclear-armed missiles. In 1986 a Russian submarine carrying sixteen missiles, each armed with two nuclear warheads, sank off the coast of Bermuda. Another Russian submarine, *Komsomolets*, sank in the Norwegian Sea in 1989. One hundred eighteen soldiers died when *Kursk* sank in 2000."

Anna continued, "There have been accidents involving French and British submarines as well. It is also possible that other accidents are not reported unless someone else finds out about them."

"What is going to happen to the sunken nuclear submarines?"

Anna said, "It is a problem we must address soon. Otherwise they might start leaking plutonium and other radioactive substances whose effects we may not know but we don't believe it is going to be beneficial to our children or the fish. We should make a petition to the United Nations to ban nuclear weapons in submarines."

I agreed. I suggested that our children should write letters to our representatives to introduce bills to ban such weapons in future, particularly since there are no safe ways to retrieve them from the ocean floor.

It was important for me to move on because the road from Cheyenne to Laramie gets covered with snow sometimes early and at other times late in the season. It is rather unpredictable. I have driven on this road in the past but I had never walked. I was on the road at seven in the morning. I was huffing and puffing in less than fifteen minutes. It was windy and I had a steady climb to almost 8,400 feet. I was not in a hurry. My journey was for fun and not for reaching any destination. I was excited and free. I had already walked more than half the distance and I knew in my heart that I would finish. At least I had always finished anything that I had started in the past.

However, I had never experienced such hardships in the past even during the entire neurosurgery residency.

Anna came along. "Hi. What's up?"

"Just having fun with the wind on my back and bracing myself to not fall as the wind pushes the sign on my shoulder."

Anna was in front and she was moving slow and would scoot her feet every so often to avoid getting wet from the dripping of my sweat from my forehead. I didn't care.

"It seems that we need very little stuff in life," said Anna. "We have almost everything we need in our backpacks."

I agreed. I washed my clothes daily and I had an extra set in my pack in case I was to get wet before the driver arrived. I had my water pouch and a banana and couple of power bars.

"So how come you own so much stuff?" Anna continued. "Hoarding is an illness, you know." I agreed. "Many people who hoard things actually have dementia of the frontal and temporal lobes." I agreed. "You have saved stuff in your garage that you don't use."

I said, "But the cord for the four-prong drier that I had used in the past is valuable and I may need it in future. The extra hose that I have saved may be needed if I move to a bigger house."

"How about all those brooms and mops, for that matter all those pieces of two-by-fours, the cans of paint that are more than five years old?"

"Well, I thought I might need them."

"How about all those articles in your office about leprosy, and malaria and Dengue fever etc? How about all those pants and shirts and suits that won't fit you?"

"All right, I get the point. I might need some cognitive behavior treatment."

"Don't you remember reading Dr. R. Frost saying in *Cognitive and Behavioral Treatment of Compulsive Hoarding* that hoarders apply emotions to a range of things that others would consider worthless? Where most people see an empty roll of toilet paper, they see art supplies."

I promised to give away my clothes that I didn't wear and the utensils that I didn't use for cooking to some refugee facility. Anna stopped scolding.

I had walked almost eight miles. I sat down and Anna sat in front of me all crunched up and short. Gatorade tasted good. I swished my mouth and spat a little. Anna wanted me to feel better after all that scolding. "So, do you remember some of the stuff from *Wit and Witticism*?"

"No. Who wrote it?"

"Well, it was published by National Federation of the Blind."

I smiled because I vaguely remembered reading it. "So tell me something from it."

"Maybe I will on another day."

I rested my head on the backpack on the grass next to the shoulder of the interstate. Cars whizzed by as Anna said, "So what did the rabbit say when it jumped into a hole full of water? Oh, well!" We both laughed.

I was ready to go and I moved on till the support van arrived to pick me up for lunch. I thought it was lot more difficult to walk here than it was when I came through Pine Bluff. Anna was panting with me. Well, the highest point in Nebraska was only 5,500 feet and here we are getting close to 7,500 feet. We drove back to Cheyenne to eat lunch. It was only fourteen miles from where I had stopped. After lunch I walked a little past Buford and that was halfway to Laramie. Next day I walked past Laramie.

Reminiscing Honduras

I told a story about my work at Honduras.

It was summertime at San Pedro Sula. My excitement was sunk by the unctuous feeling I developed as I walked through the sign that said "Emergencia Para Ninos." It is not the feeling one gets while walking into the pyramid in Egypt in a half-bent position. That is a feeling of discomfort and apprehension. This was a sense of anger that was generated in me by some perfidious characters that sit in the government and have not necessarily stolen the health of the children but have done nothing to prevent the agony and distress in the face of the women of Honduras who bore these children. The corrupt government does not provide proper nourishment or facilities for the people of the country. I wept. I didn't want my colleague doctor to see me.

Children were lying in stretchers. The air-conditioning unit was held up by chicken wire. The curtains had pictures of Donald Duck and Porky Pig and on another wall there were pictures of Michael Jordan and some *Baywatch* girls.

All the children were suffering from very serious illnesses and I was there to help reduce the suffering of a few. I told God that the task was too much for me.

Then we moved under a sign that said "Biennvenidos Sala Emergencia." I saw a man lying on a stretcher with an intravenous line going into a vein in his right hand; the bottle hung from a nail hammered into the grout on the wall. The left hand was frail with a bleeding wound below the elbow and a bandage covered a gash on the forehead. The nurse explained that someone had attacked him after he got paid and stole his money and during the process had hit him with a machete.

Another man was lying who had a gunshot injury to his left side that had gone through and through without injuring any internal organs. The nurse asked him to take a shower with a hose that was attached on the side of the wall in the corner next to a drain. He was told to go up for surgery after he took a shower and was cleaned up.

We wanted to start the day with a simple case. No sooner had we walked a few feet than we saw few policemen walk in under a sign "Cierren La Puerta" and throw a man on the floor. They asked us to determine if the man was still alive. He was blue. He was not breathing and his bowels were poking out of him through the hole where he was shot. My Honduran colleague told the nurses to place a cover on him. We moved on.

I spent several weeks working. Our neurosurgical organization had taken the responsibility to develop the neurosurgical program. I had the opportunity to work with one of the kindest doctors I have ever met. Dr. Ena always had a positive attitude and she was full of energy. She is a true energy bar.

Anna said that she was going to throw up after learning about the conditions and the suffering. I said that I almost did. I have read many papers written by evolution biologists. I do not believe Neanderthals were more violent than us, though they possibly had less judgment, thinking power and ability to predict actions than us because they had a smaller frontal lobe. Although the idea that the frontal lobe enlarged disproportionately during hominid evolution makes intuitive sense but the behavior seen here certainly does not testify to that fact.

There was some construction on the road just outside the university near Laramie. So we took a ride around the place to find the road that went towards Interstate 80 west. As I rested in the car Ms. P called the radio and the TV station to generate some publicity. Someone from the other side said that there was "someone always doing something crazy around here with bicycles or on motorcycles." The radio station didn't think that walking across the country for the prevention of violence was much of news in that particular Western state. Ms. P was disappointed. I said life goes on.

I went ahead and ate a twenty-six-ounce steak and some greens and a large cheese-coated potato. I already had about half a pint of whiskey. I was asleep even through O'Reiley's yelling at someone on the TV next door. Next morning I started punctually at seven in the morning. I thought that sometimes the steam coming from the truckers' engines was so hot that my skin almost felt scalded as they bathed me with the hot air that exuded from the exhaust pipes.

I felt that the trucks got swallowed by the mountainous Interstate 80 as they went past me and I couldn't see them anymore past the curves on the road ahead of me. I kept on singing, "Yes, I can. Yes, I can," or at least that is what

I heard the trucks were saying as they passed me. I remembered being in trains in India when I was a child. The noise made by the train as it ran over the track actually always said to me whatever I had wanted it to say as though I knew the rhyme.

Today I talked a lot about my grandfather to Anna. I thought Anna was a good conversationalist. She always asked me questions and then let me talk. I talked some but then I often just yelled at my ex-wife. I told her that I missed her. I always wanted to be married for fifty years. But now I won't live long enough to accomplish that. For some reason I felt that as though that time frame was some sort of a yardstick for measuring life's achievements. I felt that I had failed somehow in this important area. "It is not important," said Anna. "Move on. You will miss out if you don't go with the flow of life."

I wanted to make love to my wife right then. I called Ms. P on the cell phone. She was driving the support van at this point. It didn't work. She had Verizon and I had Sprint. In this area they didn't communicate. I walked in frustration till the opportune time. "She wouldn't do it on the road anyway. You are sweaty and smelly," she said.

I concurred. "But I feel hot."

"That's exactly my point," she said. "Cool down in a shower first, then you will not stay hot any longer but we can be sweaty together!" I liked the idea. I almost fell off the mountain with a thunderous explosion. It wasn't even dark outside.

We slept well at Laramie that night. We backtracked to a motel to Laramie for the night again and started the next morning from the spot where I had stopped walking the night before. I hadn't realized how agitated the umbilical chakra can get being on the road talking to my woman friend all day.

The wind was strong and cold in the morning. It came to torment me through a hollow in the mountain that was made to build the interstate. At times I just ran because the wind pushed me downhill. Then I slowed down so that I wouldn't ruin my knees. I felt like a motorcycle whose front wheels were up in the air and as though I was balancing on my back wheels. By now I had become quite an expert in going up and down the ramps of different exits and I knew exactly how to carry on the task of entering the traffic without fear. I was always amazed at my tolerance of heat and exhaustion. I never felt the need to express it verbally. It was evident to anyone else who looked at me. At least that is what Mr. W, my preacher, had said when he was driving the support van.

Anna said that pain, suffering and death are facts of life and I shouldn't worry about it. I asked Anna if she thought that those who die of cancer are actually in a better position to arrange for death. "Yes," she said. She continued with a gasp. She had to take a breath. This is a high mountain pass. "It is all in the attitude."

"It is difficult to have a good attitude when we face the inevitable and that our vulnerability is brought to the foreground."

"However, look at it this way," she said. "You have time to talk to the family about the meaning of life. Family gets a chance to share and relive all the joys. Love is warmer when the toaster is on a timer without any numbers and no one really knows when it will click off. There is an opportunity to set the financial affairs straight. The voice of the little granddaughter is sweeter.

"All this is possible when we truly believe Reinhold Niebuhr's beautiful Serenity Prayer, 'the serenity to accept what cannot be changed, courage to accept what should be changed, and wisdom to distinguish one from the other.' When you die in an accident there is no time to grieve with the family. No one is prepared. Although you are dying, death is really a matter of preparation for the living." I couldn't agree more with her at this time although the subject was grim.

We both sat down for a while to cool off. I was dripping sweat on her. Anna often liked to say the last word. "You know death does not have to be a crisis and it is an event much like birth. It is a turning point and fulfillment of the spiritual journey that you have been longing."

The cars and trucks went past me as I lay with my right ankle resting on my left knee bent at a right angle with the left foot flat on the grass.

We both sang L. Larson's "Come Down, Oh Love Divine."

Come down, O love divine; seek out this soul of mine
And visit it your own ardor glowing:
O Comforter, draw near, within my heart appear,
And kindle it, Your Holy flame bestowing.

I had dozed off for a few minutes. When I woke up I was at the same place and a long journey lay still ahead of me, though I had wished it to have had become a little shorter.

The days seemed to pass rather quickly at times when I played with Anna or just kept mumbling to myself. I thought of calling the man that I had met on

US 50. He was bicycling from L.A. to D.C. He had said that most people were nice to him. It was only an occasional person that called him names. He had enough water in his thermos so he didn't have to stop where he was not welcome.

My phone didn't work until Elk Mountain exit. Here Ms. P met me. Then we drove about three miles to a restaurant for lunch. Many people had signed a guest book. The owner lady said that most people who came there are hunters but a few came there to just to get away from stress. I saw two persons fly fishing in a piece of water as we drove by to get back on the interstate. "Hey, did you guys catch anything yet," I yelled. "No, nothing yet." There was a big cooler and possibly a game warden in shouting distance. Fishermen usually are afraid to say it loud if they have caught more than the quota or undersize fish. We moved on to the exit.

It took me two days to walk to Rawlins. My knees and my hips hurt a little bit but they always got better in the evening when I emptied some Jim Beam into my system. However, I always felt that I drank for medicinal purposes only. After all, I did not take any other medicine during the entire time that I was on the road. However, I had to cater to my feet daily with iodine and puncture at least a few quarter-size blisters until now. Now the calluses were forming and I had a run of good days with my feet. It might appear to some people that I have been talking a bit much about my feet. Anna said it was perfectly fine.

By the time I finished my walk I had three layers of blisters under and to the side of my feet. Some of them started out as a little irritation but soon became the size of quarters lying side by side. But I accepted them though not happily. I knew that they didn't have very long to live. I was waiting for the day when my feet would be normal again.

I ran into a man who said he was an atheist. He was fine to talk to for a while but always was critical of everything. "God didn't do anything for me. My friends help me. I don't need God to join any group like you do. You go to church and I have the same effect at home."

"Where will you go when you die?"

"Same place as you. You just imagine all this heaven and baloney."

I had a hard time. I suggested Eugene O'Neill's *Long Days Journey into Night*. Tyrone said "When you deny God, you deny sanity. When you deny God you deny hope."

"I think God helps us to forgive and sometimes we need to learn to forgive ourselves."

"Forgive ourselves for what?"

I struck a bad chord. "Well, for one thing that is important."

"And what is that?"

"Well, for not being able to love or quick to anger or to think that this is all there is in life; is to try to make money and spend all the days worrying about success and how to be powerful. Or just day-to-day living, sleeping, buying food and driving to work. I think God gives us humility and it is one of the hardest things to learn.

"I am sure that I enjoy being recognized and secretly I wish that I was famous. I sometimes forget that God has a purpose in me. God gives us joy and happiness unless we are pessimistic and doomed by our own desires like the last chorus of Oedipus, 'Call no man happy until he is dead.'"

It was late and lunchtime was over. I said, "You know we all have several parts to our personality. I may appear religious but some of my behaviors are not quite consistent with superficial religiosity. Duke Ellington put together 'A concert of sacred music' but sometimes the religious fervor in many cases was inconsistent with his sybaritic private life."

"That's right," he said. If you consider life to be the bread when you soak it in olive oil with balsamic vinegar life becomes enjoyable. But you know that the dark vinegar makes a swirling river around the 'almost clear' oil. Good luck," he said as I left to bake in the sun.

"Don't you worry, God will take care of me and He will transform me into a different person by the time this walk is over. I am banking on it."

I was in a great mood to chat. "Anna, do you know that Captain Meriwether Lewis was shot by friendly fire much like the way it happened to General Jackson? Lewis didn't die when Private Pierre Cruzatte shot him in the thigh mistaking him for an elk. Sergeant York had already died from appendicitis or an unknown illness. Although both Lewis and Clark were generously rewarded for their great achievement by President Jefferson, William Clark did not get the captain's commission that Lewis had recommended. Lewis was only thirty-three years old when he undertook the expedition and after all this accomplishment he got himself into debt buying land which caused him great depression. He committed suicide when President James Madison refused to reimburse him for expenses that the president felt were for personal gain."

Anna was by my side and we moved briskly. I adjusted the backpack every so often. I lifted my shirt at times to get some air on my belly as the trucks passed by. My sides were getting chafed from the strap of the backpack. At first I thought it was because of my muffin shape at the waist but as I checked the muffins from my sides had melted and I had dark bruises from the tension and the pressure of the wind pushing the pack tearing against my torso. My body was burnt and dry at places. Part of me looked like a monkey-puzzle tree (it looks like a pine tree with thorny bark). Dr. Archibald Menses, surgeon and a naturalist on Captain George Vancouver's around-the-world voyage (1791-1795) brought the seeds from Chile.

At times I wanted to walk naked. I was hot and melting. But I was afraid that I would get arrested for exposing myself. I didn't want Anna to think less of me. I really was never bored but to others it might appear that way at times. I chewed gum. I spat. I peed on hot rocks to see the smoke and sometimes I was just excited from feeling my own body by walking funny. This was a long walk and I had plenty time for just about everything. Anna said she knew how the bird of paradise came to the West. "OK, Anna, you might as well say it."

"They grew wild in the Eastern Cape of Good Hope. Francis Mason found them in 1795 and sent them as a gift to Empress Catherine of Russia."

I was ready to quit. I knew that the next day would be about the same in distance but I hoped that I would be stronger and more excited.

Walk Getting More Difficult

The walk from Rawlings was tiring. It was dry and dust blew in a haphazard manner but at times I could see the circular motion of dust balls at a distance like little tornadoes that swirled for a while a mile or so away from me. I sucked on my water tube every so often not because I was thirsty but because I wanted my load to get lighter. And I moved along to complete today's journey. I knew that I wouldn't make it to Wimsatter but I never worried about being in any city at any particular time. I knew that I would arrive at the next big city in appropriate time and I was predestined to accomplish the task. Therefore I had no anxiety or stress about it. There was no race and certainly no prize at the end except the joy of accomplishment. I knew that my God was walking with me.

There is an area that I had to walk through when the exits were more than twenty-five miles apart. A part of the road to Rock Springs also went through a desert. It is here that Anna had asked me as to why I chose this path and not through Montana. I had explained that this was a bit shorter and I wouldn't have had to climb the high mountains of Montana.

"You won't get to see the dino bones," said Anna.

I told her that I had been to several museums of natural history and had learnt a bit about those animals. But the most interesting of all was reading about them in the *American Scientist* volume 94 by Dr. Keith Stewart Thompson. In 1787 Timothy Matlack and Dr. Caspar Wister (Wisteria fame) had presented an account of a large thigh bone that was found near Woodbury Creek in Glocester County, New Jersey.

The specimen had been missing ever since. In March 1856 Joseph Leidy of Philadelphia wrote a paper describing and naming four kinds of reptilian teeth that were discovered in Judith River region of Montana.

The first-ever description of a dinosaur fossil (Plot had submitted a drawing) was by Robert Plot, the first director of Ashmolean Museum at

Oxford in his *Natural History of Oxfordshire* of 1677. It was the distal end of the femur and it had been found in the village of Cornwell. Plot called it a thigh bone of a human giant. In 1772, Richard Brookes, a naturalist, turned Plot's figure upside down and noting a startling resemblance to male genitalia gave its first formal name: Scrotum Humanum. Probably, because of this notoriety, the original specimen had disappeared.

Anna thought I was tired and told me to drink a Red Bull. Although the interstate is named 80 it is actually 30 west. We watched a few antelopes at distance. They grazed without looking up. I was no threat to them. The vista was getting wider with an occasional building scattered throughout the land for drilling oil and gas. I thought everything belonged to Sinclair.

"Anna, I really want to be more involved with our local Rotary but my plate seems to be full all the time."

Anna was listening. "So what's holding you?"

"Nothing really! I just think that there is a lot of politics within the club, particularly when such should not exist. I don't think we really follow in the Rotary what we say, 'Will it be beneficial to all concerned. Will it build goodwill and friendship?'"

Anna said, "Louisville has come a long way. It is almost an international town. Just wait a few more years then more people will be sincere and when they say, 'nice to see you' they will really mean it."

"Anna, I have to improve too. I often find myself bearing a grudge towards those that I thought had slighted me. Somehow, I feel as though I have to remind them of the hurt they caused me."

Anna told me a story. "There was a man who had come to a distant land and had started a business and raised a family. He had found that several persons refused to give him opportunities in a very subtle manner. But he succeeded and gave up the fight and gave all his wealth away to help the children of those that rejected him. The fellows that resented the foreigner's success became more angry and jealous." Anna continued, "You don't have to follow Lady Macbeth's dictum in life, 'Look like an innocent flower but be a serpent underneath it.' It is frustrating and agonizing when you do a good day's work and not get paid the same as others. But remember those that are angry or hateful are not your problem." I almost felt like Anna was pontificating. What does she know? Somehow she understood what I was thinking. "Hey, women didn't get to vote until fourteen years after the death of Susan B. Anthony." I acquiesced. I said I was going to be patient.

Anna knew when to change the topic. "So who is Uncle Sam?"

I knew this one. I didn't like to appear dumb in front of her. I retorted, "Samuel Wilson was a meat supplier during the War of 1812 and people grew fond of him for obvious reason."

I had eaten a large breakfast this morning as I did every morning but I felt particularly hungry rather early despite the consumption of a huge amount of food earlier.

I always listened to my body. My support van arrived and I gorged myself while reading *A Tramp Abroad* by Mark Twain. It seemed appropriate for the occasion. Anna sat by the side while I read loudly. "Sometimes there was only the width of the road between the imposing precipices on the right and the clear cool water on the left with its shoals of uncatchable fishes skimming about through the bars of sun and shadow." Anna and I both agreed that we needed some shade but there were no trees on the road we were walking and we couldn't find any cool water on the road. As a matter of fact we were heading towards the Red Desert.

I wanted to dream that I was at sea sailing towards Dubrovnik. The blue-green water of the Aegean Sea enticed me to jump overboard. I got pulled in by the gentle touch of a mermaid who stayed on her belly on two large flotillas and I felt cool and warm both at the same time. My heart pounced when I found myself on the white sand. Many scantily clad women came to check on me. Some placed their cheeks on my chest to see if I was breathing. I held my breath so that I would feel their touch longer. Some just lay there and others touched the forehead as though to wipe the beads of perspiration that occurs when the forbidden fruit is eaten the first time. The gentle waves soothed me and my profile got covered with the sand and I became hidden in the water as my back dug deeper into the sand as the water retreated under me. I didn't know what was going on. I thought maybe the heat was getting to me and I was hallucinating.

I always like to eat a lot. I imagined that one of the universities that specialize in cooking had invited me to give a talk about the effect of food on mood after I had finished my walk. I began speaking. I told Anna that I was really imagining this and so I wanted her to hear my speech.

"I want to begin by saying that this is a rather disputed subject and I am not an expert by a long shot. I was asked to participate because I ate a lot recently, almost 9,500 calories daily, and stayed in a good mood almost always. What

I am going to tell you is not medical advice. Only your doctor can give you advice. I am just a regular citizen that knows a bit about food and mood. There are many diets that are touted to be the best. Many of the promoters have passed on while others who did not follow all the instructions have lived longer. This is much like the doctor who went to a town and asked some of the citizens as to what was the common illness prevalent in that town. The folks said that they didn't know because no one had died there for many years except the doctors who had come in the past. So the doctor made sure that he didn't starve!

"In general certain rules are helpful:

(a) Eating breakfast is important
(b) Eating regularly and not being on the run. Enjoy and take time to chew.
(c)Eat smaller portions and more frequently
(d) Exercise regularly—something such as walking, running, lifting weights, going up or down steps are very helpful.

"Certain foods and exercise help produce Happy Hormones. There are hormones in our blood that make us hungry and there are those that make us satisfied. Satisfaction comes from an area of the brain less than one centimeter in lateral hypothalamus called the Satiety Center.

"In the late ˙40s experiments in rats showed that damage to this area can make rats eat till they explode. It has a human counterpart called Prader Willis syndrome.

"Dieting without exercise is like trying to make words with Q without using the U. Exercise produces encephalin and endorphins that are opiate-like substances produced by the body and thus may be a factor to produce the well-known runner's high!

"There are eight essential amino acids and three essential fatty acids that we find in our food as nutrients. Nutrients are precursors to neurotransmitters. There are a lot of complicated chemical reactions that occur in the liver and the brain to make us happy from the chemical point of view. What I am going to tell you today is about the acronym SMILE TODAY. This is my original and the rest is borrowed knowledge which we all have to have to graduate.

S—Serotonin
M—Methionine
I–Isoleucine
L—Lysine
E—Epinephrine

T—Tryptophan
O—Oolong Tea
D—Dopamine
A—Acetyl Choline (keeps brain computers clean)
Y—Yams (for fiber—regular BM)

"We can try to remember the amino acids or the hormones but sometimes trying to remember too much causes stress. Oolong tea increases metabolism. Caffeine in moderation produces alertness. Red wine in moderation has been found to be helpful in managing good health. Too much of it deprives us of the benefits of antioxidants. Mushrooms have antioxidants. Apples are good for us because they have both kinds of fibers, soluble (lowers blood sugar) as well as insoluble (regulates bowels). Regular bowel movements are necessary and important because this is a satisfying event in the lives of many persons and thus SMILE TODAY includes yam. Much like Ahh! I could have had a V-8!

"In general anything that is good for the heart is good for the brain. Another general rule is that any food that looks like the prostate is good for men—garlic, tomato, beets (in moderation), onions, mushrooms, and even Brussels sprouts!

"Eating carbohydrates release insulin—released insulin—clears the sugar and other amino acids except tryptophan that goes to brain—produces serotonin—reduces pain, makes us calm—decreases appetite—and in large quantity produces sleep.

"Healthy carbohydrates are whole-grain bread, crackers, pasta, rice, cereal, and fruits. Fruit juices are also good for us. However all this has to be taken in moderation, otherwise they will make us gain weight. The rule is to burn what we eat, otherwise it is stored as fat.

"Proteins, meat, milk, eggs, cheese, fish and beans produce tyrosine, and other amino acids that increase production of dopamine, epinephrine and nor-epinephrine, which are all needed for aggressive activities, alertness and energy.

"Fruits, nuts, and green leafy vegetables are good sources for vitamins and iron as well.

"None of the diets have been found to cure any illness although certain kinds of diets will aggravate certain illness e.g. eating pea nuts when some one has nut allergy, high purine diet in cases of gout, too much carbohydrate in case of diabetes etc. Taking high doses of vitamins has not been found to be particularly beneficial. However, in some cases it can be harmful.

"Comfort food—Chocolate has sugar, fat, phenyl ethylamine and caffeine. Sugar releases serotonin, fat and phenyl ethylamine produce endorphin-like substance and caffeine is a stimulant and thus they produce happiness!

"Large meals that are high in fat cause sluggishness. Though it is commonly believed that a heavy diet causes less flow of blood to the brain in reality the brain has a system set up that prevents any other organ from stealing its blood. It is possibly slower absorption, sense of fullness, production of alcohol and serotonin that slows us down.

"When I was walking across the country I ate almost every two hours and I also ate very large amounts of protein during the day and carbohydrates at night for resting and catch-up energy. A good night's sleep is essential for good mood when the acetylcholine (A) of SMILE TODAY cleans up the brain computer by deleting rarely but mostly repositioning the files of the awakening time in special places in the brain so that next day before the test when the epinephrine (E) of SMILE calls on it, it will open up without a drag on the RAM!

"At this time a lot of work is being done with glucagon, incretin (sugar and type-2 diabetes), leptin (appetite suppressant), ghrelin (hunger hormone), and cholecystokinin (satiation hormone)

"Ghrelin levels in blood spike before meals and drop afterwards. It is produced by the stomach cells. It stimulates the pituitary to release growth hormone and thus the insulin cycle begins.

"Leptin is produced by fat cells and supposed to suppress appetite. Some of these hormones have been discovered within the last ten years.

"So if you want to be HAPPY and be in good mood:

"Eat lots of protein for energy and alertness and carbohydrate for energy and sluggishness, chocolate to feel loved by the endorphins release and some fruits and fibers for your bowels, but most importantly go and exercise to burn up what you ate, otherwise you will be sad that you gained weight and sadness will prevent you from fulfilling the acronym SMILE TODAY!"

Anna was silent for quite some time after listening to my speech. I couldn't stand it after a while. I wanted to tell her about some violent acts that I had seen in Nepal while I was working there.

"Self-inflicted burns are not an uncommon event in Nepal. Several women every year ignite themselves with gasoline or kerosene as a way to escape the agony of dependency, body-image concerns, dowry threats and possibly some type of guilt related to not loving the person that they have married. Although uncommon in the United States, the situation still occurs in sufficient numbers for the surgical residents rotating through the burn unit to learn to be sensitive to the subject. In the Louisville area it is more common among the African American population."

"Are you doing something to reduce this type of violence?" asked Anna.

"I don't know if we are doing anything directly but I think our program is making the children aware that we must create a support group for everyone. My understanding has been that on many occasions there is significant underlying depression or schizophrenia that drives the persons to participate in such impulsive acts."

There were a few birds that went ahead of me and gossiped loudly. I heard them but couldn't understand the accent. Anna went away for a while. The cloud moved in. I hoped it would rain. It didn't. One minute I was singing the doxology and the next minute I was being weak and relishing the spirit of the body. Anna said that was normal for a man who has been on the road for such a long time. The road stayed straight with a few shining water spots that were shimmering ahead of me. However, as I got closer the water spots moved away. I knew that the sun and the clouds were teasing me. All this walking has been quite a turning point for me in my life. I think the business of operating on heads and for that matter on any part of the body has been very stressful. Now I can stop or lie down if I want without harming anyone else.

I still remember my professor, "Handle adversity with discipline and aplomb. That is the only way you will be successful." I thought I did enough of that already. Anna said, "Well, look at Bernie Barker. The guy is the oldest male stripper according to the *Guinness Book of World Records*. He dances with a G-string on him and makes a ton of money at O'Malley's Ocean Pub in Hollywood Beach, Florida. All the women flock to his show and stick dollar bills under his string. He was an engineer at nuclear power plants for many years."

"I think that's a lot of fun." We are about the same age and I thought maybe I ought to try that out.

"Aren't you a bartender?" Anna asked.

"Yes, ma'am, I sure am."

Anna didn't know that I had worked at a cadaver party. That is the name given to the party for the medical and dental students after they graduate from their anatomy courses. I made almost forty dollars in tips on my first night even though I worked only from eight in the evening till two in the morning. I remember serving many Long Island Teas to young students who lost track of time. As I was driving a few of them home in the wee hours of the morning one of them asked, what do you do in the day time? I said I was a neurosurgeon and I couldn't make it as a doctor and so I work as a bartender at night! One of the students made a noise like he was going to throw up either because of what he just heard or the Long Island Tea was reaching his brain. I told him to be sure and open the window so the fresh air would dissipate the feeling of upchucking. Actually, I didn't want my car to smell bad. I did tell them to tell their parents next day that a neurosurgeon who was working as a bartender drove them home twenty miles out of his way! I thought that would help the parents to understand the level of inebriation of these prospective doctors when they left the party the previous evening. I did offer to return some of my tips but they graciously declined.

I remember going to the track next day. I bet all that money on a horse that I thought was going to win for sure. The horse was not as confident as I was of him. He didn't perform to my expectation.

I was telling Anna about my visit to the Grand Canyon. She always was a good listener.

"I had been to the north rim and also to the south rim. What I thought was funny was that when I made the reservation to stay one night in the bottom of the canyon I had to call the Xanterra folks two years ahead and they wanted to know what I wanted for breakfast and dinner so that everything could be charged on my American Express card at that time. They said that in case I thought that I wouldn't make the trip owing to some conflicts in schedule they would refund the money up to three days prior to the actual trip.

"I had walked down and watched some people climbing rocks and felt that they were lot more courageous than me. I recalled standing on a limestone promontory and looking down into this colossal hole and reflecting on my size in the macrocosm. The beautiful sunset and the Kaibab Limestone cap rock and the spectacular pastel color just dazzled me. I praised God for my eyesight and the ability to enjoy nature in full bloom. Many tourists go down the rim to see Havasupai or Havasu falls which splurges its blue-green water into a cavity. The once prolific Havasupai Reservation does not exist in its full capacity today. This is almost two thousand feet below the rim and there are creeks where there is drinkable water though some of them have too much lime.

"I always try to remember some of the things I see because I don't have a camera on many occasions. On such occasions I think of my childhood when I didn't have paper for writing and so I had to remember everything. I had to erase my slate to make room to write new things all the time."

Wind was blowing a lot of dust so I was trying to walk keeping my head down. My sunglasses were already fixed such that most of the dust particles found a barrier of aluminum foil on the side rims before they could hurt my eyes. One thing I did for myself before I left Louisville and that is I prepared myself for most of the possible injuries. I knew that I would be alone and I knew that if I sustained any kind of injury I would have a hard time finishing my walk.

There was nothing in Wimsatter except an unattractive-looking gas station and sandwiches that were at least seven days old. The wind blew the dry dust on my face. There were no tourists and so the place looked rather remote and desolate. "How often does the food guy come here from Rocksprings?"

The gas man said, "Usually once a week."

Ms. G had driven here by now so that we could have lunch together. We were hungry. We had to eat the little sausages that come in small cans and some Spam.

Later on that day my hands and feet were swollen, like a tick that had sucked all night on a puppy's neck, from all that extra salt I ate. That was our only food that day. I had a hard time sleeping that night though we had driven to a Motel 8 that was about thirty miles behind us. This was one of those days when I could not make it to any exit where I could find a decent place to sleep. Rocksprings was too far still.

It was here that I was looking for the Traveler's tree, that I had seen in Madagascar or Madagasay as it is called these days. It is almost ninety feet tall and looks like a palm tree with large banana-like leaves and each leaf holds almost a quart of rain water at its base. Unfortunately there was no such tree to give me shade or water.

An interesting encounter with a truck driver happened today to make the day interesting. I was still not quite at Wimsatter and I was walking and sweating quite a bit. I saw a truck that pulled over just ahead of me. I walked past the cab window when the driver said, "Where are you going? What is SPAVA?" After I explained to him he said, "I am going to Seattle and then to Portland. Come on in. I have air-conditioning. I am from Russia."

A chill ran down my spine. "No, I need to walk the distance. I have promised to the children."

"You will have fun. We will talk and the time will pass." I declined and continued walking. After a few minutes he drove away.

He reminded me of a story I had heard long time ago. How someone got enticed to get inside a truck and then he was raped and thrown into a ravine. His body was not found for two months. I did not have much of an appetite on this day. Just before I fell asleep I remembered that Bram Stoker had written in *Dracula* that "Knowledge is stronger than memory and we should not trust the weaker."

Next morning I realized why the area is called a desert. It was cold. The wind blew hard and mean. It tried to drag me towards the mountains at the horizon through the vast openness. There were scrubby bushes on both sides of the road that resisted being uprooted by the demonic sneezes that sprayed them unpredictably. It seemed as though the arms of the bushes were being pulled up by force as they resisted and they were unclothed by the dusty hands of the gusts of circling whirls. The whole area felt half-asleep and eerie. I felt that there was something secretive in the air. I saw a large rabbit that ran between the bushes. The shoulders of the interstate were covered with a thin layer of sandy soil and the grass beyond the six feet of concrete was scant and dry and strewn with pebbles of different colors. I wanted to move on.

I remained excited about my journey with the vision of the ocean that lay ahead of me. I just recognized that I have not had much time to talk to many people about SPAVA except the persons who waited at our tables. During the evenings when I had stopped walking for the day I had no energy for chitchat and in the mornings I was in a rush to get to the road to start the day. Mr. B, a Chinese gentleman, was extremely nice to me and had told me that he was a student at the University at Laramie. He was learning business and wanted me to write him a letter after I would finish my walk. I told him that I would.

I was in a reminiscent mood and I told Anna about my friend Dr. R. "He was a loving man. Every night around 9 p.m. he came to the hospital to read

EEGs. He always paged me to invite me to sit with him while he read the tests. These encounters developed into a wonderful friendship that I cherish very much even today. The knowledge that I acquired through his acquaintance helped me immensely during my neurosurgical practice. One day while I was working, a nurse, who later became my wife, had asked me to arrange a date between her and my friend, Dr. R.

"I did not tell Dr. R about this exciting opportunity that was to come his way but I did tell the requesting lady that Dr. R was not interested but I was. It was after ten years during a dinner at our house that I told my friend and my wife the truth. We laughed and he congratulated me at my skill of finding the woman of my dreams."

"Hey, you were getting ready to tell me about a girl by the name of Munna."

"I knew Munna. She was a sweet girl with a smile like Mona Lisa when I knew her. I had asked her to review a book that I had written. Munna had said that there is a lot of truth in that book that I wrote but part of it was possibly my imagination. She thought that since I could not decipher between the two enough to draw a line to separate, it was good that I created a bridge connecting the two with love."

Anna was listening. "Have you told your professors that you loved them?"

I said, "Let me tell you what I wrote for the *Bulletin of American Association of Neurosurgeons* when the committee had asked the membership to write about incidents or people that either changed their lives or got them interested in neurosurgery.

"I knew I wanted to be a neurosurgeon ever since I was ten years old and I had confided that to my grandfather while sitting on a mat on the field in front of our house. He was a physician who taught me to love and be disciplined. In early '60s I had read Dr. Spurling's book and thought that it would be fun to be with him and thus I came to Louisville, Kentucky. Here I met Dr. Richard Roth, neurologist, who introduced me to Dr. Charles Wilson, professor at University of Kentucky. Dr. Spurling had long retired when I had arrived. I had read his book and actually didn't know when he had retired. Dr. Wilson had instructed me during rounds that I must not participate in small talk and that I should be extremely diligent in learning details. He showed compassion and kindness. He had accepted me to join him at San Francisco as one of his residents.

"Unfortunately, the laws of the land discriminated against foreign-born physicians and he couldn't train me for the entire duration. He helped me to go to Ohio State University where I worked with Dr. W. E. Hunt, Dr. John Meagher and Dr. Martin P. Sayers. Those were the best years of my life. They taught me persistence, tolerance and the rules of survival during the most trying times. We worked often eighteen-hour days with minimum food and sleep. Jack always loaned me twenty dollars at the end of the month because I needed grocery money. I never returned it. They were master surgeons in the operating rooms and the finest clinicians. My dream had come true. They had helped me to understand love, compassion, hard work and seeing triumph even when I was sad and wept for my patients. They were giants because they truly loved the residents and their patients. When my father had met Dr. Hunt for the first time and enquired about my abilities as a prospective surgeon I still remember him saying 'He is eminently educable.' He had said to us on many occasions 'advance on a wide front' as he opened the arachnoids along the optic nerve and if by chance something bled during an operation he often called for Dr. Hiroshe Abe, who was a resident in neurology. No matter what Dr. Abe always bowed and said 'very nice, very nice.' Dr. Hunt just loved to hear that. I loved my professors."

Albert Einstein wrote, "The wonderful things you learn in schools and colleges are the work of many generations produced by enthusiastic effort and infinite labor…and all this is put in to your hands as your inheritance in order that you may receive it, honor it, add to it, and one day faithfully hand it over to your children." I told Anna that one time when I was teaching the SPAVA curriculum in an eleventh grade class one of the students had said to me, "Dr. Tim, you only teach about people who have died," and then I told him to tell us something about him so that we can learn from it and honor that act. Many children do not understand the value of the persons who have gone before us so that we can enjoy the freedom and knowledge we have today.

Munna and Ashoke

We had called it quits early that day. I was lying down on the grass away from the shoulder. I wanted Anna to hear about Munna. I remembered her and the story that she had told me:

I was born in Ohio. My parents had emigrated from India. Ashoke and I usually sat at the table, on the balcony, overlooking the street in the center of Thamel, just next to Katmandu Guesthouse. We spent a couple of months here every year to assist in the medical services. I started coming here to learn a bit of tropical dermatology and also to share my knowledge of management of cancers around the head and neck area. This opportunity came about through the national organization of my specialty, to volunteer in a country of my choice. We did not see too many melanomas here although every one of us is vigilant about spotting this aggressive type of cancer. We always drank beer and ate lots of Indian and Thai food and of course Momos either fried or steamed. I liked the pot stickers filled with pork or vegetables. This is actually a Tibetan dish. I enjoy eating food from different countries. Some days I enjoyed eating Newari food. The spices used to cook these dishes are similar to those that are used in cooking Indian food. Dal or lentil soup is the same. Kwati is a tasty soup made from of different beans and is usually followed by Samay Baji. It is a ritual dish of flattened rice, roasted meat, smoked fish, boiled eggs and black soybeans. There is of course achar (chutney), tarkari (vegetables), sukuti (hot and spicy concoction of dried meat roasted on fire) and meat curries.

It was one of those evenings when I was feeling bubbly and was telling Ashoke that I had just reconnected with a guy after many years. This joy brought a lot of memories back and there was a queue in my brain but some thoughts were impatient and wanted to break the line though not for any special reason. Our waiter was very gentle which is characteristic of most people of Nepalese origin. He had noticed that we had finished our beer and wanted to know if we wanted a refill. I looked at Ashoke. He knew what I wanted. So he nodded yes. That is the custom in Nepal. Men usually speak up when they are with a woman as though they are in charge!

By the way, before we go any further let me introduce Ashoke to you. He was a surgeon from Louisville, Kentucky. He came here to help with the surgical program and I met him here one afternoon during lunchtime at a restaurant across the street from the University Hospital. I was sitting at a table to his side but slightly in front of him in a restaurant. The owner of the restaurant hires only those who are hearing and speech impaired. It became apparent to me from the tone of his voice that Ashoke was not aware of the fact that his server was challenged in the area of hearing and speech. Our eyes met. He greeted and asked if I would join him since we were both by ourselves. 'Are you a doctor in the hospital too?' I nodded in the affirmative. Since then we met for dinner almost every day after work .It was convenient as we both stayed at the same hotel and this way neither of us had to eat alone.

I met this guy that I am going to call BB when we were in high school. We lived in a small town and there wasn't that much to do except go to the drive-in movies. Sometimes we had a root beer float. We sometimes hung out at BB's farm. We sat next to the creek or watched the chickens. There wasn't that much common between us except the fact that we were both young. His father had helped him to buy a '59 Thunderbird and he loved to drive it around. We tried to study together but often it didn't work out owing to the fact that BB would get too excited and he would try to kiss me everywhere. I was a little bit afraid to go all the way and had to push him away. He would pout and sometimes would yell at me. I was afraid something might go wrong since each time he would kiss me he poked me above my waist with his body. He was a bit taller than I was. BB liked the fact that I was his girlfriend. I did not know if he liked me or liked himself for having me by his side.

The teachers liked me too. I enjoyed the status. I had overheard the boys' talk about his prowess. You know what! Don't you? At that time I felt that I possessed something special. Just after we graduated from high school BB got drafted. It was not even a month that he was to leave for Hawaii. Two nights before his departure his parents were gone for a couple of hours and we were together when he insisted and I gave in to him thinking maybe that was the best prize I could give him. It didn't last long. That was my first and by looking at his face when it all ended on my stomach I wondered if he knew what he was doing. I didn't understand why he said sorry. After about a year when I was in college I wrote him a "Dear John" letter. I did not include a return address.

After a couple of months I stopped by to his mother's house to return the friendship ring he had given me and also to explain that we have different plans in life. His mother treated me real distant and handed me a letter that she had opened although it was addressed to me. BB called me an "N—r" woman. I drove home more alone than when I had gone to visit. I always felt that I had given away too much of myself and now I felt that it was taken from me. I sobbed in solitude.

Surely, you are not going to talk about him.

No, but I had to tell you this as a prelude to the next array of events that took place. I was bummed out and didn't want to talk anymore. So I asked Ashoke as to what he has been doing. He agreed to read me the book he was writing a bit every day. "I want to tell you, Munna, by chance if I don't finish it for some reason I want you to finish it for me from what you have heard from me." I agreed.

Although the menu was primarily for the tourists coming from the West they had Tawkhaaa on the menu. I ordered the dish. It is a jellied meat curry that is served cold. It was delicious and it tasted great with beer. It was only later that I modified the dish and served with hot red pepper jelly as an additive on the plate. The story that Ashoke began after this was just as appetizing.

I looked at myself one day in the mirror and suddenly realized that I had grown old. I practiced as a surgeon for more than twenty-five years. But now as I looked back I wondered where did those years go? My marriage had just ended after twenty-five years of exuberant life. I always knew that the Taj Mahal was one of the greatest examples of expression of conjugal love. But then in reality it is only a mausoleum!

I expressed my joy during living. I didn't think that it mattered about love after I am dead? At this age, this time I felt that I was alone. My spouse had found a new dog more exciting. I went past the colorful fire hydrants only with wishful imagination because I couldn't raise my leg. My hip hurt to raise my legs. Her departure made me feel more impotent than I possibly could have been. I looked at my children. They had their own lives.

I shaved off my moustache. It was a kind of gray rough which had bordered narrow bald fairways. I trimmed my eyebrows that were beginning to look like a couple of hamsters' backs after they had wild sex. I started dating different women. My daughter cautioned me. "Dad, pace yourself!" I had dinner companions. I went to the movies and dinner frequently with women I barely knew. We went to see operas and ballet. I watched *Anna Karenina* performed with exquisite movements and heart-wrenching music but I got angry. I knew exactly why. It was for the same reason that I have been angry with Madame Bovary, Josephine, Gretchen, and even Daisy from *The Great Gatsby*. I even laughed at times to disguise my true feelings. But my inside was empty. I needed something more than just sex and sleep. My daughter called me at dinnertime most nights. "Dad, I don't want you to have dinner with the Red Baron every night."

"I don't love you anymore" is the last thing I had heard as I remembered. And those words reverberated in my head like a boomerang that just did not stop. I would yell out every so often, but how could she have not loved me after twenty-five years? This question bothered me forever. How could I have not been lovable? She was my soul mate. My love! I loved her body, her mind and all. There were times when I asked her funny questions in jest during intimacy knowing full well what the answer would be. Then I would say, "OK, why don't we start again and make marks on the carpet with a pen below the bed so we wouldn't forget to count as to how many times we screamed." We would fall asleep in absolute exhaustion. I connected all the dots of the exciting times in the car, in the barn, even in a loft next to the pilots' cabin inside a 747.

I vividly remember the times we had spent in the garden together and planted hedges in the rain. How about the time when we just lain on the couch and listened to the raindrops hitting the window of the sunroom? How about the time we just admired the frog that stuck to the glass and was catching bugs? I had never seen a frog's stomach before that. The frog didn't have a belly button of course. For some reason I had to think about it. Whenever I was with her I felt like a child at times; forgetful, demanding, loving and hoping and clinging on. "I tried hard but just couldn't love you," kept humming in my ears. I used to scream while driving on the expressway when no one else was in the car after she left. I talked to myself and often answered what I thought the response should have been but wasn't actually so. I got over all this slowly though unwillingly. I did not want anything to change. I am one of those that sit at the same seat in church for twenty-eight years. If I am late and I find someone else is sitting at my usual place I feel like I have not been to church at all! I am one of those that like to park in the same spot in the hospital parking lot as though it is my very own place and even get a little annoyed if someone else parks at my self-designated spot.

I was beginning to realize why Kawabata Yasunari received the Nobel Prize for literature. His childhood loneliness and preoccupation with death helped him write novels such as *Snow Country*. I understood the sadness of losing parents as a child and why it took him twelve years to write the book that I believe was a great cathartic. Finding peace was my motto too. So I read only selected chapters from the Old Testament because it seemed to me that the God of Jeremiah was too strong a dad with rules. I needed the love of the God of the New Testament.

My mind was like the third-class compartment of a train at Calcutta, totally cluttered and everyone trying to find a seat with a stuffed suitcase in hand. Different thoughts ran through my mind like the thousands of passengers erratically bumping against one another on the platforms. I needed to be focused. I needed fulfillment. I wanted a renewal of spirit. I looked for double rainbows in my yard every day when there wasn't even one.

My daughter informed me about the identity of the true Red Baron, Manfred Richthofen. "Dad, do you know why the pizza guys made him the savior of the lonesome? He was a combat pilot who allegedly shot down seventy-nine British and one Belgian plane while fighting for the Imperial Air Service. His successor as commander of the fighter group was Hermann Goring." I didn't understand why someone would want him to be a dinner companion. I thought that I wasn't that brave.

I read Bertrand Russell's *Conquest of Happiness* again. I needed a Siddhartha. I needed that mind of Siddhartha when it could say that he loved the rock because it represented the past, present and the future all at the same time. Govinda realized that peace was within and he didn't have to hunt for it. I watched Bronco Billy and wanted to be the doctor that helped Clint Eastwood as he fixed the torn tent. I bought a gun belt and walked around in my house wearing it and listening to John Lenin and the Beatles.

My friends were supportive and gave me many ideas. They said I should travel. Some suggested that I place an ad in the paper citing my qualifications and someone just right would pop up in my life. I agreed with the former and found the latter rather distasteful yet funny. I didn't want to be merchandise in the meat market. I gave notice to my patients that I would retire. When my office staff informed me that my patients didn't want me to retire I felt important. My patients started calling me and telling me how important I was in their life and that I was irreplaceable. It made me feel good for the time. I realized all the more that I needed to retire because I was falling in love with myself. I wanted someone else to love me beside myself.

I restrained myself from buying a red convertible. I hated gold chains. But I got a small tattoo on my left shoulder. I didn't tell anyone that it was one of those washable kinds that went away after seven showers. I felt that I was in. I drank whiskey and smoked cigars. I had time to read *Crime and Punishment again*. I saw *Les Miserables* and *Don Giovanni*. I read and reread the Psalms. I learnt about Kashf (Arabic meaning is revelation), a very meaningful word in Sufism (Islamic mysticism). It is the privileged inner knowledge that is acquired from direct vision of God and personal experience.

The truths revealed by attaining Kashf cannot be transmitted to someone who has not had a similar experience. It is about finding peace based on the principle of faith that is different from Ilm (knowledge) based on theology and logic. I stuck to my faith.

The initial conversions to Islam in India happened because of the message of peace from the Sufi saints. This message had inspired the Bhakti movement. Liberal Islam had instituted many Hindu customs. Many Sufi saints were known both by Hindu and Muslim names, e.g. Pir Patho as Raj Gopichand. I started reading more about the fundamentalists in religions. I wrote to the prime minister of India protesting when the Shahi Imam of Jama Masjid called for jihad in favor of Osama Bin Laden. I knew that Mrs. Indira Gandhi had created the Shahi Imam to garner the Muslim votes.

Since the time of Muhammad, the Imams, called Muftis and Qazis, have been paid by the state to interpret the Sharia to common Muslim. This is much like in the Catholic churches where only the priest reads the Bible. I had once asked one of the stewards in Pakistani airlines to explain to me the Urdu prayer that is recited from the Koran each time as the plane takes off. He told me that only special people can do that and he was not allowed to explain it to me.

Incidentally, the long beard, headgear and borkha with which Islam is associated today have no Koranic sanctions. Montgomery Watt explained in his book, *What Is Islam*, that around the eighth century, Christian Europe became conscious of Islam as its greatest enemy. Christendom had to bolster confidence by placing the enemy in the most unfavorable light possible. The image created in the twelfth and thirteenth centuries continued to dominate

European thinking about Islam… (That)…it was a religion of violence, spread by the sword, it is a religion without ascetics, gaining adherents by pandering to their sexual appetites.

The Hindu priests and the Muslim clerics alike performed social ceremonies and accepted gifts and thus making the rituals more important than the religion. When I was real young I might have attended a circumcision party. I didn't know what was being cut off till I was much older. I had read about Christian fundamentalists in Eastern Kentucky. I recalled that a man called Mr. Hensley had some sort of revelation while standing on White Mountain and then started a church with believers that believed handling a serpent would demonstrate true faith. Many persons have died during anointing when folks have handled rattlesnakes with emotional exuberance. The rattlesnake, not being much of a friend to the Christians, have bitten them in self-defense and for that matter they would probably bite a Muslim just as well! In South India there is a temple where cobras are worshipped as they have been coming out of their dens for centuries to drink milk placed in special containers at a certain time of the day.

I wanted to tell Anna that my father used to tell me that the "more you read the appetite for reading would grow." He said that if I hadn't read Omar Khyaam I would have never missed Hafez, the great Sufi mystic.

I remembered from Hafez: "The portals of the heaven will open up, and with that will come unfastened all the complicated knots of our life. But will this be really possible? The path may not be open to the vain, self-styled men of religion, but have faith in your God and the right path will show up."

I looked up and saw a big streak of white wool across the sky. I figured it was some sort of jet practicing warfare or such. Anna asked me if I have ever been to Cape Canaveral. I answered in the affirmative. "Do you know anything about jet engines?" I said no. "Jet propulsion engines by definition produce combustion inside and the combustion products produce a thrust sending the products rearward." She said that the Australians, Russians and the Americans are all trying to develop an engine called Scramjet that takes in air from the atmosphere and then compress it enough to burn while traveling six or seven times the speed of sound. If it works then they don't have to carry oxidizer on board like the conventional rocket engine. It will save fuel and may be a lighter payload.

So I said, "What kind of engine was that one that we just saw in the sky?"

"I don't know," she said. I had read Chuck Yeager's book that he wrote after being the first man to have traveled faster than the speed of sound in a jet in 1947.

Ashoke continued:

I went fishing. I even caught some big salmon at Seward. I had met a woman friend! I began exercising and began to make myself feel good. I became politically active. I started writing letters to the senators and congressmen. I started using the recycling bin. I didn't mind picking up the trash can lying upside down thrown across the street after the garbage man had left. I didn't drive fast enough to be awarded tickets anymore. I smiled even if someone left the turning signals on forever. I remained calm when someone changed lanes in front of me without turning on the turn signal light.

I went to work in Nepal for months and took time out to walk in the mountains. I met some of the Sadhus. I mailed pictures, to my friends, of Sadhus with their faces painted and wisps of smoke rising from the chillum (the container that houses Ganja). "You are compensating for the sadness. Write about the times you felt loved," said Madhu Baba. "Then you will find peace." He was a Sadhu who had no worldly possessions now though at one time he was wealthy. "Happiness is a mindset. I think the way to achieve it is to reach a stage in life when all needs and wants are conquered," he told me. "You have to feel what Omar Khyaam felt and then give it up by making a choice and not lose it owing to bad luck. It has to be a spontaneous event. It has to be a destination, the last stop of the train of life."

I went to my old high school and found out the address of my teachers who were still alive and wrote them thank-you notes. I bought a burial insurance. I began to admire myself when I walked out of the shower. I was beginning to feel alive again.

I was cynical. I was critical. I was admiring and complimenting yet full of contradictions all within a matter of minutes. It was a fun time at San Diego at the Naval Hospital. The uniform, the salute and the martinis were fun. I jotted down the times in my life when I laughed loud and made someone else laugh with me.

The lieutenant commander, Nurse Jennifer, held the retractor while I operated on a subdural hematoma (a blood clot inside the head) of a young soldier. Later we drank beer and went our separate ways but somehow I felt that something more should have happened. But nothing did. I seemed to think for some reason that I should have been found sexually attractive to almost everyone.

I grew. But it was not of my doing. I called my older brother and told him that if anytime in my life I needed a mother it was at this moment. He said, "You have to be your own mother. Find out what is nurturing and go with it. Write it down." I started writing about the times when I felt most nurtured. This is what I wrote. It transformed me. I learnt to love again. At times I felt like a child.

I remembered that a long time ago I had written a note to a girl saying that I loved her. She was my Allison in Peyton Place and I was Norman. She was sweet. She confided in me that she had gone "all the way" once. I didn't care. She made me feel whole. I had met one of her uncles quite some time back. He was kind of a curmudgeonly sort of a fellow. He had strong opinions and always ended his comments with some verse from the Bible. He wanted me to know that he was a very religious man. His religiosity was thought by some to be inconsistent with his colorful private life but no one questioned his sincerity. He often spoke to me about Daniel's ability to interpret dreams and Abraham's faith. I told him that he should include Job in his armamentarium. He had said to me once, "Ash, I am glad you are a Christian. It really don't matter that your skin is little dark. You will go to heaven." I was always happy to be reassured about my final destination, particularly since I felt that I had not earned the currency for the passage yet.

He knew that Jesus was the Savior. However, sometimes during the evenings he had to make sure that some of "them colored folks didn't get the wrong idea that they are going to heaven with us folks." I don't believe he included me in the "us folks" although he had said differently earlier. I recall asking him once if he thought Jesus needed any help during the nights when he stood with others wearing funny white clothes. "Don't mock me," I recall hearing. "That's the trouble with you foreigners. I show you my friendship and you think everyone should be free to do anything they want." John referred to anyone with a darker skin as a foreigner.

He believed that America is for white folks only. I tried not to bring up the topic of equality and freedom for discussion with him. He thought that God overlooked little peccadilloes like drinking, smoking and a little fun with women. He looks at the big picture for folks like us. "We fought them wars. We freed the world, you know. Isn't that the reason that you are here, far away from your native country and all?" On such special occasions I always agreed with John.

He and his buddy had owned a liquor store once in the past. "Some foreigner had the audacity to tell me that I was charging twenty percent more than the liquor store down the road. You know where I told him to go. He had no idea that this is a free country and we can charge whatever we want. Now, I don't know what happened and all, but the guy who owned the other store was some sort of a shenanigan I guess, because the folks that used to come to my store got religion or such. So I just let him have all the drinking customers. It ain't good for you anyway. I think real money is in tobacco and ginseng, you know, from the real business point and everything."

He had graduated from high school. He got drafted and went to Vietnam. "We should have never tried to have helped them sons of bi—s," he carried on. "Two years of my life are gone. I know that I was a helicopter door gunner and all. I don't remember much of it though. Some of it just in bits and pieces like a jigsaw puzzle. I was a kid. For some reason there is a fog or something in my memory. Some of my other buddies have some kind of a vision and they get all sweaty and nervous. The doc calls it flashback Vietnam syndrome. I am glad I don't have that.

"My dad used to have something like that and he had never been outside the country. They thought he had bad blood or something. He used to walk funny too like he was walking on them hot coals like folks in your country do.

"Yeah, I smoked a little and maybe drunk a bit too. The army doctor was one of your kind, you know, a foreigner, and he told me I had the claps. I told him that my problem was from 'Orange Yellow,' the stuff that we had not knowed about yet. Anyway he wasn't much of a doctor. I got better from some penicillin shot he gave me but even now they say I have a stricture or something. In my younger days I could take down the bark of a tree from the force of my piss, you know what I mean. Now I couldn't move a piece of sliding jelly in my toilet bowl. I was a young man but I couldn't act like one."

He was disgusted at the doctor. The government is going by what the doctor has put on the record and not taking responsibility. John always thought he was well traveled because he had seen the Far East on account of having been to Vietnam and Saigon a couple of times. "Them women got no class," he said. He confided in me that one time after he had smoked pot, "I had wild sex. I tell you I was a bloody raging maniac. I just could not be satisfied and it seemed like I could do it forever. I don't remember what all I did." He giggled. He had some problem with the tip of his tongue after that. He told the doctor that he might have bit it during excitement and fear while sitting in the foxholes. "He did a blood test and gave me a shot of penicillin." He always reminded me that he had been in real combat. "You might have been a commander or such in the reserve unit but it ain't like being there you know." I didn't disagree.

John came home. He was a hero in his town. He fought for his country and more importantly he was alive and well. Two of his buddies from the neighboring town weren't so lucky. He had gone all the way only once before his call to duty. He found his old girlfriend. He confided in her that he has been saving himself in eager anticipation of this moment. He had received a citation for some heroic acts. He began to believe that the impressive writing on the citation is a true representation of what he had actually done.

Everyone talked about his great performance during the war. Different stores had different stories, one trying to outdo the other. He was the coveted young man of the town. He was fully immersed and re-baptized. He felt clean and real proud.

He gave speeches about being an American. He said that we should try to show everyone why we Americans are the greatest. We Americans have made the world free. He fell in love with himself and his girlfriend too. He was soon married.

He joined a church. He sang in the choir. He raised his arms and swayed and sang in animated fashion with his eyes closed, "Everything else is sinking sand." He learnt the Proverbs. He quoted Reverend Billy Graham, "If you find a perfect church join it because it won't be perfect after that." He was a born-again Christian. He taught a Sunday school class and often discussed about the morality of our youth. He recited, "I am the resurrection and life…never die." He came to all the potluck dinners and shook everyone's hands and told everyone that they looked good and they were all blessed. He invited the pastor to come to Sunday dinner in his home every so often. He had a Bible study every Wednesday in his house and they discussed the Good Samaritan and read the Ecclesiastes and discussed why Numbers should not be a subject of discussion in modern-day living.

They drank orange juice and coffee during the class and praised the Lord together in Christian brotherhood. The discussion was always lively, particularly since the pastor always said, "Christianity is the best religion in the world. The Bible is the only book about the only true God. Only our leader was the son of God. It is the centripetal force in other religions whereas we are centrifugal and drawn to God personally because He chose us. 'We are' because of God. Look what God can do by studying the life of Paul. Remember he was Saul. We have hope, brothers and sisters! God's peace is with you."

The pastor believed that drinking, smoking, gambling and dancing were not to be condoned. John was busy recruiting new members to the church. He was in charge of the welcoming committee. They were responsible for finding out who had moved in the general neighborhood and then tell them about the happenings in this church. Proselytizing was an important part of the job. John wanted to "save" everyone. They prayed for the Hindus, Buddhists and the Muslims. It was generally felt that "these heathens" were not going to heaven because the Bible didn't say that they could and that they were kind of "pagan like."

The congregation was large and they had one black member. Everyone kind of made an effort to say good morning to Sam and his family. It was the Christian thing to do. Everyone was making an effort to integrate. Busing had just been made mandatory. The church was being progressive. A few thought that Sam, Wauneta and Letuwan were little different but wanted them to feel part of everything. John knew that Wauneta was going to bring a vegetable and a meat dish for one of their first potluck dinners. Some of the busy active women of the church had confided to John with apprehension that kale and chitlins wouldn't go very well with the other items for the meal, but when it turned out to be fried chicken and broccoli someone had said, "Shoot, they are almost like us." The morning service often began with the reading of "The Lord is my shepherd." The music was exquisite. The children had a glow on their faces. This was an active and vibrant place of worship.

John was offered a job in Chicago as an undercover cop. But he liked being the local policeman. The city council thought that it would be real good to have little extra protection and John was offered the job. He was following in his father's footsteps. He had a side business of pruning trees. He called himself a tree surgeon. He thought he could make some extra three to four hundred dollars every week on top of his salary of fifteen thousand dollars per year. He thought that was more than his dad made and he certainly was comfortable. He could have made a little more money if he had taken the out-of-town job. He resisted.

He wanted to enjoy Amy. He hadn't been home but a couple of years. He had put on a little weight since his marriage and felt settled. He believed in

"Man should eat and drink...love," as it is said in the Ecclesiastes. He had married Amy out of a self-imposed obligation. He thought that since he was the first one to have taken her it was only right that he should marry her. "Boy, if you mess around with a girl, you better be ready to marry her. Someone may do the same to your sister," Bubba had told him. His father was a Christian man and all! John liked sex and Amy was there. And that was that.

John was real pleased the way his life was going. Amy had learnt that the way to a man's heart was through his stomach. Amy obliged in every way. They bathed and showered together. They spent time at the local motel sometimes. John thought that going to the motel at times added excitement to their life. It felt like as though he was cheating. That was fun. Chris, the manager, knew not to charge Officer John any hourly rate. They made out in the drive-in movies and at times even in his police office. He kept his uniform on most of the times because he liked being the boss. One time he stood on his chair with his gun cocked when Amy made him feel real good. He soon got Amy pregnant. They had a boy, Jonathan. He was baptized and John introduced him to the church community. John remained active in his commitment to the society. He raised Jonathan with the help of Amy. Mary Joe had come along soon after.

John's sister, Dorothy, had walked in front of an oncoming train. Bubba didn't cry at the funeral. "Crying is not what big men do," Bubba had said to John when he was whimpering. She was always kind of shy and afraid of everything, Bubba had said to him. She tried to tell John once that she hurt between her legs a lot. John was young. He told his mom to take her to see Doc Burns. He didn't understand what could be wrong with Sis. "There is nothing wrong with you, young lady, and don't you try to sass me," his dad would often yell at her. "Going to the doctor was a big waste of money. They don't do anything any way. They will probably give her a penicillin shot and charge me twenty bucks," Bubba had said.

John was only ten years old. But he thought that it was real funny that dad was real sweet to her and sat her on his lap and everything. But Sis just didn't want to do that. Sometimes Bubba picked her up from school and took her to picnics all by herself. He wanted to spend more time with his daughter. He had learnt about spending more time with children after reading some psychology magazine called *Red Book* that one of the employees in the office read all the time. It seemed that Betty had little to say in things of this nature. There was some grumbling in town after Dorothy's death but none dared to talk much when they were in Bubba's hearing range, the town sheriff.

It was about a year after the death of their daughter that Bubba had come down with some sort of an illness for which he had to retire. Doc Burns had told John that his dad had come down with some illness that affected his mind. It was believed that he had contracted some form of insanity on account of his blood getting poisoned or such. He had to make several overnight trips to different states in the past. Bubba had explained to them that the trips were related to the "law." "I have to go to southern Kentucky for a couple of days, hon, to get a few items of legal nature ironed out, you hear," his dad would say before he left. It was decided that from all that hard work that the sheriff had to do his brain was afflicted with a condition of going mad. Doc Burns was asked by the city council to sign a paper saying that this condition was related to work so he could retire on work-related disability.

He had trouble getting around and at times he screamed with pain from his shin areas. They said that he saw things walking or swimming in front of him. He was found dead, lying on the road, face down outside his house. It was decided that he had fallen off the roof while trying to clean gutters during a cold February day in Indiana. He had a clump of leaves in his right hand. One of the windows from the dormer was open.

John went to the funeral with his mother. Neighbors told him that "Bubba looks real good. Boy, grow up like him and be a real man." The preacher read a glowing eulogy depicting him almost like a saint, "much like St. Francis of Assisi." He was described as a "community leader, with high morals who loved everyone and could not even hurt an animal. He had lived his life without a blemish. He loved his family and dedicated his life to maintain law and order in the community where he had grown up."

John just stood there holding his mother's hand. He hadn't quite fathomed what actually just happened or what was to become of him. He couldn't even cry although his mother kept on wiping her eyes every so often. John didn't exactly know who Assisi was because that sort of thing was not taught in the schools. But one of his classmates had a picture of a man with different animals that were all eating from the same plate. He remembered that lions, donkeys and chickens were all together just hanging around this man. There was written in small print at the bottom of the picture St. Francis of Assisi.

But he knew that his dad was not like that at all. As a matter of fact his dad hated animals. He had a gerbil once. It used to try to hide at different places in the house. One Sunday morning as they were all getting ready for church in a hurry he heard this huge thud and a hateful yelling. "This bloody rat damn near killed me." Everyone ran to the bathroom to find Bubba half naked lying on the floor on his side. He had fallen off the toilet with his pants down and Gyro was lying flattened next to him. He said that as he was reading the paper in a relaxed mode he felt something fuzzy crawling near his ankle and it scared him to death. In his startle he jumped up but owing to his pants being down to his ankles he fell down and felt something fuzzy and juicy underneath his buttocks.

As he scraped this saucy object with the fingers of his right hand he found Gyro, who was not moving except a bit near his moustache. And had a subdued look in one eye and the other eye socket was empty.

The day didn't go very well. Bubba had to take a shower again, change all his clothes and they were late for church. John felt sorry for Gyro, who was probably hiding behind the toilet next to the vent just for fun. He knew that Bubba must have scared Gyro to go berserk although he might have said that he was quietly reading the paper. Betty would often have to turn on loud music outside the bathroom whenever they had guests to camouflage Bubba's noisy behavior on occasions when Bubba would have to use the bathroom. John buried Gyro next to a peony bush. He had seen ants on the plants in the past and he thought that if the ants would eat up the meat he could recover the bones and save them for show and tell the following Friday. Unfortunately, it was July and there were no ants near the peony bushes. On Friday morning when he quickly dug up near the stick that he had placed as a marker for the grave site he saw a lot of maggots and that gave him the "willies." He just didn't bother anymore. He didn't have anything to show but he told everyone that Gyro had died and he wanted to observe a little silence like they do in church sometime.

He remembered that his mom had gotten him a rabbit for Easter. He had named it Peter. He loved Peter and walked everywhere in the neighborhood holding him next to his chest. He enjoyed the soft fur and the fact that Peter ate from his hand. He felt Peter's heartbeat against his chest. He sometimes wished that he and Peter could be one. He would let Peter loose in the grass and Peter would run. Peter would sit and munch next to the dandelions but he would always come back for the sliced carrots that John would offer. He mostly liked Peter's nose and moustache. He always felt warm when he held Peter and they were friends.

Whenever John spoke Peter seemed to listen and sometimes blinked when he got tired of looking. John tried to look inside Peter's eyes and wondered why they were red and shiny yet Peter didn't seem to be uncomfortable.

He remembered that he had pink eye once and he was really miserable and he had to stay home from school for a couple of days. He used to lay his book bag on the deck after he got off the bus and always ran to Peter's cage first before he came inside the house. But one day when he came home from school he could not find Peter in the cage. He found Peter on a stick resting against the back fence lying limp with eyes closed and a blood-stained mouth. In the evening he had asked Bubba if he knew that Peter was dead. Bubba said that the rabbit was too destructive and he had to fix him.

John went to his room and wept on the pillow and didn't eat dinner that night. Bubba sometimes came home for lunch. This was a special lunch day because he had gotten an afternoon "nookie." He felt dissatisfied despite the surprise gift. He was not happy the way "Betty did the things," he thought in his mind. Being raised in the environment where he was he didn't know how to communicate with his lover but he did know how to pout.

As he was zipping his pants he saw this rabbit enjoying himself in the lettuce patch that was just outside his cage. The cage had gotten unlatched somehow. The scene of this enjoyment infuriated Bubba. At one moment it even seemed to him that Peter looked directly towards him and wiggled its nose and moustache as though to tease him for his impotence. This just did it for him. He pithed the rabbit for making fun of him.

He always thought that it was Bettie's fault that he couldn't arouse her. He thought that she was a woman and "it is not my problem that she can't come" and that was that. He thought that it was kind of funny that no sooner did he get close to her he always got wet and became limp. Betty was a preacher's daughter and had grown up in a small town. She didn't know what actually an orgasmic experience was when she got married. She only knew the word. Her mother had told her, "If you just wait for your husband then sex would be fine because you wouldn't know anything different." She had masturbated a little bit when she was in high school. She always used Crisco and she used a little bit of lipstick for color on her fingers. She sometimes used her mom's vibrator. These were short-lasting projects, just "getting the rocks off" kind of experiences. She wanted more. She had anticipated something of longer duration after the matrimonial experience that her mother had promised her.

She had imagined that the sexual experience had the potential of engendering an amorous assimilation of fluids that would lead to an ascent to expanses beyond her body's capacity to withhold. Her feelings would break the bank with a bang so to say! She thought that she would encase the male genitalia inside her much like a baguette or samosa enclosing a tasty meat. As she would meld while dipping in a deep fryer the intensity of the heat would pop the morsels open with a sound and a spark both of which would be startling. For many years she thought that Bubba knew what he was doing. But no one made any noise except Bubba's snoring that followed shortly after the fondling.

She knew that a man had to be satisfied to keep tame. She had seen some pictures of male organs in dirty magazines once. She had talked with some of the women and they had told her to try to play with herself in "that special area just before the entrance to the vagina." One of them even told her, "You are a preacher's daughter, so think of one reason why God gave that little honey to us. So use it to keep it alive." One of them had told her, "Honey, ride them like a horse, that will get you there." Bubba wasn't there long enough.

At times after Bubba left she would light a candle. She would lie on her side and look at herself in the mirror and then take a little warm margarine and rub herself until her whole body would tingle. When she would get all curly and everything she would push in a condom-fitted dildo into herself and squeeze it during her spasmodic ecstasy till she became all flushed in her neck and her back would feel hot. She then just rolled over in her sweaty body and fell asleep. She had heard the word "intercourse" and it bothered her that she could not find out what it meant in her marriage. Bubba had never been inside her except for a few seconds. She wondered if it would be more fun to be able to scream in ecstasy. She wanted an opportunity to scream. She wanted someone to f… her brains out and lie beside her to hear the soft sound of her satisfaction.

She wanted to moan and groan and then wanted to be held and caressed. She wanted to feel the way she had imagined some of the women felt in the few novels that she had read. She had never smoked cigarettes but someone had told her that smoking was no fun in the dark caves because you couldn't see the smoke. She wanted to see the smoke from her mouth during a raging spasmodic orgasmic explosion. She secretly resented Bubba for his failure to deliver one thing she needed most. As happens in many lives, one makes excuses and accepts substitutions. Betty lived with Bubba as though she was in love. Betty wanted a feeling of amorous togetherness, a joyful understanding, a sense of warmth and fulfillment of being together. She imagined herself to be the rainbow after the rain in her life so that she could shine and bring joy to her husband.

Betty went to the local ball games. She tried to raise money to clothe deprived children during Christmas. She tried to fill a couple of wishes from the Angel Tree. She volunteered in the hospital cafeteria where everyone came to eat on Sundays after church service. It is where you were seen if you had gone to church and everyone said they were glad to see you. It was the Morrison's of the time. Food was good and cheap.

Betty kept herself busy. She cooked and went to the grocery and did everything that was expected of her. She ironed everyone's clothes in her family. She took care of a small garden where Bubba raised lettuce. She helped with the homework of the children.

She remained active in the women's group where they chatted once a week and disseminated information to one another.

She didn't understand why they needed a newspaper. Everybody knew what was going on in town. Everyone knew what everyone else was doing. They participated in activities of "doing good" through the church. The women played pinochle and drank iced tea. They sometimes visited the "shut-ins." They usually went shopping at Woolworth and sometimes they went to Indianapolis or Terra Haute to shop at Sears. Almost all the women sewed. All of them had a Singer's machine. Needlepoint and making quilts was a big to-do and everyone had a project for the winter months, when driving was hazardous. Pickup trucks were the common modes of transportation. Many of them had stickers that said, "If you love America then Honk," "God made me and God made no junk or duplicates." There were many others with different aphorisms and admonitions such as, "If life is too easy, you ain't living it," "Don't be knocking if you see it rocking," "If you ate carrots, you will have better vision and maybe see Jesus" and "God has no power failure." It was only the outsiders whose trucks said, "Ditch the bitch. Let's go fishing."

John and Dorothy played together in the sand box when they were small. There was only a difference of two years between them. Bubba had made them a swing in the backyard. It was nothing fancy but functional. John often gave the push and Dorothy loved it. Soon they were playing in the creek just in the yonder behind the house. They tried to catch little minnows and whenever they were successful they kept them in little jelly jars. They made couple of holes in the lid. They always let them go after a day. "Sis, we don't know what to feed them fishes," said John.

They threw rocks to see who could throw the furthest. They talked silly at times and teased each other at times too but always just for fun. They were real close. They walked in the woods behind their school sometimes. There was a bit of woods behind the neighbor's house that they liked to walk through.

They walked through dogwoods and redbuds and a few thorny bushes. The bushes had no names. They picked the morning glories that always climbed the bushes. Dorothy picked an occasional stick and pretended that it was a protective cane. John liked walking through the woods for the spirit of adventure though they had trampled these grounds many times. Dorothy had seen the beady eyes of a copperhead once. John knew those brown camouflaged little snakes in the summertime. He stirred the leaves and the sticks on the ground and the snake went on its way. There were few sycamores that were higher than the rest of the trees. They always had some broken branches. The ground was covered with vines, wild strawberries and in some areas white mushrooms grew next to some old rotting wood. Dorothy beamed whenever John would say, "Sis, you are really clever, you know."

John didn't know mushrooms and so they never ate them. They had cleaned an area next to some holly bushes and wild rhododendrons for camping out during those special nights of the early fall when there were no bugs or snakes outside. They heard the leaves fall on the roof of their tent. John was brave. But it was Dorothy who had always said, "I will take care of any problems." The trees made weird shadows on the walls of the tent in the night. The dogs barked on occasions for reasons that they could not imagine. Dorothy always thought that some dogs let other dogs know when they were getting ready to take a nap. The frogs argued in the creek nearby and the crickets chatted through the evening while the two children fell into deep slumber.

Dorothy knew where the moth lived in the pine and juniper trees. But they were no bother outside in the moonlit sky. There was a large persimmon tree. They picked the persimmons from the ground after the first frost and Betty made them persimmon pudding and homemade whipped cream. John just loved the taste of it and he always had seconds. Dorothy sometimes had ticks in her hair and John would always make sure that they were all removed properly. John had heard that he could really get sick from the tick bites. They played hide and go seek. They loved each other and John always thought that he loved his sister more than anyone else.

Dorothy was good in math and always helped John, though he was older. Dorothy helped Betty do things around the house. She had a little standing stool in the kitchen. Betty got it for her one Easter. They colored the eggs together in kitchen. Betty always told her to learn to cook. "Someday you will have a man and men like women that can cook." Dorothy knew how to peel potatoes. "Mom, you peel the whole apple in one piece. I wish I could do that." They made apple butter together and Dorothy had already learnt how to make the pie crust from scratch. She still had plenty time to play.

Something happened to Dorothy and Betty didn't know what to do about it. Dorothy kind of stopped playing and just didn't like to come out of her room much. She began to hate going to school. She often had stomachaches. Betty had noticed a little sore between the legs when she was helping Betty one day for a special bath. Dorothy said, "I hurt it while playing." She was scared. She seemed sad. She didn't want to talk. Bubba thought she was just "ornery."

The job in Chicago turned out to be one of the most exciting events in John's life. He had been divorced almost a year. He still didn't have a steady girlfriend. He wasn't sure what he wanted to do with his life at this point and time. He called up his friends in Gary, Indiana. They made him the connection. He came over for the interview and got the job. He was told that he was going to be an undercover cop. He didn't have much experience with this sort of work. He wasn't told much about his present assignment except that he would know in bits and pieces. Someone will use the word Rudy and that would be his key contact and that Rudy would find him in the Greyhound bus station at Louisville, Kentucky. One afternoon John was just sitting outside the restroom and had barely dozed off after having smoked some pot at the projects when he was aroused by a disheveled fellow who held a knife at his throat while dragging him into the storage room. John was very strong but he was caught off guard. He noticed that he was being watched by three fellows who did not try to help him. The man mumbled he was Rudy and asked him to stay calm. John retired from the police force in Chicago. He bought a small home and lived in Mitchell, Indiana, where Betty also had lived after Bubba's death. John said to me that after all these years he has learnt the values of many Buddhists' ways. "Resolve to be tender with the young, compassionate with the aged, sympathetic with the striving, and tolerant of the weak and wrong, because sometime in your life you will have been all of these."

I told Anna that I loved her. Anna blushed. The cloud above was gone. I played tricks with Anna as I walked. And at one time I had bent down and touched her. You know it, she bent with me! We played and she entertained me as I marched on to the next exit. I was becoming quite an expert having walked on many interstates. At the end of the day I seem to talk louder to Anna because I feel like all day I am sitting in the front row of Indy 500. Ms. G told me that she had a flat tire. She was an expert by now because she had one of the tires fixed once outside Mound City, Missouri.

I Share More About Myself with Anna

It was a few years back when we were at the Katmandu Guest House. I think this is when Nuevo livro da Vida began. On September 15 there were only about thirty people in the large plane going from Detroit to Amsterdam. This was only four days after we were attacked by the Muslim extremists from different countries. The tears were still fresh in our eyes. I was walking down the aisle when our eyes met. We had not seen each other in ten years. I had met her for the first time at Half Moon Island. We were both enjoying the waddling walk of the chinstrap penguins and commenting on the aroma of the guano when my hand touched hers. We observed the kelp gulls, snowy sheathbills and looked for the Antarctic terns. We walked together and now and then I purposefully bumped my hands against hers. "Crustose lichens are readily found on the rocks of this island," said the guide. We returned to the boat and drank together till the wee hours before returning to our rooms. We had been through the Lemaire Channel and to Port Lockroy. We saw the gentoo penguins and the skuas. I watched Phoebe take a bath in the hot spring of the Deception Island. She lay in the icy ocean in her swimsuit with a smile of anticipation of warmth. I clicked my camera quickly because I knew that the smile would be short-lived.

As we went through Drake Passage into Cape Horn we were swaying and swinging erratically on forty-foot waves. I believe the ship doctor ran out of Phenergan injections. Phoebe and I were among the few that were not sick but we didn't eat anything that day. We sat under cover on the deck and watched the ocean heave and spew buckets of water on the upper decks, as we became closer. At Ushuaia I believe Phoebe ate half of a lamb and I ate a large amount of the Argentinean beef that was cooking on an open pit. She was excited and I hoped that it was not all because of the tasty food. We watched the January moon through our stateroom window play hide and seek with the clouds under the canopy of a gray sky. Our passion made us sweaty and then we both fell asleep with our bodies melded together as the motion of waves of the ocean caressed us into oblivion. When I woke up Phoebe was still asleep. My knee was where I had dreamed it to be. One of my dreams was fulfilled. I always wanted to wake up with my lover by my side and me between her legs. I watched her secretly, a beautiful Yakshi with thin lips and rounded bosoms that had matured with age and made her look much like the statues of women on the walls of the Khajuraho temple. I brought some coffee and we reminisced about the wonderful days we had spent together. "I know you are going to hop into bed with someone else when you return home but I will remember you." I was tearful. It was here at Tierra del Fuego that I thought I fell in love again. In the midst of immense happiness I was sad. I wanted to remain a burning candle with its glow but instead I felt I was getting spent.

I remembered reading what Matthew Arnold had said:

From the soul's subterranean depth up borne
As from an infinitely distant land,
Come airs, and floating echoes, and convey
A melancholy into all our day.

I wanted to perform Arty (Hindi) to this special day with lamps burning camphor and basil. But I couldn't. We sailed towards Buenos Aires. The intimacy grew like a veil around us as the clouds draped the moon every so often and the sounds of Phoebe's laughter and my guffawing reverberated from the walls.

Anna was spell-bound. She spoke. "So what happened after that?"

"Before you know it you will be in Idaho."

"I want to hear the story."

I believed her. I had learnt resilience as a child. You will certainly lose some of the times. Everybody does. But you must regroup and see how you can do better. I can still hear Grandpa saying that to me. I felt that at this time in my life I needed Avalokita (Sanskrit). He is the earthly manifestation of the self-born, eternal Buddha, Amitava. He guards the world during the time of departure of historical Buddha, Gautama, and the appearance of the future Buddha, Maitreya. Avalokita protects against shipwreck, fire, assassins, thugs and beasts. He is the creator of the fourth world, which is the actual universe in which we live. He supremely exemplifies Bodhisattva's resolve to postpone his own Buddhahood until every being on earth receives emancipation.

My life moved on an auxochrome while I remained the electron that never formed a covalent bond. I sometimes lit up, though never as bright as halogen but most times remained a negative electromagnetic force so much so that I needed to see a psychiatrist. My colleagues sometimes treated me as an apocryphal creature but my "shrink" truly helped me. Get a plant, kind of like a fern that grows in India called Aspidistra and study it, she said. I investigated and found this cast-iron plant, as it is commonly called, after much effort. However, the effort paid off. It grew in a prolific fashion in the planter and I learnt that the evergreen pointed leaves tolerate extremes of temperature, dust, smoke and harsh conditions and still produce beautiful solitary purple flowers. I stopped thinking that life was over. I had ended a relationship that had stifled me. Years passed and I didn't even know it. I accepted an opportunity to work at Katmandu two months every year as a volunteer. I became a changed man, free from my own prison. There was nobody to stamp "denied" on my prison record as happened numerous times to Morgan Freeman in *Shawshank Redemption*. I was free. Ad Majorem Dei Glorium!

We could hardly take eyes of each other. Neither of us talked about the years gone by or the reasons why we didn't keep in touch although every so often I would try to talk about it. But Phoebe just placed her index finger in front of my lips. Phoebe and I sat in the guest house lobby and we drank San Miguel. We kept count of the bottles by making marks on the napkin because I was afraid they would charge me more than we drank if no one kept track of the bottles. We held hands. We talked about our plans. She had come to assist in the critical care nursing area in the same hospital where I was working. We recited poetry from Longfellow's "Ode to Duty":

Me this uncharted freedom tires;
I feel the weight of chance desires;
My hopes no more much change their name,
I long for a repose that is ever the same.

"How do you differentiate between courage and fortitude?" asked Phoebe. I wasn't sure. But Tom Brokow in *The Greatest Generation* makes a distinction. Physical courage, he said, represents acts that accomplish bravery during war or fighting a bear may be, but fortitude represents moral courage. It is the willingness of an individual to suffer personal anguish or loss for the sake of greater good. I thought the sacrifice my grandpa and my dad had made during the non-cooperation movement to drive the British demonstrated a great amount of fortitude. I didn't want to talk about such stuffy subjects at this time though.

"Who restored Colonial Williamsburg?"

"John D. Rockefeller," quipped Phoebe.

"OK, who was the president when Gutzon Borglum started carving Mount Rushmore in 1927?"

"Calvin Coolidge" was the quick answer. That was enough for me. I didn't want to pose any more Jeopardy questions. This is how we spent most days after work. We didn't drink any water all day and in the evening made up for it by drinking beer. We operated together and moved to the level of being from just acquainted to intimate. We touched each other effortlessly.

Phoebe said, "Did you know that John Quincy Adams was a diplomat, Harvard professor, secretary of state, president and then a congressman from Massachusetts?" I listened. "Have you seen the movie *Amistad*?" I shook my head from side to side and then Phoebe continued. She knows everything about movies. John Q. Adams with his eloquence defended the slaves who had gained their freedom by capturing the vessel *Creole*. "All the southern members of the committee resigned after that. Fifty-four slaves led by Cinque had revolted on the *Amistad* and were arrested. It was John Q. Adams who successfully pleaded their case before the court and won their freedom."

It was my turn. "Did you know that George Drouillard and John Colter were cartographers, hunters and sign language experts that could communicate with the Indians and possibly are the most forgotten and unsung heroes with the Lewis and Clark expedition? In 1817, Colter only carrying a thirty-pound pack walked through 500 miles of snow-covered mountains to view what was to be designated as Yellowstone National Park."

We had finished twelve beers by now. "OK," I said, "I am going to ask the last question." My competitive spirit just wanted to win. "Which movie has the line, 'You can run but can't hide'?"

"*River of No Return*" was the instant answer. I gave up. "By the way you know I am having trouble sleeping after being with you all day."

I said, "How come?" She didn't answer. Usually she went to the left side of the staircase and I to the right to get to our separate rooms. "Do you want to make the wrong turn or the right turn today?" I asked wishfully. She made the right turn.

As our bodies touched each other Phoebe said, "I think submission is one of the most important human traits. It requires trust, love and forgiveness." I thought that was a good start. The night was short. The rooms are not well insulated for sound. A few times I had to kiss Phoebe hard so our neighbors won't be awakened. We both laughed at our jubilation. "I have to lie down now," she said after sitting for a while and soon she was asleep.

The morning light had just sneaked through the window when I found myself lying on my back with my right ankle resting on left knee folded up reciting George Seferis (The Bodley Head Limited, London, 1966):

They told us, you will conquer when you submit,
We submitted and found dust and ashes.
They told us, you will conquer when you love,
We loved and found dust and ashes.
They told us, you will conquer when you give up your life,
We gave up our lives and found dust and ashes.
It was time to go to work!

Mr. S, the manager, sat with us in the evening. He said, "Jung Bahadur established the Rana dynasty in Nepal and became the ruler and the prime minister for life after killing Gagan Singh. He remained a friend of the British."

"How did Nepal stay away from being a British dynasty?"

"That is a good question. It is possibly because Jung Bahadur kept peace here and when there was mutiny in India in 1857, he sent Gurkha soldiers to aid the British. In 1970 King Birendra married a woman from the Rana family, who became his queen."

"Don't many Nepali men have more than one wife?" Anna asked. She was getting tired of listening.

"Jung Bahadur tried to abolish 'suttee' but it was so ingrained in the culture that three of his widows sacrificed themselves after his death."

"No! More than likely the neighbors forced the women."

"I will introduce you to my dad tomorrow. He owns the business. The Beatles stayed here, you know."

"I know. Thanks for letting me sit with you."

"I wanted to welcome you. Namaste!"

We both ate chicken pakodas and fried rice and continued our evening interlude. Phoebe is a voracious reader. "I was thinking of James Jones; he must have been such an eccentric. Here he writes this great book about a charming soldier, *Here to Eternity* and then leaves America to live in Paris. Why is that?"

"I don't know," she said.

"The guy gets a bronze medal and a Purple Heart during the attack at Pearl Harbor and then leaves the country but returns to New York as an old man."

"Henry James left the United States too to live in England."

"I read some of his stuff," I chimed in.

Phoebe said, "Let's not drink any more today." We picked up some filtered water in the lobby on the way to our room. She didn't use the room on the left anymore. We were in love. Now I clearly remembered Grandpa talking about Jaydev's Meghdoot, when the cloud messenger carried messages to the lovers in the distant land but now I was able to send my own messages again!

Grandpa and I often lay in our field in front of our house outside Calcutta. "Grandpa, why do the clouds have different shapes?" He said that a famous poet of India wrote that different clouds carry different messages to their lovers in distant lands and during the process some remain smiling and robust while some others become tired and have the appearance of having lost weight. Some of the others become rain and bring joy.

My Grandpa Leaves Me

Anna wanted to know more about my grandpa. "I am getting tired of bits and pieces. Just tell me the details." I said OK.

I gazed at the field and the street beyond as I sat on the cement seat inside the window of the second floor with my face stuck to the steel bars. The place was full of people. But I couldn't see. Salt water ran down my cheeks in waves much like the wailing of the big waves at the Outer Banks of North Carolina. My nose was running too. There was a candle in my room. It was lit at one time but a harsh wind had killed its light. I felt totally alone in this world. Sadness and I both gazed at the sky. Sorrow had enveloped me with its cold prickly hands. I couldn't breathe through its "non-holey" net and I kept choking. It was still dark outside. The only sound I heard was of my whimpering and everything else was muffled. I was the retinue of my grandfather. My very being was with him. I didn't know what was to happen now. Is this possible? I really had not experienced any loss before this.

We went to bed together that night as we always did those days. Grandma was busy cleaning up. We went upstairs and sneaked inside the mosquito net. I always jumped up and down to make sure that there were no mosquitoes inside.

Grandpa always lay down for a minute or two. Then he sat up and closed his eyes to pray. I always calmed down by then. We had a routine and a rhythm. Then Grandpa would tell me some stories. I always fell asleep before the story ended. I knew that because on the subsequent nights I had to always remind him that I only heard so far into the previous night's story.

Sometimes Grandpa would stick his hand out of the net to get a glass of water that was kept on his side. I remember one time he had to take several drinks because I was really into the story. I had asked him why our neighbor Jaguda had only one hand. "One day someone had seen a tiger in our neighborhood," Grandpa started. "Everybody was a little apprehensive. Most people started going back into their house before it got dark. Some carried a flashlight and some others carried a torch made of burning lard at the end of a bamboo stick. But Jagu (he didn't call him Jaguda because DA means older brother and Jaguda was only fifteen years or so older than I was at that time) had more courage than anyone else did. He bought a goat and tied it to a pole every night. He sat on a small maachan or platform that he had built just next to the pole. He did not have a gun but he did have an axe that he normally used to split wood.

"Everyone in our village thought Jaguda didn't fit the criteria of a normal youth," he continued. "He was rather insouciant. He often just worked in the rice field and then sat next to the train station and played his flute. He built a fire and cooked a potato or a squirrel and ate them all by himself. He had a great knack with the slingshot. He could knock down a mango or even a coconut. Sometimes this got him into trouble. He spoke very little." Grandpa said the only time he had heard him speak was when he was hallucinating from black water fever. "Jagu after recovering from cerebral malaria developed an arrogance and attitude that was not common in that part of the village. Most importantly, he didn't smile and no one had heard him laugh. Some people thought he must have a deep sorrow hidden inside him and he was not strong enough yet to expel it from his system.

"One day, during the full moon of August, just about the time when the monsoon had ended, Jagu did the strangest thing. He dug the ground next to the maachan about ten feet deep and covered it up with banana leaves. He tied the goat on the opposite side of the hidden ground hole. He had slathered himself with different paints and wore a sorcerer's hat."

At this point I asked Grandpa how Jaguda knew what a sorcerer's hat should look like. "That is a whole new story. Let me just tell you about this now." I let him continue.

"It was just about the twilight time. Jagu cavorted down the field in most ecstatic glee and cawed like an unhappy crow. Then he sat on the maachan, ate a carp from a cawl that he had brought with him. He lighted incense and lay down. He had tied the axe to his right leg with two little strips of string so that he could pull the axe out of its halter as fast as Mat Dillon could draw his gun in *Gun Smoke*. The goat was enjoying himself with all these banana leaves. Soon it became dark and Jagu had fallen asleep after all this activity. The goat was quiet. The August moon was full. There was a gentle breeze.

147

Suddenly there was a scratch in the silence. The goat started hissing like its voice was too heavy to make a sound. It started pulling at the pole and Jagu's maachan started shaking. Jagu couldn't believe that he could actually look into the tiger's eyes. It was stalking the goat. It stealthily moved forward and then it jumped.

"It fell in the hole and as it was just about getting ready to jump the other wall Jagu split its skull open with the axe. But as the tiger fell Jagu got pulled in with the axe and the right paw of the tiger dug into his left arm. When he came to me his arm was too mangled. So I had to amputate part of it to save the good part.

"The mayor came and honored Jagu. Jagu got a government job in the office. Now he is an important man but he is particular about making sure that children have opportunities to play in safe places. He planted mangoes, leachy and guava trees in the common field area. There was a slingshot next to every tree for anyone who wanted to try his or her skill. Jaguda was the referee for the annual slingshot championship."

Grandpa said that sometimes a dramatic event such as this has to happen in life to take away sadness. "Goddess Demeter continuously mourned the loss of her daughter, Persephone. However, she smiled for the first time at the mocking jests of the maiden, Iambi. Her sadness was taken away by a happy event. Jaguda was happy when I saw him. I never learnt what made him sad in the past. I was sure happy to see him laugh and he still played his flute while lying on the grass next to the train station just beyond our field."

Tonight, Grandpa didn't tell me a story. Just after praying with his folded hands he fell down to his pillow. He did not speak again. I did not know what happened. There was a lantern in the hallway. I took it and ran to my grandmother. Soon I was ushered into another room. All I could hear was wailing and crying. My grandpa had prayed to God and had held me last in his hands before he had passed on!

There were hundreds of people that came to pay their last respects to Dactarbabu (Mr. Doctor). Our courtyard and the field were full of his patients, friends and those that loved him. This was 1957, March 14. I was twelve and my grandpa was only sixty-two when we got separated but I know now that he has traveled with me everywhere. I told myself silently that I will visit all the different places that he talked about and more. I wanted him to be with me and help me. I look at the map of the world and wonder where Grandpa would like to go next.

Anna and I Discuss History and Grandpa

Today Anna and I talked about Stonewall Jackson. I didn't know as much about him but I knew that he was one of the greatest commanders in American history. Anna said I needed to learn devotion to duty and honesty from his actions. "How come?"

"Well, he was a strong Unionist until Virginia was threatened and then he joined the Confederacy. His greatest achievement was the Shenandoah Valley campaign where he blocked the advance of a bigger and more capable army. He went on to prove that he was one of the most valuable generals that fought with Lee against McClellan and then at Cedar Mountain he had won. Jackson had almost entered into General Joseph Hooker's unprotected area of offensive when friendly fire from the confederate soldiers shattered his left arm. On May 10, 1863, he died of the complications of pneumonia after the amputation. It is believed that he had passed away quietly after saying: 'Let us cross over the river and rest under the shade of the trees.'"

I told Anna that I had visited Lexington, Virginia, where Jackson is laid to rest. "He is one of my heroes and he means as much to me as does Thomas Jefferson. His actual name was also Thomas Jackson."

Anna wanted to know more about my relationship with Grandpa. Anna knew that he was my hero too. I started my journey on May 10 as well.

I recited from Lord Byron:
"So, we'll go no more a-roving
So late into the night,
Though the heart be still as loving,
And the moon be still as bright.
For the sword outwears its sheath,
And the soul wears out the breast,
And the heart must pause to breathe,
And Love itself have rest.

Though the night was made for loving,
And the day returns too soon,
Yet we'll go no more a-roving
By the light of the moon."

Grandpa was my friend and I was his shadow. Grandpa said that I did not have to go to school. So I learnt mathematics, English, Bengali and Sanskrit from him. We left early in the mornings in a palanquin to see patients. Well, he did. I was just his companion. We traveled on dirt roads on the shoulders of four people sometimes for hours. They chanted some rhythmical songs to organize their steps and we moved most of the time, at a pretty good clip. We carried boiled water in a large clay container that kept the water cold. We also had some chappatis and rolls. Sometimes when it rained we had to stop under a mango tree or a banyan tree. The Palkidars (those who carried the palanquin) always made sure that we were safe from any lightning strikes. Grandpa's bicycle was strapped on the top of the palanquin. We talked. Mostly I talked and Grandpa listened. He would close his eyes soon after we would take off, particularly on the days following the nights during which he had poor sleep owing to multiple interruptions.

I did not know this at first that he was tired because often he didn't get enough sleep. I thought he was just tired because he was older. He was almost six times older than I was at that time. I was good at multiplication. It was customary in India to memorize the multiplication tables. It was believed to have helped us with math as we studied further. I don't believe it did any good for me except that I know what are sixteen times sixteen or for that matter even twenty-five times twenty-five. I know that in college this attitude hampered me. What I mean is that I developed a habit of memorizing instead of understanding. My grades were OK and everybody thought that I was good in math. But I knew better than that. Thank God, I remembered Grandpa telling me, "You will know you are growing when you know your limitations. It doesn't mean that you don't expect the best from yourself but don't fool yourself into thinking that you know something when in reality you don't. Admit and say I don't know. Then you will learn."

He took a breather. "Sometimes in life we begin to believe ourselves without knowing the truth. We can at times make others think that we are smarter than we actually are but it is much harder to fool ourselves."

One night I woke up because I heard a lot of conversation downstairs. I heard Grandpa telling some people that he didn't want to go. It was a hot summer that year in that village where I lived about fifteen miles outside Calcutta. We didn't have electricity inside the house at that time. I saw Grandma was lying next to me and fanning me with a fan made of dried palm leaves. She seemed disturbed and told me not to talk. I understood. She was trying to hear the conversation through the closed door.

Soon thereafter Grandpa left in his horse carriage. It was already late in the morning when I saw him come through the door. Grandma was weeping when she saw him. "You don't have to do this. I think you should fight a little more," said Grandma. Grandpa didn't respond. He usually didn't disagree with Grandma in front of me. He was the only doctor in a fifteen-mile radius.

As he sat down on the flat bed downstairs sipping his tea I came and sat next to him. I was curious as to what he was doing during the night. "I was forced to go to treat a wounded dacoit," he continued. "They came, blindfolded me, hooked up the horse to the carriage and drove my carriage to their hiding place. I had to treat a person who was bleeding from a gash from a sword near his shoulder. I had to pack the stitches, needles and whatever else was necessary in a hurry in the light of the lantern downstairs because they told me that I had to get done before daybreak. One of the dacoits brought me back blindfolded. Then the dacoit left!"

Grandpa stopped to drink his tea and take a bite of a toast. I was excited. I asked him where they lived and how come he didn't turn them in. Grandpa didn't answer directly. He asked me if I knew why we never had theft or armed robbery in our house. He reminded me that a patient and a doctor have a special relationship and that trust is sacred. It really didn't matter what the patient did for a living, honest or dishonest. "My job is to treat the problem and not judge anything else. Befriending a thief is just as important as befriending an honest man. That way you will always be protected." He said life is about love and everybody has it but some are afraid to show it. He told me that on many nights he had to go to people's houses to deliver babies. He said usually Dai's (women who are expert in delivering babies and have learnt by experience much like midwives) deliver but sometimes when there is a problem someone usually came and got him.

We didn't have a telephone in our house those days. Grandpa could wake up at the first knock even before the thump on the door had time to make a sound! That's why I never knew what he did during the night. "Sometimes I have to go during the night when someone has a bad stomachache or lot of vomiting or high fever from typhoid fever or malaria." Grandpa stopped.

We didn't have electricity in the house but that didn't deter us from reading in the evening. Every child in Bengal I believe learnt the story of VidyaSagar, who became a famous scholar because of his aptitude for reading. He came from a poor family and his mother had him stand in the street lights and read every evening.

Reading was emphasized as the most important way to get ahead in life. "Once you learn the taste of reading you will want to read more," Grandpa often said.

Grandpa's timing was impeccable. After I finished talking for a while and would just keep rambling he assigned me tasks. Although he wrote on paper and prescription pads I did not have paper to write on till I was almost eight years old. "If you write on paper your mind does not remember it. So write on the slate with a chalk and then wipe it off. Next time when I ask you the same question you will try to remember what you had written on the slate because you have actually written it in your mind's memory center," he would say. I always believed Grandpa because I knew he was always on my side. Sometimes we didn't agree. He never told me, "Just do it because I know best" or "do it because I said so."

He would explain to me how he learnt from his father and how he got into trouble when he didn't listen. One time I didn't want to do math. So he said, "Every day has twenty-four hours to learn and in our case less because we don't have electricity and when evening comes even the birds go to sleep so we have to sleep. However, the bird babies are taught math by their mother during the daytime."

"How is that?" I said.

"Well, you can't sing unless you know and count the Matras (much like Do Re Mi Far except in India it is Sa, Re, Ga, Ma etc.) Birds have to sing to find mates." I thought that made sense. We did have a mynah bird that could sing.

He never let me feel as though we were not on the same side. So I memorized the math tables, multiplication numbers, a lot of Rabindranath Tagore's poetry and even the newspaper headlines. He was proud of me and that is what he told everybody in front of me. And that made me feel good. I was the happiest man a little kid could be!

After we would reach our destination the palkidars would stop and Grandpa would get ready to go and see his patients on his bicycle. He then gave me tasks that he would write on pieces of paper and told me to finish those before we went back home that evening. The palkidars would entertain me and watch me while he would ride his bicycle between the rice fields carrying his black doctor bag on the carrier in the back and a bottle of water hanging from the handle. Time as one sees in a watch had no value to us. None of us had any watches. But we knew from looking at the sun and knowing the time of the month as to when approximately it would get dark. We always got back just before dark. I always had a lot to tell Grandma after we got back. I had watched cows with tika's (marked with a paint or colored powder as a symbol of worship) on their forehead that marched in procession. The donkeys that carried babies and loads of wood on their backs were always vivid in my mind as were the water-buffaloes that stared at me as though I was something unusual.

The mynah birds, the bulbul that flitted between the papaya and the mango trees made me want to fly. But I didn't get enough time to talk after I came back because it was always late and there was barely enough time to get cleaned up and have dinner. We sat on mats on the floor and Grandpa prayed and offered food to the elders who have passed on, before we started eating. Grandma smiled and loved us for being who we were then. We usually ate in the illumination of a petromax lamp. I had become an expert at eating fish and picking off bones between my fingers and teeth at an early age of six. Fish and rice was our main diet those days and of course I had to eat some vegetables as well. I loved eggplants, squash and beans. So that is what we had almost every day. We used our fingers as substitutes for forks and knives. The important lesson was never to allow food to touch above the middle of the middle finger.

One of my greatest disagreements with Grandpa was about the outhouse. I refused to go during the night. Grandma did not favor the idea of the honey bucket. We had just finished reading Rudyard Kipling's *Jungle Book*. I told Grandpa that I was afraid of snakes and the only solution would be to get me a personal Riki Tiki Tavi. Grandpa was a resourceful man. But this kind of a request can strain a man even with mighty capabilities. He sent messages to a couple of snake charmers that he knew from the past. They came to the house and placed their baskets in the courtyard. I wanted to see their snakes. They brought their flutes. The snake charmers swayed and played and soon some of the snakes slowly crept out of the baskets and stood straight up. The baskets were all covered up quickly after the snakes were put back into them at the end of the show. I didn't like the show to end. I wanted to buy the flute. Grandpa said, "That's not for sale. That is how he makes his livelihood."

It was only later that I learnt that snakes don't have ears. I was so preoccupied observing the motions of nodding and writhing that I forgot to look for the features. A few weeks later a man who raised chickens was summoned. He brought chickens thinking Grandpa wanted to buy some chickens. He didn't know that Grandma didn't allow chickens in the house. We could eat chicken eggs only in a designated place outside the house. She always felt that chickens were Muslims and ducks were Hindus. Grandpa was not enlightened enough to establish the religious persuasion of either bird to my grandma. He knew he had a limited time in this life and he never fought wars that he knew that he could not win.

Anyway, since the chicken grower had two mongooses to keep the snakes away from the barn so that his eggs wouldn't be eaten up he was enticed to give up one. It was negotiated that when they would be in heat there would be two in our house for a short period. It would be the responsibility of the chicken farmer to decide when these animals would be in heat so that there would be no suffering and frustration from conjugal separation. I was excited to have one and I knew nothing about "heat." Next day I had my very own Rakhi (it is a string band placed by the sisters on the brother's hand on brother's day as a symbol of safety) that was tied next to the outhouse. He had a long leash and he went as far as he could in different directions and often during this process of checking his reach he made his leash shorter by wrapping around the neem tree.

Walking with a friend-the first twenty-five miles

Author with a friend and Elvis

MT. Kailash

In the Himalayas

On the way to Annapurna

A yak and a friend

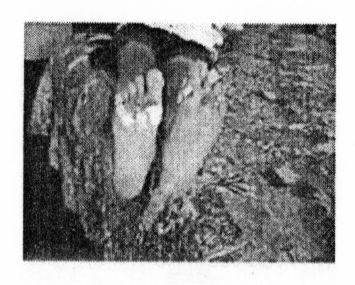

Top picture—Author's feet at Illinois
Bottom picture—Ms. G, support van driver

Tibet

Meeting a friend at Ft. Vancouver

More Wyoming

I was walking fast but Wyoming seemed never ending. By now my neck and arms were like Melba toast. I mean the color and not the consistency.

If there would have been a fire alarm sensitive to smoke as it is in my kitchen it would have been triggered, I think. I saw many gator skins on the road and on the shoulders. Most people in this part of the country drive about ninety miles an hour. I just didn't want someone to have a blowout next to me. He would surely run over me then with an out-of-control car or truck. Sometimes I had to walk with my head down for a long time owing to the wind.

The wind was strong and I was afraid that my hat would get blown away from my head. It was clipped to my T-shirt in the back. I used to wear this hat while sailing. I told Anna how much fun I had sailing at Bayfield, Wisconsin. It took us about three hours to drive up there from Marshfield. Our sailboat had a mahogany mast and it was a wooden boat made in the Far East. I bought the boat after an hour's lesson. It had a four-horse motor to just get it in and out of the marina. We sailed during the day and came back home during the night. The boat was about twenty-eight feet long and was just the right size for our family of four. We cooked on shore and then put the jib up and sometimes the genoa and the boat would heel and we would warn the children to hold on because they sat on the front deck. And we would loosen the cleats here and pull the rope on the opposite side and the boom would sweep the top of the boat with a swish and soon we would turn about again. Lake Superior is like an ocean and so we went up and down the shore towards the small islands across from Bayfield many times. I told Anna that I liked the wind then.

I told Anna that my SPAVA sign being above my pack was like a sail facing the wind. Although I was long past Nebraska but I never could forget the wind. In the afternoon cold wind started blowing from the west at times. I sat on the roadside and read some of the letters that the students from Ms. Mantooth's class had written to me. They were letters of love and inspiration from the children. "You are an American and we know you can do it." Some others had drawn pictures of Kentucky and then Oregon and joined the two states saying "We are praying for you." And others said, "You have perseverance." How could I disappoint these children and not finish?

By the time that I had walked almost halfway between Lincoln and York I was dealing with severe sunburns and needed extra protection. So I took my undershirt and got it wet and placed it on my head in a manner that my face stuck out through the neck hole. I applied forty-five-plus sun blocker and of course my bra with long sleeves and Capri pants that stopped at my socks.

Anna had saved my life once already. She had pushed me to the side with her heels when this crazy guy skidded so close to me that he almost ran over me. It was about midday. Anna was too short on the ground and I figured her heels must have been on my buttocks. The backpack swung in a jerky fashion and my back began to hurt. But I knew that in the evening Jim Beam would soothe my pain.

I was walking on high grounds and desert. I was talking about the mountains and how far they were from me at times and real close at other times as the roads were built by dynamiting the hills. Every so often I used my binoculars to see if I could spot any animals. I saw some rabbits and free-range cows. Most of this part of Wyoming was pretty desolate. I saw a car pass me that had some people who seemed to have had shaved heads and they were wearing saffron-colored clothes. I presumed they were Buddhist monks possibly traveling to one of the cities for a conference or such.

So I told Anna about the time I visited Mt. T'ai in Shantung province of China. The slopes of Mt. T'ai are covered with temples and shrines dedicated to a pantheon of minor deities. The mountain is associated with beliefs of Taoism. It was also considered to be the source of Yang (male) principle, source of life. Some believed that the souls of men returned here for judgment. Just at this moment I saw a big dust ball ahead of me that crossed the highway while whirling at a fast pace and I forgot my chain of thought. So I continued with the story of Grandpa that I was talking about.

It was some time in late 1949 early morning when I was reading the English newspaper loudly. Grandpa wanted everyone to hear my reading capability. Of course no one was supposed to criticize. This was an exercise in "look how great is my grandson"! I didn't understand too many words but I could read well. Getting a dictionary and looking up the meaning of at least ten words every day usually followed the reading. We often had fun with words such as knave, knife, and knew, gnu and gnat. He made learning fun by teaching me about wildebeest but he pronounced it as "wild-beast" so that I won't forget.

He knew a lot about tigers and he thought Shere Khan was funny. He said that the royal Bengal tiger was the most majestic animal. It was important to do something to protect them. He said that the population growth in India is going to take away all the living space for the animals unless someone makes an effort to preserve them. The newspaper provided the backdrop to discuss Mr. Nehru, prime minister of India at that time. There was a lot of discussion about the United States and the end of the Second War and what effects that would have on different countries. He said that the United States was going to be the one of the most powerful nations in the world because the constitution of the country is based on democratic principles.

He loved the fact that the Achuut or the untouchable class in India was going to be abolished. "I think it is terrible to consider another human being untouchable because he participates in a profession that no one else wants to do," he continued. "Gandhi might have united India to drive the British, which is not any meager achievement, but the greatest accomplishment is his acceptance of this segregated class and calling them Harijan or God's children. This act alone will raise India's prestige in the world."

People that did not believe in egoism or upstarts were friends of Grandpa and people with generosity and altruism surrounded me. Grandpa did not like aggression and always spoke softly when someone would yell. His gestures were kind and his personality emanated acceptance. He is yelling because most Indians talk loud and he thinks his words are most important. So let him finish, he often said when the conversation led to a shouting match.

It seemed that the egalitarian ethos was always present in the substance of the conversation although not evident in all the actions of our family. I did not see any homeless person that was provided a place to stay in our house even though there was plenty of room for someone to sleep behind the courtyard. However, if someone ever came in hungry Grandma had them sit down on the outside courtyard and they were served a meal after the family finished eating.

Often there were women and children that were hungry that came by to our house. Although Grandpa might have believed in avoiding the term "untouchable," Grandma was a different matter. The persons who cleaned the outhouse only come at a certain time of the day to avoid being in Grandma's path of vision. After they cleaned the toilets one of them then carried a big drum on the head. I had Grandpa take me to the place where all this was dumped. The pond of night soil announced itself from its aromatic exuberance long before we arrived at the scene of execution! I never wanted to see it again.

This was a time soon after the partition. We would have big debates in our waiting room about Mahatma Gandhi and Mr. Mohammed Jinnah. There were strong opinions against the partition of India by the British. I felt strong feelings of nationalism in the crowd. Sometimes Grandpa had to stop people from deriding each other when there was disagreement. This was my study hall. I didn't have any specific books to read on these days.

"Jinnah might have been a brilliant student and called to the bar at London at the age of nineteen after graduating from Bombay; he should have never been allowed to join the Calcutta session of the Indian National Congress in 1906," said one of our guests. "He was too much influenced by the liberalism policies of William Gladstone, the prime minister of England in 1892."\

"But Jinnah didn't join the All India Muslim League because he wanted to unite the Muslims and the Hindus," said another.

"As a matter of fact it was Gopal Gokhale, the great Maharashtra leader, called him the ambassador of Hindu-Muslim unity, hoping Jinnah would unite the country's religious differences," continued Grandpa. "Jinnah went away to England because he was frustrated that the Hindus and Muslims couldn't share views. In March 1940 at Lahore, the League adopted the idea of Pakistan, a separate state for Muslims. When the British decided that they had no choice but leave the Indian subcontinent Jinnah dealt not only with the British but with men of such stature as Nehru and Gandhi. British chose the easy way out. Don't meddle in someone else's fight. It was not their fight anymore. They didn't have a dog in that fight. In 1947 India and Pakistan got separated."

Many Muslims had homes in our neighboring villages. All the children played together but grown-ups rarely sat and talked. Most of the conversation took place standing. There was evidence of discomfort or at least lack of effort to be anything more than cordial between Hindus and Muslims, the way I remember it. Nobody knew who it should be to ask the other to sit down. So nobody did. Grandpa always favored brotherhood rather than jingoism or belligerent nationalism. Grandpa said, "British guys sent soldiers to restrain Russia during the Russo-Turkish war of 1877 and they sang a song:

"'We don't want to fight, yet by jingo, if we do
We've got the ships, we've got the men,
And got the money too!'

"Now we have driven the British out and let us not waste valuable time calling one another names. Rest of the world is going to watch to see what we do with our independence."

Grandpa didn't care who came and sat on our flat bed in the living room. It was our library. People are our books and they all have different covers. That is what he always told me. He honored every book that came in through the door!

At one time only a few persons of Hindu origin spoke to my grandpa in private but nobody could shun him. He was the only doctor and a friend of the Gandhi connection in that neighborhood. My uncle, older brother to my dad, was a friend to Mahatma Gandhi. It was kind of flattering for most people to have had the opportunity to participate in discussions with people of different class (as they were thought those days) under one roof which was not their own. Soon everyone felt comfortable and sat and argued till tea ran out and Grandma summoned Grandpa inside. This was usually the cue to go about one another's business and discussion time was over.

It was imperative that I read the English as well as the Bengali newspaper. I would have to give a verbal report to Grandpa of what I had read either during travel or at home. "The people of India are extremely intelligent and the British knew it," he continued. "But they were greedy so they hung around this long. One day India will rise and no one will be able to contain the spirit of India. Indians will serve in every important organization and India will be a great nation again. The British might have tarnished our image. But gold will not remain tarnished for ever. If you are educated, intelligent, courageous and respectful of others you will always succeed. India and United States were both British colonies. The difference is that in the US they are British people that escaped and we were conquered. It was the best deal for the British when people moved out to the United States. They didn't have to feed the ones who were disgruntled. They could send the criminals to till the grounds in America. They could steal all the goods from India, refine them and sell the items as their own at a high price."

In the warm afternoons we often took naps for about an hour. I gave my reports prior to falling asleep. I gave reports on Ramakrishna, Swami Vivekananda, Dadavai Naoroji, Sister Nivedita and many others on different occasions. Dadavai Naoroji was the first Indian to sit in the House of Commons. Then I fell asleep. Learning about the great leaders of India and abroad was part of the daily assignment.

In the afternoons we went to the dispensary. This was across our courtyard. The courtyard was kept clean by brooming and washing with a substance called Phenyl. It had an aromatic smell that drove flies away and produced a milky appearance as it was splattered by the fast-moving broom. The dispensary was a large room with benches for the patients to sit. The furniture was primitive (I consider now but I thought differently then) but was adequate for the occasion. A desk and a chair adorned the room next to a window. This was Grandpa's chair. The window behind him remained open for air to flow to keep him cool during hot days. A fan made of dried palm leaf was placed on his desk that he used every so often to get rid of flies or to fan himself just to get the air moving. Another chair was placed just to his right for the patient to sit. There was a bench on the other side for prospective patients to sit. Everyone could hear and see what was being done to another.

Medical examination and history taking was a communal occasion. There was no such thing as HIPPA, and everybody knew about everyone else's problem except for the problems related to genitals. Those were examined behind a wall with no doors but a curtain that fell far short of the floor. Anyone who had to walk behind the door always came out with a guilty face. A large aluminum bowl filled with soap and water (a red soap called carbolic) for Grandpa to wash his hands was on one side of the table. The towel that he used to dry his hands was washed every day by Swagirma (our maid who lived in a room attached to the barn).

Nankumama (Nanku was his name. Mama is a common word used to honor someone older ascribing him the title of maternal uncle. In India everyone is a brother or an uncle), the compounder (as he was called because he compounded many fluids and powders), sat on another side next to a lot of bottles partially filled with different colored liquids. He was more like a mixologist. He did not have any certificate on the wall. Grandpa just knew that he could do the job. I remember that most people returned even when afflicted with a different illness and that made me realize that they had to have survived the previous course of dispensed chemicals. Grandpa knew his pharmacology well.

Grandpa never told me if anyone had died from the medicine that was dispensed. And I doubted that. Most people those days that died were usually from the illness or from inadequate medications. The commonest male problems that were diagnosed behind the wall were hydrocele. Most of them didn't need to go behind the walls because the object of examination was easily visible through the dhotis' or lungis (about three yards of material sewn like a gigantic skirt that is tied to a knot around the waist). It was usually worn by the Muslims. Grandpa had a flashlight (called a torch in India because the British called it so) that he shone through the back of the gigantic appurtenances to distinguish between water and blood. Almost all of these were the result of Filariasis caused by mosquito bites. I was frightened of this condition as a child.

It was many years later when I was teaching in England that I had an opportunity to visit the pathology laboratory of Bartholomew Hospital when I saw the picture of a man whose body parts were of such size that there was a little boy who walked underneath him carrying it in a basket on his head. I never did see such during my childhood. I think Grandpa would have sent that one for an operation long before it could reach that stage.

I never stayed in his chamber (doctoring room) room too long. The room was always full. Many persons coughed and then they would clear their throat and go outside to spit. There was a sign for people to not spit in our courtyard. They had to walk to the hibiscus tree on the side and expel whatever was in their mouth. The hibiscus tree was very forgiving and energized. It never drooped. It used the degraded saliva as the fertilizer that was given to it and made beautiful red flowers that Grandma used during worship of Lord Shiva. I am sure that Lord Shiva didn't care as long as the flowers were not wilted. The system worked well.

Grandpa examined the patients while sitting on his chair. He felt the stomach, the chest and looked at different parts and used his stethoscope to listen to the front and the back. Sometimes he would get up to examine women behind a curtain that hid a bench on which lay a leathered cushion that had seen better days. We never wiped anything between patients like we do now. I think the patients had about thirty seconds to talk.

Now and then he would get aggravated and tell everyone to be quiet because he could not hear whatever he was trying to hear. He would write bunch of Latin words on a piece of paper and the patient would take it to Nankumama, who would prepare the concoction and send them home with instructions.

One time he was very upset because everyone was talking. He was trying to listen to a boy's chest. He had a large stomach. Grandpa said he couldn't hear the boy's heart sound. He was moving the stethoscope back and forth. I just happened to walk in and I heard the patient's dad tell him, "Dactarbabu, you do not have the ear pieces in your ears. They are around your neck." No one laughed. I left.

He told me later that the boy had too many worms. I lay down immediately and had him feel my stomach. He said I might have one or two but he couldn't be certain. He said that he only knew to treat when people got many! Most children in our village had worms. He told me that worms get in the body when we walk barefoot. I did not go out barefoot again. For a long time I was kind of skinny with a big stomach. I was beginning to look like one of our calves. Its back was kind of arched and had developed funny hooves. "It's from eating too many clovers that you get 'flounders,'" said Grandpa. My nails were okay and I didn't eat any clovers except a few while sitting on the field at times. I kind of twiddled it between my teeth and then spat them out. He gave me a capsule to swallow. Next morning I couldn't believe what I saw that was inside of me.

One evening we went to see a Jatra (a theatrical performance in the neighborhood under a canopy of tarpaulin) when the Mahabharata (the great Indian epic) was being enacted in Bharat Natyam (Indian national dance style). There was a lot of motion of the eyes, hands and swaying of the head. The actor was expressing the wrath of one brother on the other with every motion possible. The other brother was not reacting the way he was supposed to have been at that time. In those days no one memorized their parts and therefore I could hear the guys reading from the background. We had front seats. Suddenly, a fight broke out and the guy who was reading got angry and told the actor that "If you know your stuff then you could be a better actor." The actor yelled back, "If I could hear you then it would be better." Trouble was that a hailstorm had started and the patter-patter noise on the tarpaulin was interfering with his hearing. The rain washed the faces of the actors and made streaks of dripping make-up exposing a woman to be a man. It was customary for men to dress as women during the performances. The drama was put on hold.

We went home when the rain stopped without knowing how the play ended. Grandpa said that he already knew the ending and he didn't have to see it. He seemed stressed. I asked him if it was difficult to practice medicine. He said, "It is much like the drama we had seen where the actors perform with eyes, hands and ears except in medicine there is no one to prompt the part. We just have to know the stuff and be able to hear the information even through the noise of a hailstorm," he continued.

Giddha is a traditional pastoral dance performed by the women of Punjab at harvest time. There was going to be a Punjabi cultural festival in Bengal and he would take me to it. He wanted me to appreciate the harmony of graceful hand motions accented by melodious music from an area a bit north of us. "It will uplift our spirits and make you proud of our culture," he promised. I was excited.

I felt that I was absolutely free when I was walking across the country. I sometimes ran on the shoulders of the expressway with my backpack and the sign attached to my pack, although the Walk for Kids sign dragged me a little bit. But I felt that no one was watching me as the cars passed by at high speed and the trucks always made a big whizzing sound whenever they went past me. It seemed at times a few passengers would turn around in their back seats to see if I was of stable mind and behavior. I don't know if few people had reported me to the state police on their cell phones. However, the police did stop every so often to check on me. I appreciated that.

I often practiced T'ai Chi exercise while walking. T'ai Chi is believed to be the union of two primary aspects of cosmos, yang and yin. It seemed to help me to relax while I walked making rhythmic, deliberate movements of my arms and legs along the road enjoying the scenery and ignoring the noisy trucks. Anna told me that T'ai Chi was practiced in China in the third century and by the fifth century monks at the Buddhist monastery were performing exercises emulating the five creatures much like the five elements, bear, bird, monkey, deer and tiger. The snake was added later. I believe studies performed on this subject in some Western university have shown development of better balance through practice of T'ai Chi in the older population.

There was an editorial I had read, I believe, in early 1956 that generated vitriolic discussion among the people present in our waiting room. All the older guys liked me to read and then they talked because most of the time I did not understand what I was reading. "The Americans have created great disturbance in the peace process of Indo-China," wrote the editor. "The Geneva Conference of 1954 attended by the representatives of Cambodia, China, France, Laos, England, United States, USSR, the Viet Minh (North Vietnamese) and the state of Vietnam (South Vietnamese) helped create the Geneva Accord. After the defeat of the French garrison at Dien Bien Phu on May 1954 an agreement was reached between the French, Cambodian, Laotian and Vietnamese that there would be a cease-fire line between the 17th parallel.

"The French did exactly what the British did to India, basically split Vietnam," I continued reading. "Three hundred days were allowed for troop withdrawal and the communists and guerrilla troops were to leave Cambodia and Laos. Then free elections were to be held. It was stipulated explicitly that the partition line was not to be accepted as a territorial line. India, Poland and Canada were responsible for execution of this agreement as supervisors of this project. The Final Declaration, as I understood, stipulated that all Vietnamese election was to be held under the supervision of the committee before July 1956 in an attempt to reunify the country.

"This was a step to induce Viet Minh to accept a temporary regrouping because they occupied three-fourths of the country on the eve of this conference. United States reneged in its guarantee to the pledge. South Vietnam also withheld their approval and the Final Declaration was not signed.

"The U.S. government undertook to build a separate anti-Communist state in South Vietnam. United States supported South Vietnam's refusal to hold nationwide elections." I stopped to take a break. Most people here did not like the French. France had a colony, just forty miles outside Calcutta, a place called Chandannagar. They left the place without much of a fight because the British next door had borne the discomfort for both.

Grandpa had assigned me to read about Edmund Burke, a great orator who spoke the truth under trying circumstances to impeach Warren Hastings. I was also asked to read about Joseph Goebbels, an orator who had deviated from the facts so much as the propaganda minister that he began to believe his own lies. "I want you to understand that this man actually didn't hate Jews at first. All his high school teachers were Jews. The good in him was made rotten by misdirected nationalism and greed for power. He had a clubfoot and people compared him to the Devil. He became one."

Grandpa had stopped to take a breath. "We must honor our convictions. But we must recognize if it is going to harm others. In that case we should regroup," he quipped. "Remember that all hate crimes are usually committed by people who are afraid to compete. It is because either they are inept or incompetent. The perpetrators must put someone else down either for the features, physical appearance or race to make their interests look better. It is a mind of hate. I have seen it. I believe we have to wait for it to die. You cannot reason with them. It is their core that is at odds with their capability. It is their vulnerable and deceitful character that is at stake. They of course have no integrity but they can't afford to expose their own deficient raw hide." Grandpa took a drink of water. We had to go. The palkidars were ready for us.

I was doing my math on the slate while listening to rhythmic melodious singing by the palkidars, "*Raghupati Raghab Raja Ram, Patit Pavan Sita Ram*" (Ram was the greatest king and husband of Sita). I could occasionally hear them breathe hard in between the sounds of rhythmical motions of the feet. I saw a Lingam (a black rock, a phallic symbol representing Lord Shiva) covered with vermilion paint in the trunk of a tree. I noticed a woman worshipping. She had her head bowed. Her head was covered with a fold of her sari and she was kneeling down. I asked Grandpa about Lord Shiva.

"He is the god of creation and destruction. He is the Nataraja, dancing the final dance. He is also called the NeelKantha (in Sanskrit it means the blue throat). At first there was Brahma, then came Vishnu and Shiva is a later god. We will read more about them later. But let me tell you about Shiva. He is the god who carries the trident in his hand. His eyes are red and he has dreadlocks. His hair is adorned with a crescent moon and the Ganges River. The people believe that he indulges in Ganja or Hashish. The Shaivites believe that he is a great ascetic (deerskin in his hand for sleeping and a garland of skulls) and the symbol of sensuality. The bull Nandi is his mount and mascot.

"That is one of the reasons why the Hindus worship the cow. His female consort has many manifestations. She is known as Uma, Durga, Parvati, and Kali. In reality it is the concept of Sakti (supreme goddess) that is most important in this relationship. The divine couple with their sons, Ganesha (elephant-headed) and Skanda (six heads) lives at Mt. Kailash. Of course these are based on faith. Nobody has actually seen them."

Grandpa was on a speaking mode. "Much like our Christian friend believes in Father, Son and the Holy Ghost, almost all the religions have a trinity. We have Brahma, Vishnu and Shiva. Shiva has three eyes. The third eye bestows inward vision but it can cause destruction when focused outward."

I asked him to continue. "The legend has it that the Gods decided to get Amrita (nectar) for everlasting life from the bottom of the cosmic ocean. They did not want the Amrita to fall in the hands of the Asur (demons). But to churn this cosmic ocean the mighty Himalayas volunteered to be the pivot and the great snake was chosen to be the rope. The demons volunteered to assist during the churning thinking that they will fool the Gods when the nectar arrives. The demons held the tail and the Gods held the head of the snake. During the process of churning poison came up that was about to destroy the earth. The only way it could have been removed was for someone to swallow it. Lord Shiva lay down at Mt. Kailash and swallowed the poison to prevent destruction of the earth. That's why his throat is blue. Mt. Kailash is a holy mountain for the Hindus as well as the Buddhists."

Grandpa said that a river was needed to purify and to cool the earth down after all this. "So Ganges, the holy river of heaven, was summoned but it could only come down to earth if someone could break its fall. It is Shiva's dreadlocks that paved the way from heaven to the Himalayas by making a meandering path."

Grandpa said that the origin of Ayurveda might have some relation to the above story. Ayurveda has been available from about 5000 B.C. from the Vedic times. According to some experts of the Vedas the medicines have been available to us, the Aryans (we are darker variety Caucasoid, Europeans are the lighter color variety Caucasians) from the description in the Atharva Veda. It was not until much later that I learnt at the University of North Carolina that the "canine teeth appearance" distinguished us (north India) as Caucasoid. The legend has it that a Hindu God, Dhanwantri, was the end product of the churning of the ocean and he evolved holding a jar of nectar when the churning stopped.

The renowned names of physicians knowledgeable of Ayurvedic principles were Atreya in 800 B.C. That was before the invasion of India by Alexander the Great. Charaka in 200 A.D., Susruta and Bagbhatta, to name a few, were known to have been fine physicians in the subcontinent.

Atreya was a famous teacher at Taxilla University in India, Susruta was a famous surgeon and Charaka was a physician. Ramayana (Hindu epic) has mention of Ayurvedic drugs. The principles of Ayurveda were based on the understanding that the body did not work well if there was a problem of Vata (air), Pitta (bile) and Kapha (mucus). It still holds true partially if we look at body function in a simplistic way. During those years I didn't know about my bile. Everyone else seemed to be spitting and I knew that there was something wrong with the mucus or air system.

By the time Grandpa returned I usually finished my math or whatever he had asked me to do. We played ticktacktoe or dots and squares. Sometimes we played Ludo (Snakes and Ladders) as well. Sometimes I won. But at times I came down from the head of the snake at the top to the tail and lost the game. Grandpa didn't care if he won or lost.

The days we came home early I played soccer or volleyball in our field next to the house. The neighborhood kids had some game going on every day. They weren't so busy. Well, they didn't have a companion like I did. I wasn't any good in the sports. One of the local bullies would place me in the opposite team, which already had a couple of other inept players. This way he would be assured of winning.

I wasn't as good a kicker as most of the other boys. Moreover, I was afraid to jump up to hit the ball towards the goalkeeper with my head. I always knew when some boys kicked me on the shin on purpose rather than kicking the ball. It is not because Kesta missed the ball or such, although he always made it look like an accident. I played anyway. I had a couple of friends who understood that I just wanted to be one of the guys although I was smaller than the most. Grandpa watched us play sometimes. Mostly he read the paper.

I sometimes felt that if Grandpa hadn't been sitting within sight the bullies would have punched me out or thrown me out of the game. At times when I kicked the ball it went straight out instead of being in the middle. I often wondered if the shoes were the wrong size for me. I thought I should have done better than the way I usually performed. The boys thought otherwise. I was a little better as a volleyball player. I didn't play at the net because I wasn't tall enough. But I could punch the ball and make it fall in between the players. Everybody said that I knew how to find a hole in the game. This boosted my ego. Grandpa didn't play any sports. But he sometimes played badminton with me. He didn't like to run too much. I think he was too tired most of the time.

I believe Faulkner said, "Memory believes before knowing remembers." I fully remember that Grandpa had said, "I have given you an A and it does not matter what grade others give you." I always told myself that it was OK that

I wasn't as good as I could have been. I came and told my grandpa about the experiences in sports. He always told me to have fun. "Don't worry about how they treat you. You have no control on that. But you have control on yourself. It is OK to be angry and admit it before acting out. It is a good idea to acknowledge our feelings. Then we may not have to act out."

Idaho Not Far

It rained a bit today as I was walking towards Pocatello. There was very little cloud above me and it cleared quite rapidly. There was not much electrical activity in the air as I had experienced in Indiana and Nebraska. I dried quickly as the air was warm. I was talking about Ben Franklin and his kite experiments. But Anna corrected me and told me that William Sturgeon from Lancashire had performed five hundred kite observations.

Sturgeon had established that in serene weather the atmosphere is invariably charged positively with respect to the Earth, and becomes more positive with increasing altitude. I was on a high area but I knew not to worry unless my hair stood up in the wake of a storm. I remembered reading in my physics class that he was the first person to have devised a seven-ounce magnet that held up nine pounds of iron using the current from a single cell.

I rested for a while on a rock and changed my clothes. My mind was continuously moving from one area to other. I figured it must have been the Red Bull I drank daily.

"So what do you think of boxing?"

I knew that Anna was needling me. "You know that I think boxing is a violent sport. In 1997 the AMA published a position statement saying that 'all forms of boxing are a public demonstration of interpersonal violence which is unique among sporting activities.'

"Victory in boxing is obtained by inflicting on the opponent such a measure of physical injury that the opponent is unable to continue, or falls on the floor unconscious, delirious or bleeding from the face. I think there was a time when people didn't know the damage it caused to the brain. I personally think John L. (Sullivan) was the greatest symbol of bare-knuckle boxing era. He fought one seventy-five-round knockout with Jake Kilrain at Mississippi in 1889 and that was the last heavyweight title bout under London Prize ring rules. I believe he became an alcoholic and then recovered and became an advocate of prohibition. Many boxers have sustained significant brain injuries and some have become reformed peacemakers when their intellect has been lost by the trauma. Mickey Walker, who had studied architecture and was also a pugilist, eventually was diagnosed with Parkinson's disease."

Anna made fun of me and said, "So what do you really think about it?" I didn't answer.

By now I had crossed the Mississippi and Missouri and I was telling Anna that these two together were the longest river in the world. But Anna corrected me and told me that the White Nile from Lake Victoria, Uganda, and the Blue Nile from Lake Tana of Ethiopia join together in Sudan to form the Nile that runs a distance of 5,500 kilometers or a bit more from its source to drain into the Mediterranean Sea along the coast of Egypt and have the distinct fame of being the longest river in the world. I bowed.

During the evenings about three times every week Grandpa taught a class in our inside courtyard. All the neighborhood children came with their chalks and slates and sat on the floor. We had a papaya tree on one corner of the courtyard. There was an elevated cement platform built like a parapet in another end where basil plants surrounded a Lingam. Grandpa taught math and English to the group. He had a blackboard and some chalks.

No one sat next to the papaya tree because the tree did not forgive a sudden jar on the trunk from a sleepy head. This had the potential of a bruised head from a falling papaya. My job was to keep the lanterns and a petromax lamp lit for proper illumination. We always had a clay oil lamp burning from a wick next to the Lingam. One time during the study period there was a disruption because a cobra happened to glide into the class. It was dealt with very quickly and the study proceeded without any further interruption. Grandpa poured small amounts of carbolic acid on the edges prior to subsequent classes to avoid such surprises.

We had a routine in our life most of the days. A lot depended on other people though. Our plans would get interrupted when someone would show up to take Grandpa somewhere for sudden illness or such. One day we were sitting in our patio and grandpa was sad because one of his women patients had died the night before. She had puerperal fever subsequent to giving birth to a baby. He believed that it could have been prevented. He didn't get called until the baby was born. Mother and the baby had high fever. "Maybe with proper precaution of boiled water, iodine and hand washing we could have done something," he said. Grandpa always read about people.

Dr. Philip Semmelweis was a Hungarian doctor but was trained in Vienna. He introduced the concept of antisepsis. But nobody believed him. The older German doctors didn't like his theory. He had a mental breakdown because his colleagues treated him unkindly. But ultimately Joseph Lister honored him. It is not uncommon in life for people to not agree with you. If you believe something is right you just have to stick to it.

He often complained that he did not have all the medicines he needed. "America and England have lot more facilities available. It is going to take time for us to catch up." He told me to get the atlas and we looked up where different countries in Europe were located. He asked me to memorize the capitals of many nations. I did. There were times when he would show me how to draw the maps of different countries. "I wanted to see many places. But it won't happen in this lifetime. But you can see them for me," he said. I told him that whenever I went places he would travel in my heart. He hugged me.

We got interrupted because a man brought a little boy on his arms bleeding in his shorts. We went together inside our dispensary. He examined the boy after washing his hands. As he painted iodine the boy started screaming more. The boy was about my age. He had a gash next to his penis. I watched with awe and nervousness. The whole thing was almost hanging loose from the top. "Has he urinated since this happened?" Grandpa asked. The man nodded in affirmative. Grandpa injected some medicine all around it and then took out some catgut sutures and sewed it all up. He placed a dressing with iodine and wrote a prescription. Nankumama filled it. "I injected numbing medicine and gave him sulfadiazine powder so that he won't get an infection," said Grandpa.

This was the first time I had seen Grandpa perform an operation. The boy was playing with a stick with the top of a can attached to its other end. He was rolling it on the road and walking but the wheel (top of the can) hit a rock and the end of the stick cut into him, his father said. I had one of those "sticks and can" toys that I had made hammering a nail into a stick. I threw mine out before I went inside the house after watching this. Later on during the evening Grandpa showed me a picture from his anatomy book depicting the path of the urine as it travels through the penis. Soon after I went to the bathroom and inspected my penis to make sure that it was like the picture I had just seen. I was pleased with myself.

I remembered later in life that Grandpa had said to me that it is important to be pleased with ourselves. "Otherwise," he had said, "it causes anxiety and dissatisfaction in life with unimportant issues. Later psychiatrists ask lots of questions to establish the cause and we have to pay him for telling us what we should have known anyway."

On Saturdays there was a cricket game in our field. Usually the older boys played. Sometimes they let me play as well. I liked to hold the red cricket balls. It is very masculine. It is smooth with rough stitches. It is slick yet hard. It bounces when thrown but stops when it runs out of momentum. The parchment over the bat envelopes treated willow wood. The wood is soaked in linseed oil to make it pliable. The batsman nodded saying he was ready and the bowler ran to pitch the ball from the opposite stumps (wickets). Another batsman stood near the bowler. The bowler bowled and I ran to gather it after the batsman had hit it. Sometimes when the batsmen would miss and one of the three stumps behind him would be knocked down the wicket keeper always yelled to the umpire "How is that?" The umpire raised his pointing finger acknowledging that the batsman's turn was finished. I had to hurry to throw the ball because the batsman ran to the other stumps as soon as he had hit the ball to score a point. The total points or runs at the end of the game determined the winner.

"So, how did it go?" Grandpa asked.

"OK, but I like to play marbles with my friends. That's great!" Under the Bel tree (it is a gummy fruit that is usually used as a laxative) I played marbles. I was good at flipping; my thumb could also bend quite a bit backwards and I could hit accurately at a distance. I had all the qualities needed for a good marble player. Grandpa said that I had good coordination.

We got up early every day when I lived with Grandpa. It used to get pretty warm in the mornings as the sun came up. During my childhood we brushed our teeth using a twig from the neem tree and at times we just used the ash that was in the stove to rub on our teeth to make them shiny. All of us had shiny teeth. Later on neem toothpaste was available and that is what we used. Neither Grandpa nor I had any cavities.

Many people in India have problems with their gums and they end up losing their teeth. We rinsed our mouth after every meal and massaged our gums before going to bed. We didn't get a tube well inside our courtyard until I was almost ten years old. We used well water and the maids washed our dishes in the pond behind the house. Then they were re-washed with the well water. Our well water would sometimes develop an odor. So every month Grandpa put some potassium permanganate powder in it. It would make the water red but then it would clear up. It was kept covered to prevent the kids from falling into it.

My cousin lowered me into it once while I sat inside a bucket. I strongly believe, if Grandma hadn't come over and started yelling he would have drowned me because he wasn't strong enough to rewind the handle and I was already under the water and screaming. It would not have been on purpose of course. He was my age and we were just playing. Grandpa had told us not to hang around the well. We didn't follow the orders because we both liked to throw rocks in it to hear the sound "dib." And sometimes it sounded "dib, dib." That's when we both threw rocks at the same time. But eventually we grew out of the need to hear that sound.

In the mornings we saw everybody. All the cousins and the uncles and aunts lived in the same complex but in different parts of the house much like birds on a tree. Everyone flew to different places to work during the day but in the night all were back to the same safety net, Grandpa's den. All the uncles and I addressed Grandmother as "Mother." Nobody ever told me any different. I thought she was my mother for the longest time. I was not smart enough to figure out why Grandpa was my mother's husband. I guess I never felt the need or the urge to solve such a complicated issue. I always felt loved. So what difference did it make?

Every night before bedtime Grandma gave Grandpa a black pill and I got a glass of warm milk. We didn't have a refrigerator. The milk had to be boiled to be sure that it could not transmit tuberculosis or brucellosis or anything else for that matter. I always wanted to trade my milk for that pill that Grandma got out of the cabinet. But Grandpa didn't want to hear about it. Grandma always kept that pill under lock and key. Every Saturday morning Grandpa and I walked about a mile to a shop. I have forgotten the name of the store now but I recall that it had a sign that depicted something related to the government. I stood outside and played with the goats on the street while Grandpa stood in a line.

Occasionally, a droopy-eyed cow hung around the store. It was not until I was in medical school that I understood that the pill Grandpa was taking was opium. Opium was rationed and he could have only enough for seven days at a time. He went home and gave the package to Grandma for safekeeping. I never asked him and he never told me anything about it except that it was his sleeping pill. It was only later that I realized that the goats and the cows were opium addicts, because everybody threw the envelope made of palm leaf that housed the opium on the streets before they went into the store, and the animals had gotten used to eating them.

Grandpa always took it only at night. Later on I decided that there must have been truth to his saying as to why the mosquitoes did not affect him as much. The first half of the night the master is too full to feel the mosquito and in the second half the mosquito is too full to bite the master, he said. I believe the mosquitoes sucked the blood from him all right but fell down drunk from the opium. Therefore they could not inject him with the parasite from their salivary glands, which is essential to transmit illness. In the early mornings I often saw one or two mosquitoes lying on the floor on his side of the mosquito net that were still kind of breathing funny! I always squashed them.

I helped Grandmother with some fun things such as making butter at home. I loved the aroma of fresh butter. We sometimes listened to the radio. It was a big box and it often made a lot of sixty-cycle noise that to me sounded like many bugs were fighting inside. We had to go to the local hardware store across the railroad track to get it fixed. The store was next to the main road where there were electric poles. The store owner had some kind of a wire hooked up to the street light. For some reason every month on a Monday he had to unhook it real early in the morning because he said the electrical inspector might get confused when he comes to check the lights. The inspector supposedly had never seen a radio. Ramuda (hardware man) never invited the inspector to learn about the radio either. Grandpa always smiled when Ramuda told me that.

Later on Grandpa said that William Shockley and two other persons, John Bardeen and Walter Brattain, had received the Nobel Prize for Physics for discovering the transistor. "This will make the radios much better and smaller." He said, "Dr. Shockley was a graduate of California Institute of Technology and Harvard University. Maybe someday you will go there too. I am not too sure about Dr. Shockley's theory that the intelligence of the black people is less on the standardized intelligence test because of genetic weakness. Black people have been subjugated and their growth and spirit has been stunted. I don't know for sure but I feel that Dr. Shockley is possibly British and then went to school in America." We later learnt that Dr. Shockley was born in London.

This is what we did all the time. If we had a question we tried to look up the answer then because we knew we would forget otherwise. Sometimes it took us days because there was no library in our village. "Don't procrastinate if at all possible," he always said. "If I died and hadn't learnt when I had a chance I may be left with a desire. When I die I want to feel satisfied and be free of all desires, needs and wants. I just want to thank God for all his gifts." He stopped.

Grandpa read all the time. That is whenever I was not talking to him. I had just read in the newspaper about the American television. He said, "Television sounds to me like a radio with a picture of the person talking. I won't be surprised if the Americans come up with a picture where you will be able to almost smell or touch the speaker. It might take a while. Sir Isaac Shoenberg (Jewish, Russian) is the inventor of the first high-definition television. This was used by BBC for their first high-definition telecast. We probably won't have a TV here in my lifetime," he noted.

Television did not become available to the general public almost till 1970 in India. He thought God blesses everyone but there may be a little tilt towards some people. "You know if I had to pick a race that God has blessed the most; it will have to be the Jews. Hitler tried to kill them. You can't kill all the God's favorite children. They were freed from slavery and God had split the Red Sea or built a bridge of some kind so that they could come across to new land of freedom. Music, science, business and finance are all the areas where Jews have excelled. America could not have made atom bomb without the German Jewish scientists. But the Jewish race has been persecuted. Even Shakespeare made fun of a Jew in *Merchant of Venice*. We will read the story sometime later.

"But I want to tell you something about these Americans and their policies. Mr. Joseph Kennedy was the ambassador for the United States in England and he discouraged Mr. Roosevelt, the American president, to get involved in Europe when the Germans were killing the Jews. Six million of them were killed just because they are Jews. There was a Hungarian Jew, Theodore Karman, who developed the rocket engine. He was working at California Institute of Technology. I think the folks from CIT subsequently helped in the development of the National Aeronautics and Space Administration Jet

Propulsion laboratory. May be someday you will go to America and see and learn from these people.

"Mr. Henry Ford, the man who developed the concept of assembly line to make Ford cars in America, would not hire Jews in his factory at first." I didn't understand all this and so I asked him about karma.

The law of karma explains the inequalities in life according to Hindu belief. Our actions today will determine our life tomorrow. When I grew older this made tremendous sense about responsibility and the consequences of our actions. Grandpa was fading but continued. "This life is a Maya or Samsara and we will eventually become part of the God Brahma, otherwise we have to be reborn till all the fruits of our karma are consumed." Grandpa was getting tired. "A famous American general named Patton during the Second War believed in reincarnation much like I do. The difference is that I don't know what I was in previous life but Patton seemed to have known about his previous life."

We took a tea break. Grandma came and sat with us for a while. Then Grandpa went to see his patients and I went to play with my slingshot. My slingshot was made from guava branches. That is about as strong a wood as could have been had in our neighborhood. My friends and I went near the "Burning Ghats." That is where they usually cremated people. Grandpa and I had just recently discussed about the Tantric Sadhus that lie on the coals and meditate. We didn't see anybody. We actually sat just outside the place where they baked the bricks on the ground. Far away from where we sat garbage was being burnt and we saw the smoke drifting in the opposite direction to us. We kept our bikes at a distance from the hot ground so the tires won't be flat. We placed couple of potatoes under the hot sand and stuck a stick next to it as a marker and waited till the sticks were on fire. It usually meant the potatoes were ready. We sat and listened to the river and watched the smoke of cremation at a distance.

I hadn't quite understood the meaning of death. Death was total absence of someone from me at that time and it involved a lot of crying for those that did not die. We hadn't learnt to feel the reverence of the soul when it left the body in search of eternity. The smoke from the carcasses rose gently to the sky. We watched it ride the gentle waves of the river and shimmer in the late afternoon sun as it slowly ascended to heaven in the horizon. Darkness creeping into the twilight of the late afternoon slowly inhaled it.

Rohit, my friend, was about three years older than I was. Grandpa had treated him when he was afflicted with poliomyelitis. Grandpa said there was no cure for it. Somebody in America is working on a vaccine but we don't have it yet. India is still not free of poliomyelitis. Rohit recovered but he had one leg kind of shriveled up. He had gotten used to it. I never noticed it much. He and I talked at times about school. Since I wasn't going to school he filled me in on everything that happened in the school during the day.

Rohit had a difficult time with temper during the time we were together. His mother had died when he was young. His father did not remarry. One of his aunts (mother's sister), Anjali, lived with them. She was a child bride and had become a widow at the age of thirteen when her forty-year-old husband had died. I wasn't sure at that time how old forty really was but I knew that it was older than me and younger than Grandpa. She was married to a high-class Brahmin who had other wives in different villages. Therefore at his death five other women had become widows. Those who practiced the custom of Satti usually threw all the wives in the funeral pyre of the dead husband. But it had been repealed some time ago.

But Grandpa had told me that in some villages the custom was still practiced. Polygamy was the custom of the old days and Hindus had only one wife now. Only Muslims could have four wives. One day Rohit came home early to find his father forcing himself on Anjali. Ever since then he was easily angered. He didn't know whether he was angry because Anjali was hurt and there was nothing he could do or because he found that his father was mean and he was ashamed. He didn't have any respect for his father but he still was afraid of him. Anjali had to cover her face in front of other men as was the custom of the day because she was a widow. She wore a white sari with no color. She didn't eat onions or garlic or any meat products because it was believed that those kinds of food raised sexual desires and a widow was not supposed to have those pleasures.

His sister could play the sitar, an Indian musical instrument made from a gourd with strings, and at times she came over and performed for the neighborhood. Grandma blew the conch every evening to bring peace to our home. We went to listen to music at different festival times. Musicians from different parts of the country came to perform in a neighboring town. It was always an eclectic group of people who added a bit of classical Indian music in their repertoire. Sitar, sarod, tabla and different vocal accompaniments were part of the package that lasted all night at times.

In our house we had a horn that looked like Shofar, a Jewish ritual musical instrument made from a ram's horn. It is possible that Joshua might have used a similar instrument to call everyone. The notes from this instrument are supposed to imitate the sad notes depicting a penitential spirit preceding Yom Kippur. "Rosh Hashanah begins as a reawakening for the New Year," Grandpa continued. "It can be used for announcing good news too. But it can be like when Rambabu plays the violin every night after drinking. He is wailing for his dead wife. You won't understand now but I am going to tell you that there may be many things that can make a man very sad." Grandpa continued after taking a breath. "The two most important ones that makes a man be on his knees and ask God 'why me' are the death of a child and the death of a spouse." Grandpa became teary eyed. I hugged him.

We also had a flute. I sometimes played it trying to imitate Lord Krishna. However, the great snake never came out of the ocean to hold me up!

"So, why is it that most of the Hindu gods have all these women surrounding them? Moreover, all the women that I see in the pictures and the statues on the temples are wearing very little clothes. Is heaven full of women with no clothes on?"

Grandpa didn't have any quick answer. I heard the sound of the conch. Grandmother always blew the conch to welcome the evening before she performed Puja to the gods. I had to wait till I was twelve years old for answers to these questions. It was only then that I went to live with my dad. My father had explained that many men were involved in building the temples and the projects often took many years to complete. "The statues on the walls of Khajuraho represent the cravings of men while they were not able to be with women. The concept of heaven with Brahma lying on a lotus leaf and many women playing with him is the heaven conceived by men. The women on earth are wearing too many clothes and the men wish to see them differently. Depicting them in religious symbols adds permanency and deification and therefore you can enjoy them without feeling guilty."

Dad continued, "I don't agree with the Americans on many issues but I like the freedom of expression. I also understand that some Protestants like Baptists, and Catholic Church members feel guilty about sexual freedom. Most religious rituals induce a sense of guilt or shame to keep their members together. I will explain more as you grow older and read more about different religions. It takes a woman to make the men free. Mae West was placed in jail in New York after she performed in 'Sex.' I have read about it but I have not been to New York to see it. It took a lot of courage to perform in that play. She liberated the men by fulfilling their wish and the allied soldiers honored her during the Second War, i.e. they called their inflatable life jackets 'Mae Wests,' alluding to her hourglass figure." I know that my grandpa could have never been so liberated as to speak about this subject with me!

Grandpa really loved my grandmother. It was customary those days for women to get married very young. "How old was Grandma when she got married to you?"

"Your grandmother was married when she was twelve years old. She came to be with her mother-in-law (i.e. our house) only when she became a woman. I was only fifteen years old," said Grandpa. "We talked but didn't know at first as to what to say and she was shy. So we smiled and she giggled. She learned from your great-grand mother the customs of the home and how to operate the finances of the house. We were in separate rooms till I was eighteen years old. We learnt to love each other as time went on.

"I didn't know what love meant but slowly we started doing things for each other and began to care and listen. I believe that is love. We disagreed but never in front of others. I did what she thought was right and we talked in the evening about the day. Your grandmother waited on me in a manner such that it was never obvious and according to the custom of the day. It is that subtlety of understanding the need of the other I suppose is marital love or being sensitive. I worked outside and she stayed home and cooked and made sure that the household 'help' were doing the sort of work that they were supposed to do."

I used to see that on some evenings Grandpa would pick couple of magnolias and gardenias before he came inside the house. He gave them to Grandma in a discreet manner because it was not customary for the husband to be flirtatious in front of others. I on the other hand always noticed the quiet smile on my grandma's lips that moved just like the petal of a baby rose. Just enough to demonstrate the pleasure with slight pouting of the lip yet shy to open up fully until the proper time.

Grandpa slowly learnt that outside the house, i.e. in public, he was made to feel in charge and "man like" but in reality it was Grandma who ran the house. Grandma knew all the men and women who worked in our house. Grandpa interviewed the men face to face but Grandma asked the questions from behind the door.

She hired the women that worked in our house. When she needed jewelry the goldsmith came to the house and sat on the flat bed. Grandpa watched him weighing the gold but Grandma had already made a drawing of what she wanted and she knew exactly what she was going to pay. She spoke to the merchant from behind the door. The goldsmith could not afford to disagree with the doctor's wife, particularly someone from such high caste! I had never seen anyone argue with Grandma. But I don't believe she was unfair, although I believe the price of most merchandise was more favorable towards her than the merchant.

It was not customary for a woman to show her face to strange men when they came to the house to discuss business. It was a man's job to negotiate but the anatomy of such business negotiations was run by women! The idea was for the men in the society to feel "powerful, man like" but nothing really happened unless the women OK'd it. Although Grandma rarely went outside the house, because there was no need, when she did go shopping for saris or such she covered her head. She usually went with other women or one of the maids.

I remember one afternoon when I walked in on Grandpa. They didn't hear me. I saw through the crack of the door while I was sitting on the wall behind the porch. Grandpa was rubbing Grandmother's feet as he was lying on his side looking towards her. I moved away quickly. I was with Grandpa all the time and he never had any time to himself. I never intended to sneak up on them but I knew the inappropriateness of walking in during moments of intimacy. I quickly moved away so that they could embrace each other. They rarely had any time for that because I was always there with Grandpa.

Today was another wonderful day to walk. I slept well every night. I had developed a bit of a hip pain but I had learnt to ignore most pain and I always told myself that pills are for writing prescriptions only and not for taking. I did not take any pills during my walk except an occasional vitamin. I had walked more than thirty miles the day before.

My energy level was high and I sang and danced and argued with Anna whenever she was disagreeable. Stoicism of course is that ingredient which is needed in any extreme sport. The Stoic movement was founded in Athens by Zeno in 300 B.C. Zeno was inspired by the teachings of Socrates and Diogenes and developed the concept. I had read that stoicism helped to promote the ideal of a common humanity bound by participation in acts of common benefit and had laid the foundations of happiness, by galvanizing these with the virtues of wisdom, courage and moderation. I was flying. I could taste being in Portland, Oregon! I am not a musician but I moved my hands like Leopold Stokowski, as though I was conducting the Cincinnati Symphony. My hands were my antennae and my mind was the organ as I sensed and balanced my heart and soul with God's guidance to move forward. I was in Disney's *Fantasia* singing the melody of hope!

Love in Our Family

Whenever Grandma went out in the field or to the pond to check on us usually one of the women from the house went out as a scout and made sure that it was OK to go outside. Such was the custom and so I never questioned it. Grandpa honored her wishes to the utmost. Public display of affection was not the custom. But I learnt to see the twinkle in their eyes when they looked at each other. Grandma blushed when I said something to her about this. She usually changed the topic immediately. I addressed her as "Ma" and often hugged her and she loved it. She would then look at my face and start weeping and I did not know why until long after the death of my grandfather.

Although I went to bed with Grandpa I always woke up alone in the morning. Grandpa transported me to my bed after I fell asleep. Grandmother was always up by the time I woke up and so I never saw her lying in my spot! Grandma was absolute in charge as far as my health was concerned. I heard her tell my grandpa that "you can be doctor for all your patients but for him God and I are the only doctors that he needs." Grandpa never said a word in retaliation. I often suffered from sore throat and ear infections. Grandma had some sort of a solution that she painted in my throat. She also poured warm ghee, homemade butter, in my ears from a ladle made of betel leaf. However, if I developed a fever that lasted and her remedy failed Grandpa was summoned to give me very a painful penicillin shot in my upper leg. Most of the time my earache went away and Grandma's concoction stopped me from coughing my guts out. "I will never do anything that hurts you. I will call your grandpa to do that," said Grandma. Grandpa said nothing.

It was customary for women to not eat until the men had finished. Grandma always made sure that Grandpa was satisfied and comfortable until she started eating. It was not a form of submission to a superior but the feeling of an inner joy in the comfort of the other. It was the custom to make the men happy because in turn the women were happy as well. It was a symbiotic behavior where neither party was deprived but there was an additional effect of wholesomeness between the two.

Grandma performed Puja on a regular basis and there were special Puja when someone was sick. The regular Puja involved image worship with chanting of devotional mantras and at the end there was often a request to God usually to heal someone. The images could be a full figure or just a black rock with a streak of vermilion symbolizing Lord Shiva. Grandpa had explained that Puja were non-Vedic in origin whereas Yajna (Sanskrit for offering or sacrifice) were of Vedic origin. "I don't believe that in the Vedas God asked for a human sacrifice although the Kali worshippers developed this ritual," Grandpa continued. "In the Old Testament God had asked Abraham to sacrifice Isaac to test his faith?"

The Brahmins are the only people who can recite the correct mantras or the sacred formula to perform Yajna. This Vedic ritual is usually carried out just to honor God without asking for anything and during the performance rice and fruits are offered. I saw these rituals being performed many times during the year and Grandpa sometimes performed this while bathing in the river. He would stand waist deep in the Ganges and uttered the mantras with closed eyes and folded hands. When he would finish bathing a guru sitting at the steps of the ghat would place a vermilion tika on his forehead signifying dwij or resurrection.

I was often afflicted with boils during the summertime. Grandma usually treated them by placing heat poultice and wiping them with iodine. But I remember one episode when I had a boil as big as the hills of Ranchi (this is a hill station where folks went to escape the summer heat). This was also in an awkward place in my body. I didn't feel comfortable in exposing myself in front of my Grandma and so Grandpa was summoned. He examined me and gave a verdict that I did not like. I was extremely vigilant making sure that Grandpa wouldn't catch me when he had a knife in his hand. However, he had guessed my intentions.

One afternoon Nankumama was invited to lunch. After lunch a fight broke out between Nankumama and me. I escaped and climbed the guava tree. He ran after me and overpowered me. I was made to lie face down on his lap and then Grandpa appeared with iodine and a knife. Before I knew it my boil was lanced and the pus filled a whole cup. Although I felt better later on and my wound healed without any problem I remember expressing myself most violently towards my grandfather. I had also called Nankumama every possible unkind epithet known to me. Grandma was nowhere in sight. They forgave me and I overlooked their indiscretion too! I prayed later and asked God to not give me any more boils. A remarkable thing happened. Next summer I didn't have any more boils. This episode didn't mar the relationship between Grandpa and me. I just told him not to use the knife on me anymore. Grandpa said that I could have died if the infection had gone to my blood. He said it was his responsibility to take care of me. When I asked him who gave him the responsibility he didn't answer. I learnt that much later.

One day as we were loading our medicine chest Grandpa told me about the spleen and the liver. He showed me on my body as to where they were but what I liked most was when one day he showed me those organs in a cut-up goat at the meat shop. The butcher let me feel them in my hands. I knew at that time that I would like to feel the human organs in my hands. I didn't tell that to Grandpa at that time.

We boiled the syringes and the needles and packed them in stainless-steel cases that were boiled as well to get them ready for our journey to the villages. My job was to check the sharpness of the needles. I placed them upside down on the rack and then one by one I had to gently tug them on my nails. If any of them made a scratch on my nails I had to take the burr off by rubbing them on a smooth black rock. The needles and syringes were all used multiple times. The concept of disposable needles and syringes didn't exist and the cost would have been prohibitive too. Grandpa wiped his stethoscope with alcohol. He had a red soap dish. He washed his hands constantly.

He taught me about typhoid fever and malaria. He also told me about the diarrhea associated with cholera. I never had those illnesses but by the time I was twelve years old I could have diagnosed them just because I heard so much about them. Grandpa wore a dhoti every day. He always tucked it between his legs before he sat down to see any of his patients in fear of direct contact with infected fluids.

We were just getting ready for a nap one afternoon when a person knocked on our door with urgency. I ran to the dispensary with him and stood next to him when he examined a person who seemed very sick. He was salivating. Grandpa checked his temperature by placing a thermometer in his underarm. He has a high fever, he said. "He was sleeping outside his hut on a sunny afternoon about two days back when a dog bit him on the leg. He was fine until this morning and then he couldn't talk or swallow and goes into some kind of spasm when we offered him milk," his family said anxiously.

Grandpa got up and offered him a glass of water. As soon as the man saw the water his face went into a spasm and he kept spitting up frothy saliva. Grandpa's face became grim. He asked if they had seen the dog any more. No one seemed to know. "It would be better if you can find the dog and somehow put him in a cage to observe for next ten days. The dog possibly has rabies and the dog will die before ten days," Grandpa predicted. Grandpa washed his hands and walked outside with the brother of the patient towards the hibiscus tree so that he could be further from his earshot. "He has hydrophobia. He will probably die within next two days. We can call the Calcutta Hospital and try to find the injection that he might have to take for fourteen days in his stomach. You must not touch any of the fluids from his body nor should you allow the fluids to touch your mouth. You can catch it." Grandpa, visibly upset, stopped for a minute. They took him home.

We came across the courtyard to lie down. I was too upset. It is very difficult to be a doctor, particularly when you are the harbinger of bad news; he tried to console me. Sometimes even the shots that are supposed to save him can cause severe paralysis and damage to the brain. He answered my question before I even asked. He told me to read Ramayana, the Hindu epic. I was soon asleep.

When I was in India we had geckos on our walls that crawled and ate bugs. We didn't have screens on our windows. Geckos are our friends. They eat mosquitoes as well. They are spraying DDT in the drains and old ponds. I think it is killing the fish and some of the mosquitoes. The incidence of malaria may be a little less. Sir Ronald Ross was born in India. He was a British citizen and received the Nobel Prize for discovering the cause of malaria. The Anopheles mosquito transmits it. That's why we check in early evenings on the walls to see if there is a mosquito sitting with its behind lifted up. That's the one we don't want. Actually we don't want any of them. The mosquito is attracted by the smell of the human sweat. Dr. Ross worked in the Indian Medical Service and carried out part of his work at the School of Tropical Medicine in Calcutta but most of it in London. Grandpa stopped talking to me for a while. I was looking tired, he said.

I was always concerned about the flies and mosquitoes. Flies had easy access into the house on account of not having any screens to keep them out and so we always learnt to cover everything. I remember during my trek to Kedarnath in mid sixties the flies got the best of me. Those days there were no buses after Hardwar. It was a summer day in the mountains and I walked as long as I could. Around four in the afternoon I arrived near Rishikesh. I had no money and so I chose to stay in a Gurdwara. In these places Sikhs provide food and shelter to anyone who walks into the building. There is no expectation of money but most people give a donation. I fell asleep on the concrete floor. I knew that it was important to cover my face whenever I slept outside in India. I woke up to a humming noise only to see that I was looking at the perineum of a hundred flies that were possibly defecating on my handkerchief that I had placed as a tent to protect my mouth. As I had fallen asleep my mouth had gaped open and all the flies were enjoying their siesta on the hammock across my mouth while warm air and gurgling noise lulled them to a state of ecstasy. I spent the rest of the night sitting up and left in the early morning for NandanKanaan, Valley of Flowers, walking along the beautiful river Mondakini. It rushed down the mountain with a swishing sound just as an adolescent girl would hotdog down a steep slope on her skis. I enjoyed the occasional spray that bathed me as the river spewed water upwards in retaliation of obstructing rocks that interfered with its smooth flow of energy.

Idaho was very hot most days. I had to drink extra water on certain days. I placed my hand inside my backpack to get some gum. I found a rosary that one of my friends had given me and told me to keep it with me all the time. I did. I also wore a necklace with a cross that another friend had given me. I prayed as I handled the rosary.

"Anna, do you know anything similar to a rosary in other religions?"

"Yes. Subhah is a string of Muslim prayer beads. Each unit represents the names of God. The Muslims may recite or chant 'Glory to Allah' as they touch individual beads in succession. However, since prayer can be recited in one's heart one can carry on a conversation while moving the individual beads between fingers for praying or purification. However, I have been told that in the Muslim religion some regard the beads as pretentious and unnecessary. Buddhists chant of Buddham Saranam Gattchami is much the same except they don't use any beads."

My support van arrived. I sat for a while to rest from the hot sun. I read from Brian Andreas, *Traveling Light*: "I don't think of it as working for world peace," he said. "I think of it as just trying to get along in a really big strange family." He was talking about getting along and how to negotiate instead of getting angry.

I said, "Let's go and check on the garden," to Grandpa. He joined me and we strolled towards the garden. It was located next to the pond on the side of the soccer field. We had different vegetables that were growing. Actually some of them were doing quite well. Eggplants, tomatoes, cauliflower, peppers, onions, carrots, okra, cucumbers and pumpkins had filled the garden. The spinach was on one side with marigolds bordering the garden.

Grandpa said, "The bugs hang around the flowers and leave the spinach alone. Onions protect the other plants because it is pungent. You need to have a garden of your own." I liked the idea.

The next year he had given me a certain amount of area in the garden that was designated by a piece of paper glued to two sticks saying "A" as my very own garden. "The rain water would make the paper soggy but you get the idea," Grandpa had said. Grandpa checked on it every so often to make sure that I watered and weeded it. And when I didn't he knew it. "Garden is a responsibility much like raising a child. You have to love it, feed it and talk to it. You have to buy a lottery ticket to have a chance to win. It doesn't mean that you will win. But you will not have a chance otherwise." I loved to grow pumpkin but it took all my allotted space. "You have to decide what you want and then budget accordingly. Otherwise you have to eat only pumpkin. It is like using up all the material to make three shorts and then in winter you won't have any long pants to wear," Grandpa had explained.

It was important for us to have a garden because we didn't eat any raw salad from the vegetables that we bought at the store. It was a common practice in India to use "night soil," a euphemism for human manure, to fertilize the vegetables. This method often contaminated the vegetables with different cysts and ova of parasites. The rule in our house was that anything that could not be boiled, cooked or peeled is not to be eaten unless grown in our own yard. Despite all the precautions I often suffered from giardiasis and amebiasis. I was constantly taking Enteroquinol to control different gastrointestinal infections. Now those medicines are not prescribed as much because some studies have shown that they can cause permanent liver damage.

One day as I was working next to a tree I got stung by a wasp. So he checked it as I was screaming. He painted the area with tincture iodine and gave me a pill that made me sleepy. He said Benadryl will stop me from itching or any bad reaction. He said that wasps provision their nests with roaches that serve as food for the wasp larvae. The nests of the wasps are of paper-like material built on the ground or in branches of trees. The "paper" consists of plant materials that are regurgitated by the wasp. We went for a walk to inspect the area where the nest might have been and then to the pond. He told me about the flowers and the leaves that were covering most of our pond. We didn't kill any insects or animals unless they bothered us. "They are all part of the creation," Grandpa had said. Water hyacinth, purple flowers with blue and yellow markings, covered parts of our pond. "You will see a lot more of these in the pond next door." I already did. I just didn't know the difference between this and water lilies. "It reproduces quickly and clogs up slow-flowing streams. Water lilies have rounded floating waxy-coated leaves that contain many air spaces. The stalks arise from underwater stems that are buried in the mud."

I read the Ramayana to Grandpa during our multiple trips to see patients. The central incident of the epic is about the abduction of Sita by the demon Ravana and subsequent rescue. Sita, Rama's wife, is the symbol of Indian womanhood. Her wifely devotion, chastity and self-surrender is the goal to be reached according to Indian tradition.

Grandpa explained that Sita was the child of the Mother Earth found by King Janaka when he was plowing his field. I said, "How come the king was plowing his own field?"

Grandpa continued, "Rama won her as his bride by bending Shiva's bow and she accompanied Rama when he went into exile. Laksmana, the brother, and the great monkey god, Hanumana, was the assistant to Rama. Hanumana picked up the Himalayas and brought it over to them to find the herb that would cure Laksmana from a wound that he had sustained from an arrow of an enemy. We get a lot of medicine from the Himalayan herbs even now." He continued, "For example, quinine from the cinchona trees is used to treat malaria and rawlfia alkaloids to treat high blood pressure and many others."

I asked him to tell me about some other women that we should be proud of and try to emulate. "There are many women I can tell you about. Women bring harmony to life and the world but most nations have tried to keep them subdued.

"Let me tell you about Jhansi ki Rani (queen of Jhansi). She fought a fierce battle with the British and when it became apparent that she would be captured she jumped with her horse from the Fort of Gwalior. She died with dignity."

Grandpa continued and told me about Susan B. Anthony and the women's suffrage movement. "In America women were not allowed to vote until recently. They placed this woman in jail and the judge let her go without fining her because you can't fine someone when the principle is right.

"Nellie Ross was the first woman in the United States to serve as a governor of a state called Wyoming and she was the first woman to direct the U.S. Mint. Goldie Myerson or Golda Meir was a signatory to Israel's independence declaration and appointed minister to Moscow." Grandpa didn't live long enough to see her as the fourth prime minister of Israel.

"In England women could not be doctors until Sophia Jex-Blake successfully established a medical school for women so that women could receive M.D. and practice medicine. Gertrude Jekyll, a British woman, was possibly the most successful advocate of natural garden and she was a landscape architect." Grandpa often talked about beautiful English gardens. I chimed in about Sarojini Naidu. She was a freedom fighter from Calcutta.

"Indians are respectful of the women culturally from reading such stories as of Sita. Then of course Draupadi, the only wife the seven brothers had in Mahabharata, helps us to understand our culture. Any society that does not respect women cannot be successful because they have no peace at home. There may be a façade of organization but in reality there is a current of 'poor stitching' that builds up. Then the inner torment bursts the dam of fake sweet makeup and shows up as an ugly stitching on cheap material. I won't be surprised if India gets a woman prime minister." Grandpa had to stop to drink some water. Grandpa didn't get to see Mrs. Indira Gandhi as prime minister of India.

By now two pairs of shoes had become completely smooth from all the walking I have been doing on hot concrete. The third pair was also not protecting me from the shock of pounding the concrete. The steps were beginning to feel like as though I was walking on marbles at times. I was sitting on the roadside and thinking Rock Springs to Kemmerer took a lot of time but I always felt excited when I was about to reach the border of one state because I knew I had less left to go. I had to talk to myself about the journey and not the destination quite often because I needed convincing. I couldn't help it at times. It is like reading *War and Peace* or *The Brothers Karamazov*, you want to see how far you are from the end. I thought about Natasha for a while but I was actually dreaming of a Yakshi.

Anna asked me about Yakshi. "In the Indian mythology, Yakshas are deities that are cordial to men and are guards or custodians of treasures hidden in the earth. Kubera ruled in Alaka, a mythical Himalayan kingdom, and it is here that the Yakshas are given to worship with the serpent by the Dravidian peoples of India. Stone figures representing the female prototype on the walls of temples and doorways often jeweled in nude and seminude postures in seductive appearances have been dated from the first century before Christ."

Anna talked about the Louisiana Purchase and New Mexico. I had walked through the land of the Shoshone and Arapaho Plains Indians. The Wyoming territory was created in 1868. Anna said that the railroad was built by the encouragement of President Lincoln and he is honored everywhere. I asked Anna, "What was the Wyoming massacre about?"

She said, "It had nothing to do with Wyoming." Anna continued, "In 1778, during the war of Independence, Colonel John Butler led a force of one thousand loyalists and Iroquois allies against five thousand inhabitants of Wyoming valley of Pennsylvania and killed 360 men, women and children directly, and many others who escaped died of starvation in the woods."

On Sundays a gentleman from Calcutta came to visit us. He always hugged me and had me sit on his lap. I called him uncle although no one told me that he was my uncle. "Uncle" in India is a generic name for anyone who looks older than a brother should look like. He drank tea and chitchatted for a while and left in his car. His driver was very nice to me and let me sit inside the car for a while. During every visit I became more and more familiar and certainly very comfortable with my uncle. He asked me about my school and my studies. I ushered him to come and see my garden. I read to him from the newspaper. I showed him the books I was reading. I taught him how to hold the slingshot and fire it. I was proud when he had learnt to knock down a papaya. He sometimes brought me new shoes and clothes.

After I left the room with him to show him around, the older people always talked very softly. It is not that I wanted to hear what they were saying but I just couldn't hear them. I told him that I went to a local school for a bit but then Grandpa thought I could learn just as much at home. He thought that was great. He laughed with me when I showed him where I played hopscotch and jump. He told me that he loved me and asked me if I would like to come and visit Calcutta. I asked Grandpa to take me. Everybody seemed pleased. It was much later that I realized that I was being prepared for my independent survival in the wilderness. I was living in a habitat, much like in a place for injured animals at Nairobi, and slowly I would be ready to be "let go" to adjust to my destined environment.

I was about ten years old when Grandpa told me that the gentleman I address as uncle is actually my dad. For some reason neither did I get too excited nor did I become remorseful for missing the time with Dad. I honestly didn't know what a dad does or that anybody could be anything more than what Grandpa was to me. I never missed anything or anybody. As a matter of fact that was the first time I realized that I had never asked about my mom or dad. For me love was not a cream that I hadn't seen. I had all the milk I wanted and all the sugar in the world couldn't make my life taste any better. Grandpa said he would decide when I would go to stay with my dad. I said OK. That was that. I was too dumb and never even asked, "Where is my mom?" There was a change though.

During the subsequent visits of this gentleman I addressed him as Dad, but it sounded funny to me because I thought I was supposed to feel something. I didn't feel any different than when he was my uncle. Grandpa said, "That's great. You love him just as much." I guess Grandpa didn't want me to hate him because he wasn't my uncle anymore.

I was happy. That's all Grandpa cared about. I asked him if he ever had to call someone dad after calling him uncle for a while. He said that my experience is the first one that he knows about and it is unique. I liked that word "unique." He once told me, "You are most special and absolutely unique." I thought he was the greatest grandpa too.

On special holidays Dad bought me balloons and we went to the bazaar just looking at things. Everybody knew me in that small village as "the grandson of Dr. K." Everybody knew my dad as well. I was surprised at first but later understood the reason. No one except my friends I believe knew my name. During Dussera, light festival, we would decorate the outside of the house together, i.e. my grandmother helped a little but mostly I decorated a little with the servants that worked for us. There were fireworks that we went to see. All the neighborhood kids flew kites and I did too. I wasn't allowed to fly kites from the roof because Grandpa had treated some kids who fell off the roof and had died. I got new clothes from both my new dad and also from Grandpa.

My cousin and I played together in dirt on many days. We climbed trees and played hide and go seek. My cousin hung around Grandpa and me a lot but I knew he didn't feel right for some reason. I left the house after Grandpa's death and I went away to a school far away from home. So my cousin and I didn't see much of each other. We communicated infrequently and occasionally saw each other during the time of different Puja and social occasions, but we never spoke our heart. It was about forty years later that he spoke to me about his feelings. He was stationed at Cologne, Germany, at a British base at the time of the Bosnian war. I was alone and traveled anywhere in the world at the drop of a hat.

So when he asked me to come over for the weekend all I had to do was to buy a ticket from Louisville to Amsterdam. I caught a train from Schipool airport to Cologne, Germany, where my cousin picked me up. Dr. C, my cousin that I grew up with, and I met as brothers after many years. We drank good British whiskey and talked about old times while some folks went to bomb the Serbian soldiers, who were exterminating the Bosnian Muslims. We rejoiced at our reunion. "You know I always felt different from you when we were growing up. Now I am a doctor for the British army. I don't do much except see a few people with cold and claps. Oh! I do treat an occasional menstrual cramp among family members. In last five years I had to transfer one fellow out of the infirmary to a hospital because he developed appendicitis."

He continued, "Sometimes I see few fellows with nonspecific urethritis, and you know they all get better with ten days of Bactrim. I tell them to use a condom, but you know what I mean. Everybody is healthy in the 'soldiering' business. I play squash three times every week and I won the league. My colleague is a major. He will take you to church tomorrow. I have already invited him. I knew you wouldn't care." He took a breath. I asked him about his family. "I married a classmate of mine. She is a psychiatrist. We have two daughters more than twenty years old. They are at Cambridge this weekend for some class function. It is one of those last-minute pop-up plans that disrupt the previous ones. I wanted them to stay and meet you." I said that I was amazed that we let so many years pass between us without keeping in touch. I promised to do better.

He continued, "You know I have been angry with you all these years. I always felt that you stole the special blessing from Grandpa that was intended for me. But now I have forgiven you because I understand what happened." I told him that I didn't know that he was angry. He wanted to speak. "Whenever we played together somehow I felt that I wasn't equal and then when Grandpa came in to be with us I felt like I didn't belong. Grandpa loved me but I only felt great when you were not around. It was like he and you were like toast and melted butter. What I mean is that somehow I felt that your every pore was filled whereas with me I was the cold butter and it just wouldn't spread."

"I was terrible in sports, you know that," I said.

"You are missing the point," he continued. "I realized that you didn't have a mother and you didn't even know that. Your father came to see you once a week. You called him uncle. You called Grandma mom and nobody corrected you. But I had everything. That's why Grandpa loved you more."

I thanked him for loving me. I got up and hugged him. I know that he felt relieved to get all that built-up stress out of his system. We drove to Rotterdam and spent the day in the city and then near the ocean. We sat and watched the waves while licking on ice cream cones. We recited one of the poems that we had memorized. So we honored Grandpa by saying it together and then we laughed at the fact that we still remembered it after so many years.

I shall be telling this with a sigh
Somewhere ages and ages hence:
Two roads diverged in a wood, and I—
I took the one less traveled by,
And that has made all the difference.
—Robert Frost, "The Road Not Taken"

The day passed rather rapidly as we talked and drank. I left early next morning to catch a flight to Charlotte, North Carolina. The airplane did not sell all its seats. I started reviewing the manuscript that I thought I had lost. "Always think the best of people. Sometimes you will be wrong but most times you will be rewarded and win a friend," Grandpa had told me. Just a few months back I was teaching at Cambridge in an international school at that time during the Lent semester. Every weekend I traveled to London or to Scotland. I would have to always change trains at Peterborough to go north or west of England. One day I walked out of the train with a cup of coffee in my hand and forgot my backpack on the luggage shelf. I realized this after I arrived at the Cambridge station.

I was quite upset and my voice exhibited my emotional status rather clearly. However, the stationmaster in characteristic British non-excitatory voice asked me the name of the train. "Flying Scotsman," I said abruptly, being proud of myself for knowing that.

"All trains going north say that. I will call London. You come tomorrow at noon and hopefully we will have it here by then," he quipped confidently. Next day, I was astonished to find all my money and the manuscript inside my backpack. I thanked God and then him for our good luck. I walked into a bar to have a pint of beer to savor my good fortune.

I got my editing pencil out to give the travelogue the necessary make-over. Phoebe and I had boarded a bus at Katmandu to go to Dumre. It was here that we would board a local bus to Besisahar. The trip to Dumre took about eight hours.

It was a tourist bus that made a few essential stops for the comfort of the passengers prior to getting us to our destination. We didn't get to see much of Dumre because we had to rush to the next bus as it was already getting full. The bar for the level of comfort had been considerably lowered by now as the bus had taken a full load of chickens, goats and people and some people had already sat on the roof of the bus.

I had found an aisle seat. However, my thighs had to be placed much too close to each other to be comfortable. Just about the time when I was contemplating ways to gain some extra room Phoebe yelled out, "Look, there is a naked man!" I wanted to make sure that she was talking about someone outside the bus. She had not traveled much in the Indian subcontinent and therefore was a little excited to see a nanga sadhu. We, meaning regular Joes, have to maintain our modesty at all times. Only nanga sadhu can be naked on the roads of India. But in reality ashes drape them.

The bus took off soon after the conductor patted and thumped on the bus and yelled *"Chaloe bhai, theeksa."* The English translation would be, "Let's go, brothers; everything is okay," while he remained hanging with one hand from the steps of this overloaded moving machine. The sadhu with his ash-laden body, painted face and a head full of dreadlocks had gotten inside the bus during this time and stood by Phoebe totally buff holding a Trisul, the trident, with one hand and one of the bars on the ceiling with the other.

The bus went over a narrow blacktopped road pock marked with chuckholes and littered with people. The noise of the conductor's hands banging on the side of the bus and yelling reminded us that we were often close to shaving some people. Whenever the driver put the brakes on to stop the bus the sadhu moved forward a bit but we were all strapped to one another in our aromatic sweat. Occasionally a rooster would get excited and a goat would bleat because someone might have stepped on its hoof. This might have been an indication to the conductor that there was still some room to move. Therefore a few more persons were allowed into the imaginary cavity of the bus till the only sound I could hear was from the person who was sitting next to the standing sadhu. It was a sound of polite disgust whenever there was a jarring from slowing down to avoid a pedestrian or a chuckhole. No one got out on the way. This was the last bus to Besisahar.

Grandpa had always told me to be confident and everything would be all right. Neither of us had heard of Bob Marley then and even if we had his song "Everything Is Going to Be Alright" wasn't ready when I was a child.

Phoebe and I had planned a fourteen-day walk around the Annapurna range to see Muktinath, the temple of Lord Vishnu, and we hadn't arranged for a guide yet. The man sitting next to me spoke Hindi and I was able to express my concern in Hindi to him. He immediately volunteered to be our guide for a fee. "I have a few chores at home. I will straighten them out tonight and tomorrow early morning we will leave. I have been there twenty times and I will help you on the way." I was psyched by my new find. We discussed the finances later in private and he became our guide for the next fifteen days.

As I was getting off the bus Jadu, our guide, told me that everyone has to pay the fare except the sadhu. He is a man of God so he gets to travel for free.

We left for our journey at sunrise. The path went meandering through rice paddies and then between pine trees and eucalyptus. The path was narrow and many wet plants were full of leeches that clung to us as we walked along. Phoebe was clever and wore a panty-hose to keep the leeches away from her skin. We sang "Hai a Ho Ho, Hai a Ho, Where the nights are gay and the sun shines daily on the mountain top." The sun was up soon enough to scald our necks and make us sweat. The rainy season was just over. The grounds were still wet but the September sun still had the cooking power. We walked briskly because the path was not steep. After a short lunch break we picked up the pace along the roller coaster valley to reach Bahun Danda by three in the afternoon. Jadu had walked ahead to find a place to stay in one of the teahouses that provided a hot shower.

We were only at 4,800 feet today. I removed the leeches with a lighted match against my skin whereas Phoebe only had to take her pantyhose off to get rid off them. Their pincers cannot bite through the nylon. However, she was afflicted with a much worse problem owing to the moisture on her skin contained by the pantyhose. There were large blisters on her heels and toes with fourteen days' walk still ahead of us.

We drank the iodinated water that we had carried with us and enjoyed the lukewarm shower that sprayed in a rather non-satisfying manner through a showerhead that had most of its holes clogged by particles of unknown nature. It was still better than a cold shower. We ate rice, dal and some cooked vegetables with beans and potatoes in the candlelight. We put our socks and pants on our bedposts to dry. I looked at my watch and we were asleep soon after seven in the evening. The villages have no electricity.

Next day we left as early as possible after a quick meal of oatmeal and raisins. I drank tea and took some in my water bottle for the road. We went past Jagat, a small village where I treated many persons with different skin disorders and recommended some to see ophthalmologists at Katmandu because they had cataracts and conjunctivitis. Jadu had walked ahead of us and had informed the villagers that a doctor and a nurse were with him. Then we walked through miles of ganja fields where children were trading ganja for a pen or a writing pad or a Darth Vader toy.

Chamje had some solar plates that provided a few hours of electricity. I believe the town had a television. After a long hot climb through areas without any trees we rested for the night at Tal. We met many other trekkers on the way. Everyone had a mission. Some were walking for "just doing it." But I was walking with my grandpa and no one knew that except me and him. Here we had arrived in a place to rest for the night early enough in the afternoon to be able to shave when there was still daylight. I enjoyed the comfort of the fading sun as its rays combed through my hair while I sipped on a Fanta. I thought life was good. Grandpa nodded yes.

Joslyn and Joe, her brother, were from New Zealand. She was getting ready to go to school to be a nurse and had taken a month off to travel to Nepal. Joe had just graduated from high school. He hadn't decided yet what path he would follow in life. Then we met three Russian guys who were drinking vodka and one of them was smoking cigarettes.

The owner of the teahouse was K. Bahadur, a sherpa, who bought the place about six years ago. He had fixed it up and had arranged to have five rooms for sleeping and a small area for eating. He charged four dollars per person for sleeping and about five dollars for the food. "I am happy with the business," he said. "As long as the tourists keep coming we are all happy. We are all worried because of the Maoist violence. We have nothing against the tourists but we just don't like the police. They are all corrupt and we have to bribe to survive," he continued. He had some chickens that ran around us as we sat on the benches. They ate from the garbage pile and also the bugs around us. Two goats were tied to a rope on the grass next to the outhouse.

We watched the donkeys and the mules as they walked past us shooed by the villagers carrying dokas filled with cokes, vegetables, cigarettes and San Miguel beer. It was time to eat, said Jadu. We ate rice, dal, vegetables and a little chicken curry. We washed it down with San Miguel. Phoebe said, "We are only at six thousand feet and beer is good for us." I didn't want to disagree because I like beer too. I bought certain number of meals for Jadu as part of our arrangement.

"There will be no electricity after seven in the evening and there is a lantern at the outhouse door," said Kiran Bahadur.

Next day our plan was to walk to Chame along the Marsyanangdi River through the winding valley. At times we crossed small renegade streams that were hurrying down the mountain to meet the main river water. The water was cold and the trees were thinning out and at times the sun was much too hot for our necks and faces. It was a tiring day. We drank more water today than on the previous two days. "There are many Nepali flats today," said Jadu. He compared the path to American flat roads. He was verbose today in his warnings. "We will have a few climbs and descents today and have to go through couple of landslides. At the end of the day we will be almost at 8,500 feet."

When we reached our destination Phoebe's feet had open wounds that seeped watery fluid. The Band-Aids had gotten pushed away because the boots were firm in their efforts to maintain the shape of the feet. The rocks were sharp and they tried to squeeze and bruise the boots. It seemed as though the feet were also anxious to get out of the space that contained them. They were swollen. She elevated her feet while we drank hot tea and reminisced about our miraculous survival. It was soon after lunch that we had arrived at a landslide. It was fresh. I mean this landslide was no more than twenty-four hours old. It was muddy and we made sounds like "chop chop" with our shoes as we walked along the side of the mountain.

It was rather stressful since the path was no wider than the boots on our feet. At some places the rocks and broken limbs from trees had been laid down by nature as though it was for us to be able to walk across to complete our journey. The slightest impropriety by our feet would have landed us several hundred feet below the makeshift walkway. The backpack seemed heavier and I made sure that it didn't sway from one side to the other during my efforts of walking on this narrow-gauge path filled with sticky and slippery mud.

"How come there is no donkey shit on this path?" I was scared. I usually speak in bad language when I am scared.

"Oh, the donkeys can't walk on this narrow path. They climb another hour and half to go around the landslide. This is a shortcut," said Jadu without smiling. I sat on a rock to rest after coming across the landslide. I needed to regroup in my mind.

We started walking after a short recess. We climbed a bit for a while on a moderately steep path and soon faced a stream that we had to cross. On our left was the mountain that was being bathed by the stream that ran down the slope and on our right was straight two hundred or more feet of fall on a rocky terrain on which the water bounced and splattered to get to its destination. There were trunks of two trees that were laid across the water reaching to a place that seemed to be dry land on the opposite side. There were no bars or ropes to hold for balance. Jadu took his shoes off and walked into the cold water that was knee deep and gave us a hand as we crossed the stream.

"This is a new stream that has developed since the landslide," said Jadu. I took a picture of Phoebe walking on the narrow tree trunks with her arms in front raised for balance with an expression of fear much like the clouds before a thunderstorm. I don't believe she blinked even once while crossing. I didn't have the courage to ask her to say "cheese" or "happiness" as I clicked my camera. I was beginning to understand why Grandpa hadn't been to Muktinath and wanted me to finish his journey!

As we settled down a bit it was time to eat dinner. We had to request the meal a little early because it was prepared only after we had ordered our choice. Phoebe was getting tired of the rice and dal and ordered tomato soup and chappatis and fried eggplants. Although I thought she was being rather adventuresome in her food demands I did not volunteer my opinion. Soon after we had arrived I was summoned by Jadu to treat the cook. It was getting dark but still there was enough light to diagnose impetigo and jock itch. I had just instructed the cook to clip his fingernails and the need for frequent use of soap and water. I also gave him some of my antibiotics and a tube of Lotrimazole.

We sat in the eating area next to a lit candle and observed him cooking. The flame from the wood burning in a pit oven was swinging and swaying and burping in the darkness of the kitchen. The flame periodically reached the low ceiling of tarpaulin. The tarpaulin bore marks of the anger of fire from previous occasions and was pockmarked with black holes created by the hot tongue of the agitated flame. There was a cauldron on the large pit in which something was being cooked and the room was filled with smoke and smell of kerosene from the lamps sitting by the door. Rice was being cooked in the smaller pit next to the larger pit. There was a tap on the road across from the teahouse and a little boy brought water from it and poured it into the cauldron. We were both thrilled when the food arrived. We thanked God for another wonderful day and proceeded to eat.

I was enjoying my rice and dal but Phoebe didn't seem to be as excited about her tomato soup. "I think there is something crunchy in the soup," she said.

I was very supportive and without thinking I said, "There must be some spices." She didn't seem satisfied. She fished out something from the bottom of the soup and wanted me to check. I saw the body of a roach without the limbs in the spoon Phoebe was holding. I assumed the roach fell through the torn ceiling. I knew that Phoebe normally hates bugs and most certainly in her food but she didn't scream. I called the cooks who decided to take the bowl back and serve her some new soup which Phoebe reluctantly ate being afraid to hurt their feelings.

Next day after some steep climbs and descents we rested in a place called Upper Pisang. The air was getting thinner and trekking was becoming more and more difficult. We met a young fellow from England who was carrying two backpacks. He sat down with us with his girlfriend who had an ace bandage around her knees and was visibly limping. "What did you guys do about the crazy waterfall?" he inquired. "Deb and I went around it after we looked at it. We had to climb almost five hundred feet and in the process Deb slipped and hurt her knees."

"You think you will be able to carry two backpacks for next twelve days?" I asked expressing concern.

"I don't know. Maybe Deb will carry her load or we will try to hire someone from the village if we can."

It was a small town and there was a Gumpa about thousand feet above the city. After a short rest we climbed it and came down to sleep in town as part of the acclimatization process. Jadu had said to climb high and then sleep at a lower altitude. You won't get a headache that way. Our next stop was at Manang at eleven thousand feet. It was one of the main stops in the Nepali flat highway. They had a dispensary where I picked up some Diamox for Phoebe. It reduces headache and brain swelling. We spent an extra day here to acclimatize.

There was a long patch of the road with no trees. The sun was hot. We were drinking as much water as possible. Suddenly Phoebe developed a lot of swelling of her arms and face and she had started slowing down with her pace. I on the other hand wanted her to walk fast so that we could get out of the sun. We had walked almost ten hours on that day. I was beginning to get a headache. After a nice warm shower and hot garlic soup we both fell asleep.

Next morning we took a walk in the village. We were feeling better after taking Diamox and rest. The square cement buildings that we had seen from distance actually were houses, teashops and hospital and government offices. There was a heli-pad for emergency evacuations although only on certain days the people with broken legs and arms got airlifted. There were several small gift shops and many thatched-roof huts that adorned the entrance to Manang. There was a sense of relaxed attitude on the Manang thoroughfare. Almost everyone spent an extra day here to acclimatize and so did we. Here people got their boots repaired, shared stories and replenished the lost energy by eating an abundant amount of sweets. We were feeling better after a day of rest. Headache was gone and we were hungry, two very important signs of health in the mountains. So we ventured outside of our usual menus of rice and dal and instead ordered fried eggs, vegetables and chappatis. We drank hot tea and ate more garlic soup. It is believed that garlic soup cures headache. I believe in all good stories.

Next morning when we left I had a fever and cramps in my stomach. We were going towards high camp at almost 14,500 feet, Thorang Pedi. I soon started with colic and the end product was telltale sign of Salmonella infection.

I wished that I hadn't eaten those eggs. I had some Cipro with me and after Phoebe's confirmation of my ailment I immediately swallowed the pills. On this day we walked and walked till I thought we would never reach our destination. There were no trees after Manang and the temperature dropped precipitously by two in the afternoon.

The mountains appeared to be more jagged and the rocks appeared rather shiny and smooth on the steep slopes. There was no imminent avalanche in our path at this time. The path was extremely narrow at times. I was walking a bit slower today owing to my ailment. I remember that after we had crossed a small stream after walking on an extremely slippery narrow path we had sat down to rest on a rock. We saw a man with two horses going in the opposite direction. He went across the river rather fast and behind him were two horses walking in single file. The horse at the end was tied to the saddle and the tail of the horse in front. It appeared that he might have been showing off a bit. I watched him as he jumped on the back of the front horse and took off at a rapid pace as they proceeded to climb the side of the mountain that we had just descended.

About halfway through the climb the horse in the rear slipped from the mountain and was dangling free. It was trying desperately to get a grip of the ground in front. The man had jumped off the lead horse by now, which by instinct turned its face towards the mountain and dug its heels in the mud. This gave a few seconds to the villager to give a pull to the dangling horse. The horse moved its legs rapidly and climbed the side like Spiderman and they all went on as though nothing had happened. The villager waved at us across the rift with a smile. He knew that we were amazed at his ignorant behavior.

Although I was beginning to feel better after I had sat down to rest this incredible scene gave me some serious cramps. We caught up with Jadu. After we shared the story with Jadu he confirmed that the villager was trying to show off in front of the foreigners. The road in front of us seemed to continue forever. Some porters carrying doka on their heads were coming up the hill as we were going down. Jadu darted out in front of us and almost hit an young Israeli fellow. The Israeli fellow was kicking the pebbles down the mountain despite Jadu's warning that one of the porters might get hit and fall off the mountain.

Jadu was visibly angry. Most of the Nepalese don't like the Israelis. "They are always looking for the cheapest place to stay and they bargain in a manner that humiliates us. Most of these young men and women have served in the Israeli Army for about two years. They then come to Nepal for vacation because it is cheap over here. But some of them don't even like to spend five dollars to spend the night in a teahouse. They would walk an extra mile to see if there is a four-dollar room available."

By this time we needed to rest again to have a drink of water. We arrived at Thorong Pedi late in the afternoon. There was no hot shower there. We were beat. The energy candle within us was burnt and our sweat had dripped by our sides and had made bumpy skin tags with rows of salt on the sides. It was already getting dark and the cold air chilled our bones through the wet sweat. We were at almost 14,500 feet high in the mountains.

We had dinner at six in the evening. The teahouse was full of people. Jadu introduced the cook and we drank tea as we were apprised of the next day's climb. There were other guides and porters. Some had come across the pass and were going in the direction from which we came.

We met Josh, a Canadian man in his sixties. He said that he had slight headache and felt a little nauseous. Jadu expressed concern. "Drink more water and take a Diamox. If you are not better in the next two hours do not climb tomorrow. We will climb three thousand feet and if you have much of a headache you might get confused and fall off the mountain."

One of the porters was very sick. Jadu got him a blanket to keep him warm and placed a hot water bottle between his calves. I didn't feel much like talking. I heard someone say that he had spent a night here already and he was ready to go to lower altitude the next morning. He showed us a picture that he had taken with his digital camera. He whispered, "I was tired and cold and was just pushing my arm under the pillow before resting my head on it when something fuzzy made a funny noise and bit me. I banged on the pillow with my other fist. A small rat had found a cozy spot under the pillow when it was disturbed by my intruding fist." We saw the picture of a rat that had bled on the sheet and had the flattened appearance of a road kill. Needless to say that I knew exactly what I was going to do before going to bed.

Next morning at 4:00 we were up and ready to start our climb by 4:30. It was dark and we climbed the mountain with flashlights in our hands and some others used headlights to see the narrow winding steep path in front of us. Every so often I stopped to catch my breath and looked back only to see meandering lights of the other climbers which made me think of a slide with a cluster of fluorescent tumor cells on a dark background invading pristine snow-covered land. It was cold and windy and we were sprayed by the fleeces of snow every so often to give us a shiver through our bones. As the flashlight I held penetrated the darkness in front of me the climbing became more difficult because I began to realize the steepness of the path. I acknowledged that if

I would have seen the path earlier I possibly wouldn't have had the courage to start on this journey. By 8:30 in the morning we were in an area sheltered between the peaks of rugged and partially snow-covered mountains where we rested for a few minutes to catch up on our fluids.

We saw Josh, our Canadian acquaintance, walking in the opposite direction rather disoriented with the guide right behind him. We learnt that he was about to fall down the mountain and so the guide decided to take him down to the tea house at a lower altitude where we had started this morning. The next hour we walked through a slushy snowy path to climb to Thorong La Pass. We rested inside the hut to get away from the wind after hurriedly taking some photographs of the sign confirming the fact that we had climbed up to 17,500 feet. The wind began to howl and blew the snow towards the sky, making our visibility less and less as we marched through the white dust. It was almost 10 a.m. and we started walking down the hill to our next destination. As we walked down the gravel-strewn steep descent to Muktinath the wind died down and a glimmer of sunshine came through the cloud to energize our spirits while we sat on a flat rock to eat some food.

We soaked our eyes with the beautiful sight of reflecting sun on the snow "chaddar" of the mountains at a distance. Phoebe and I ate boiled eggs and drank some water and I felt like lying down for a while. Fatigue was my constant companion during the trip and no sooner had I lain down with the backpack under my head I was asleep.

A thunderous noise startled both of us. We sat up and saw a thick white cloud of snow across the valley rising to the sky as the top of the mountain beyond the valley hurtled down its side as a gigantic avalanche. Soon everything became quiet and peaceful again as we walked down four thousand feet occasionally chewing beef jerky or eating a Snickers bar. It almost took little over six hours to reach Muktinath. The nails of both my big toes were pushed up by blood because of the rapid descent. I walked rather slowly to the tea house where couple of San Miguel beers relieved my foot pain. A refreshing hot shower gave me the strength to walk to the government office to register our passport and trekking license, a requirement for those coming across the Thorong La pass.

Next day as we walked through the temples of Muktinath and that of Lord Shiva. I fulfilled my dream of walking with my grandpa. Now I had covered all the places that he wanted to visit but was not able to complete. It is considered a privilege for a devout Hindu to be able to visit Kedarnath, Badrinath, Pasupatinath, Muktinath and Amarnath, much like visiting Mecca by the people of Islam. This is a place considered holy by the Hindus and the Buddhists alike. Those that come for the pilgrimage take a bath in the cold water of the river and then worship at Lord Vishnu's temple, Muktinath, and also at Lord Shiva's temple next door where there is a constant flame burning from the gas in the water as it passes underneath the temple. I talked to the Indian Brahmin priest at the temple and shared with him my need to complete my grandpa's journey. We offered some flowers to the gods in his name sanctifying his wishes and also as a symbol of completion of his journey on this earth through his protégé.

I never knew that love could provide such emotional uplifting at a time when I was so overwhelmed with exhaustion and foot pain. Not only did reminiscing of my grandpa envelop me with warmth of his love but I had another reason to be ecstatic too. I often held Phoebe's hands in the mountains. This climb did not require any ice climb or special tools. Mountains have always fascinated me, maybe from the Freudian instinct. Phoebe said that the modern age of mountaineering was introduced by Jacques Balat and Michael Paccard. They climbed Mt. Blanc in France in 1786. Edward Whymper conquered the Matterhorn in 1865 and then Hillary and Tenzing climbed Mt. Everest in 1953. I had seen a documentary of the last climb when I was younger.

My Imagination While Passing the Upper Part of Utah

I was feeling somewhat accomplished about my walk across the country by now until I met a youngster who was cycling across America, starting from Los Angeles, to bring awareness for HIV-AIDS. We talked for a while. His uncle owns a business in New York and so he was going there. He was riding across each state in about five to six days. I was reminded of what my father had told me when I was a youngster. No matter what I will accomplish someone will possibly achieve much more so be grateful for the opportunity. I prayed and thanked God for being alive. I realized that as I had walked across the Continental Divide that I had entered in the zone of rivers that drained to the west, to the Columbia-Snake river system, and the others went south such as Provo, Weber, Bear and some others drained in the Colorado system.

Although I walked a bit further north of the Uinta Mountains I had secretly imagined that I would be able to see the skeleton of Uintatherium, the large primitive hoofed mammals from the Eocene age. The skull had mostly bones and very little brain. My imagination took me far away from today and by then I had walked fourteen miles. It was time for lunch.

I wanted to continue my story of India. India had become independent just nine years back. It was time to rebuild its assets and organize the resources. So many of the parents sent their children to schools where the future of India was being built. The school I went to is called The Scindia School. It is located about sixty miles south of Agra (Taj Mahal) on top of a fort and was guarded by the soldiers provided by the government of India. The soldiers were there to prevent the dacoits from kidnapping the children. Armed robbery and violence were not uncommon in this part of the country at that time. The school had all Indian teachers and one British teacher who spoke Bengali and Hindi as well as any other educated person of Indian origin. It was decided to retain the ideas and ways that were good from the British and yet imbibe within the children a patriotic spirit for the new nation. Grandpa had said, "We don't have to throw away everything British. We just have to be better Indians by adding and utilizing the best of the British. They took advantage of us but they introduced several opportunities for people. We must acknowledge that. I am a doctor from the British system." The school did just that.

We were taught everything that people learn in a school such as reading, writing, getting along, manners and sports. But the most important element of the school teaching that occurred as an undertone was to be able to be proud Indians. The elders in the country knew that the British had undermined and exploited India for almost two hundred years but now it was time to get the youth, the future force of India, going in the right direction. The most important part of the character building was teaching not to hate, not to be demoralized but to grow up as educated and well-informed free Indians of the future. My dad had said to me that it would take us at least fifty years to rebuild India. I came home during the religious holidays such as the Puja and Christmas and also during summer break. It was only during these times that I had an opportunity to see the other members of the family. I always went to see my grandma, who still lived in the house where I had spent my childhood.

As I was walking through Nebraska I often talked to Anna about *My Antonia*, by Willa Cather. I recall telling Anna about the big rattlesnake that Jim had killed and about the Bohemians. There are still many people of Czech origin that live in Nebraska and I met quite a few of them. The Shimerdas and the Burdens were often in my mind. Thank God, I did not have to face the hardship that they had to endure during the latter part of last century.

I had to drink a lot of water during this part of my walk. I noticed objects much more now than I had seen any other time when I had I traveled in the past. I was able to see the sights for much longer than I did when I traveled by car.

I saw some objects that looked like radar detectors. So I asked Anna. She told me about Cavity Magnetron that the British had devised around 1940. "The MIT Radiation Laboratory, you know, that developed most of the microwave radar systems for hunting down U-Boats, navigation and bombing was developed around this time. The radar system also helped us in air-to-air fighting," Anna continued. "All wars have led to forced developments of technology that have helped humanity in many ways. A lot of people here that perform activities that are secretive and the people that work in these areas have to sign papers saying that they will not discuss as to what projects are being worked on or what exactly they are doing."

Every October after the harvest there was a big party in Grandpa's house. The guys that worked on our rice fields brought us rice. Grandpa had made a sixty-forty deal. They kept sixty percent and lived in the farmhouse for working the fields. Many other people came on foot or on bullock carts. They had lanterns dangling from the bottom of the carts in the night. They made our field look as though it was full of swinging stars.

There were smaller lights of occasional illumination of bidis, homemade rolled tobacco leaf, or chillum. I watched the twining smoke that rose lazily in the calm air from the hot tobacco. There was a spirit of peace and gentleness among all the people. They brought rice, goats, vegetables, mustard oil and lentils. These were the gifts they had brought for Grandpa. All debts were written off. There was nothing written but that's the way everything worked. After a meal in our courtyard everyone thanked Grandpa and left just as happy as they came looking forward to a New Year. These people hadn't paid Grandpa that year or the year before when either they or their family were sick. No records were kept but those that owed Grandpa remembered it because they were hardworking honest people. They were poor but loving. I overheard Grandpa telling one family, "Don't try to pay me now. You need to buy food for your son."

Grandpa always said that we should not pray to be important or successful but ask God to give a joyful heart. Secretly during my youthful years I thought more of myself than I should have.

Now I feel joyful and fulfilled. I laughed and shook hands with people as I walked across the country and never felt exhausted though naturally tired from the exercise and the heat.

We would sometimes carry our mat to lie on the field and talk about history or anything that we thought was important. We were discussing the Battle of Plassey, a place in West Bengal, where the battle was fought in 1757. The British, under Robert Clive, had considerable difficulty establishing themselves in Bengal. The Nawab of Bengal, Siraj-ud-Dawlah was a tall powerful man with a good army. Unfortunately, his generals betrayed him and thus he lost the battle. Bribing has been in existence for thousands of years. The British exploited the weakness among the Indian soldiers. I recall Grandpa telling me the story.

"British factories were built in Bengal and many of our people lost the capacity to compete. It was the greed of some that made everyone a loser." He took a breath. I told him that I had already been to the Murshidabad museum to see the sword of the Nawab. "Murshidabad is also famous for mangoes and silk saris," he continued. "The saris that were handcrafted by the local artisans were so fine that six yards of material would fit inside a small box. The British started selling them in Manchester at a high price but the locals received next to nothing for their work. I have seen the material in the museum.

"King Herod would have been just as excited to have seen Salome peel this silk off her while twirling during the performance of her erotic dance." He had already told me the story of King Herod taking Herodius, the wife of his brother Phillip, as his own. I remember asking him if anybody threw up seeing the head of John the Baptist served on a platter. He said that unfortunately those craftsmen are extinct now.

"Let me tell you a story about greed. There is a Sanskrit saying '*Angang Galitang Palitang Mundang—Tundang.*' It means that man's desire and greed does not end even when his hair is thin, arms are withering and teeth have fallen down." He said that once a man placed ninety-nine rupees under the pillow of his neighbor to check the honesty and strength of character. "After the neighbor had discovered the unexpected money not only did he not mention that he found a surprise he actually quit eating to save money to make the amount one hundred rupees. God will always provide what we need. It is our continuous want that we have to work on." He said that there is a saying in the Bible that God never gives us a burden that we can't bear. "We are most powerful when we have control over our desires of money and material things and sexual drive. Then people can't bribe us. That makes other people crazy when they can't entice you." I didn't know about sexual drive then.

"How do you know when to say or recognize that you have enough?"

"You see, it is like this. When you pour water or a drink in a glass if you don't stop when it is full it overflows and the fluid either stains or wets the tablecloth or the rug underneath. In this case you have to see and determine when it is enough, but in our life God has given us the feeling of knowing when we should be satisfied. When we don't pay heed to God's message then we become greedy and take away the pleasures from others despite the fact that our glass is full. A child cries when it is hungry and stops crying when it is full but I was supposed to understand the fullness and recognize the need for others through love. There are some among us who are never satisfied. They are most unfortunate.

"In the Bible King David said, 'The Lord is my shepherd; I shall not want.' This is no different than our Lord Krishna talking to Arjuna about life. Life is not easy and certainly not fun all the time. But if we are believers then we have nothing to worry about. You know Prahlad, a little boy, crossed the forest every day to go to school because he believed that God walked by his side. In a similar way King David had said, 'Yea, though I walk through the valley of the shadow of death, I will fear no evil for thou art with me.' You see, Hinduism is the oldest religion and the stories are very similar in the Bible which is compilation of many books written a bit later."

Anna wanted to know more.

Mr. Majumdar was a man in his forties. He looked old with his beard. He always wore a Punjabi and salwar like pants. He was a Muslim from East Bengal. Many of my friends made fun of his appearance and called him Chacha, uncle. Grandpa did not like anyone to make fun of other people. He sometimes told us stories from the Koran. You have to be a religious person to translate the Koran but regular Muslims are allowed to discuss the stories, he said. In Islamic eschatology, it is believed that the two hostile forces Yajuj and Majuj will ravage the earth before the world comes to an end. It is believed that these are the Muslim counterparts of Gog and Magog. I was curious. "So what do they do?"

"Some are tall and some others are fat and covered with ears. They will appear in the northeast of the ancient world as ominous scouts and proceed south towards Israel drinking up the waters of the Tigris and Euphrates or the Sea of Galilee and then they will kill everyone. Then they will shoot arrows at the sky to hurt God but then Allah will fill their ears with worms and destroy them in a single night and send a flock of ravens to drown them in the sea."

Mr. Majumdar had finished his tea by now and was puffing from the hookah. "I will bring some kabob next time I come. I have to check the tube well in my house."

After he left Grandpa said, "We will talk about Gog and Magog." So he opened Revelation 20:7 and asked me to read. "And when the thousand years are expired, Satan shall be loosed out of his prison, and shall go out to deceive the nations which are in the four quarters of the earth, Gog and Magog, to gather them together to battle; the number of whom is the sand of the sea." I told him that I did not understand this at all. He said that we will talk about it another day.

Mr. Majumdar talked about Wali Allah Shah, who allegedly memorized the Koran at the age of seven and attempted to reassess Islamic theology in the light of modern changes. Aurongzeb had died in 1707. He was the last Muslim king in India and was very harsh towards the Hindus. Wali Allah thought Muslim glory could be restored if the thinking could be changed.

Grandpa did not like fanaticism. He told me that there are fanatics in all religions. Mahatma Gandhi was killed in 1948 by a fanatic Hindu. However, his great concern was the religion of Muhammad Wahhab. He introduced puritan beliefs and tried to teach people against the Sufi doctrines and was politically allied to the Saudi dynasty. Grandfather was concerned that there were so many schools in India where Muslims were taught extreme views which he was afraid in a few years would create chaos in the world. I was thinking as I was walking that he was right on many predictions. The majority of the people who tried to destroy the American buildings on 9/11 were of Saudi origin and possibly attended the schools where Muslim fanaticism is taught. Madrasas still exist.

Grandpa was always excited about different cultures. "Look at those clouds. They are the messengers carrying messages from the hearts of the people of different lands. Some will fall as rain when they come near the mountains. They may not be able to carry the message but still they will bring joy to the farmers. This is what we need to understand to have peace. All of us are God's children with different strengths."

A train went by every so often shaking our field. The field separated our house from the track. It was about a thousand yards and it is here that we played soccer and cricket. The black smoke from the engine covered the field and our chain of thought many times. I felt something in my eye. That always drove me crazy, partly because I have always been impatient and partly owing to the fact that I couldn't tolerate a moment of discomfort. Grandma washed my eyes and removed the black soot from the steam engine that had taken shelter in my eye. She knew how to flip the eyelid. At times I felt that everything was trying to get me. We came inside the house. Grandma called, "Tea and snacks."

We sat on the porch drinking tea. Grandma joined us. We saw smoke coming out of the side room of the barn. Sonali's ma lived there. Her oven was on. It was made of clay with a round hole that burnt coal and dried cow dung. She cleaned the outside of our house and took care of the cows. We had two cows so that we would have enough safe milk.

Grandma made yogurt and butter at home. It was customary to call an older maidservant as someone's mother rather than by their actual name. It was a sign of respect. It was believed in India at that time that if a woman couldn't bear a child the sense of barrenness produced a devastating psychological vacuum. It was believed that a fertile woman was happier. Therefore the latter was emphasized. In the case of those women who were not married or didn't have children they were either called by their name or as someone's daughter. It was always important to be respectful of people's age. All older persons were respected regardless of their profession.

Sonali's ma had her own garden next to the barn. Sometimes Grandma gave her food from our kitchen too. She milked the cows after washing the udders with soap. She taught me how to hold the milk bucket and also the correct method of squeezing the teats. I don't know how valuable the lesson has been in my life but it was fun anyway when I learnt it. It is a learned skill and requires a lot of strength in the fingers and thumb. I recognized that it is the gentle uniform squeeze that is important! She bathed the cows on hot days. Hot days were quite frequent. She made cow dung cakes with her hands and dried them on a dirt wall next to the hibiscus tree. She stacked them when they were dry for Grandma's assistant to pick them up to start our grill before cooking. She fed and watered the cows' bin. She swept the whole outside always early in the morning. At times she mopped the patio and the porch with Phenyl, a disinfectant like Pine-sol that allegedly reduced the chance of infection by killing bacteria. It made the area smell good. She only spoke to Grandma and that was the custom. If Grandpa spoke to her she covered her face and replied and Grandpa never looked at her face out of respect.

I had asked Grandpa why Sonali's ma ate snails. "It is a cheap source of protein. But there is a risk of Schistosomiasis, a liver fluke." He showed me a picture of a little worm from his tropical medicine book. "I have checked her. She is OK," Grandpa said. I know now that these were not escargots, what the French folks eat or what we see in fancy restaurants, and it is not the kind that flew across the table in the movie *Pretty Woman*.

She found these in our pond that was less than sanitary. But most people in India survive great challenges to the human systems. Most people of her occupation suffered from severe anemia from lack of protein. Grandma let her have some milk every day and occasional left-over meat or fish from our kitchen. She lived for many years. "It is necessary to learn to respect your subordinates," I recalled hearing from Grandpa.

The horse lived in a different compartment of the barn in a stall with dirt floor but it was covered with straw. The coachman took care of him. The animals didn't have names. He was just "horse." He was a gelding about thirteen hands. I don't believe he was anything fancy. He was ordinary like me. He was very calm tempered. Grandpa never rode him. He was strictly used for the carriage.

I had prepared myself psychologically for this demanding trip. However, I had to be careful not to get a heat stroke. I am of course aware of the stages of heat cramps, heat exhaustion and heat stroke and therefore I prepared myself adequately. I was afraid of this the most while I was walking through Idaho near Mountain Top. The heat index was unusually high and it took me many hours of walking from here to get to Boise. Cramps that occur because of excessive sweating can usually be rectified by drinking salt water so that excessive loss of chloride, potassium, and sodium are replenished. Heat exhaustion occurs when the skin gets clammy and cold and the pulse becomes rapid and weak. I never wanted to reach this stage. Therefore I had learnt to pace myself. I also changed wet clothes to avoid shivering which increases body heat. There were times when my mouth was extremely dry, eyes were red but I never reached the stage of feeling nauseated or dizzy. Anna remained engaged and kept asking me to tell her more stories.

I watched Grandpa finish his stretching exercises and recite the Surya Pronam *(Adityang Prathamang namang—).* I had learnt writing Devanagari script from him already and so I could read it as he recited. Then we took a walk. During the walk he had said that he thought we should try to go to Calcutta on my birthday in November. "This will be your tenth birthday. I will take you there."

I agreed. "How long do I have to stay?" I asked apprehensively.

"As long as you want to stay and you can come back any time you like."

I noticed that the newspaper was full of news about Tibet. The Tibetans tried to evict the Chinese delegation and in turn China is going to take over Tibet. The Dalai Lama and the other Tibetan officials are worried that the independence of Tibet will be lost. I stopped reading. A big discussion ensued.

"The issue of Tibet has been in a state of dormancy. It needs disinterment and the whole world needs to help. It will be an abomination if we just sit back. Buddhism might have started in India but Tibet is the apogee of the Buddhist culture," said the professor of English uncle.

"I am afraid the Americans won't help and certainly not the British. The Russians have no interest in that area either. There is no financial incentive. There is no commerce. It is at a high altitude where soldiers are not acclimatized to fight," said Grandpa.

The professor continued, "The world does not have to run on the Olympic motto Citius, Altius, Fortius—faster, higher and stronger, to help another. Human beings just have to be truly sensitive. I think everyone does not need to reach physically such lofty summits. But if most of us can reach such goals in our hearts then we will be truly a remarkable race."

Grandpa said that one's nature is not what one is born as, but what one is born for—is what Aristotle had said. The Greeks believed that angels guide us to become aware of our calling in life.

"I know that we should rise against the Chinese. But we are a new nation and we do not have any resources yet. I am afraid we have to watch the Chinese conquer Tibet." Grandpa was disheartened. At that time no one was allowed to visit Tibet. I told Grandpa that someday I would visit Tibet and Kailash and take him with me.

Dad came in for a surprise visit to wish me happy birthday early. He said that the Bhagwat Gita says *Karmaney Badhikarasthe Ma Faleshu Kadachana* (our responsibility is in our work and not in the result). "Hindus believe very much in predestination and Karma. But there is a twist," he continued. "The Christian free will is different from Hindu free will. Hindus believe that we are living a Maya, a dream. Our destiny has already been decided but God gives us the opportunity to try our best to do on this earth before we can meld with Brahma. But on a different note I want to say that we should watch the Chinese. They will aim for India if we do not become strong." Everyone agreed with Dad. Grandpa was not alive to see that the Dalai Lama had to escape from Tibet when China conquered Tibet. He took exile in India in 1959.

After everyone left I told Dad that I was coming to visit for a couple of days. He thought that was great. Later in life I realized that this is exactly what people do when they are getting prepared to come home from a mental institution. They come home on short visits for a trial period. After visiting with us Dad always visited my uncle across the village before leaving for Calcutta. I asked Grandpa about my dad and his family after he left.

Professor NB, my uncle, was a well-known man those days. He had been very active in the non-cooperation movement in Bengal. He had been a political prisoner and had served almost a year in British prison for civil disobedience without a trial. He had been active in the Indian National Congress. He was able to convince the local people that for the British to leave India peacefully we have to approach them peacefully. He was able to calm the people who had a penchant for aggressive behavior and he coordinated some of the movements that led to closure of the British factories. He was able to organize meetings for civil disobedience in an orderly fashion. It was the calming effect on people and the ability to disperse mass hysteria that won him his position in the society.

Jawaharlal Nehru, Mahatma Gandhi, and many other important dignitaries of the Indian movement came to visit him. The professor was involved with Sir Ashutosh Mukherjee, who became the vice-chancellor of University of Calcutta, Dr. Bidhan Roy, a prominent physician and future prime minister of Bengal, and Rabindranath Tagore, Nobel laureate for literature, in regular conversation regarding the future of Bengal in the post-independence era. "Your dad is a brother to the professor. For two years they convinced the people of Bengal to avoid wearing anything that was made in the British looms. They also avoided using British goods. Your dad had been an active participant of this movement. He wore clothes made only from handmade fabrics."

Grandpa took a break to sip his tea. "Your dad had graduated from the medical school in Calcutta and was working on a degree in public health and tropical medicine. He used to come to play volleyball in our field whenever he came to visit his brother for activities related to Indian freedom movement. Since I am a doctor in the community and this being a small community we all got to know one another. Moreover, we belong to the Congress party. We were all fighting for the cause of the independence of India.

"One day Grandma saw your dad when he was playing ball and she decided that he could be our daughter's husband. She knew his background and she thought this would unite the two educated families. She told me to talk to the professor about arranging a marriage between the families. That is how the marriage occurred. Your grandpa from dad's side had passed on and thus the older brother was the senior member of the family and therefore he would be the person responsible for negotiating marriage. This was the custom of the day.

"It is important to keep good genes in the family and not marry the close relatives. It is written in the Hindu scriptures and also in the Bible." So he opened the Bible and read from Genesis 24:2. "'And Abraham said unto his eldest servant of his house, that ruled over all that he had. Put, I pray thee, thy hand under my thigh: And I will make thee swear by the Lord, the God of heaven and the God of the earth, that thou shalt not take a wife unto my son of the daughters of the Canaanites, among whom I dwell.'" I always liked these stories because the people of these stories had servants like we did. I did not understand the part about putting the hands under the thigh before making a promise because Hindus never did that and we did not swear by the name of any God either. I told him that I was going to marry a woman from a far-away country.

I also learnt that I had an older brother and an older sister. They lived at Calcutta in my dad's house with one of my uncle's family. My aunt watched over my brother and sister. My dad worked long hours and could not have taken care of me when I was much younger. My mom had died about six months after my birth. Grandpa was breathless and tense. He waited for my response after telling me all this. It seemed that Grandpa had a charley horse in his throat and he acted like he had swallowed a whole tube of chlorophyll toothpaste. He kind of looked green. He had never told me this before. "I want to meet my brother and my sister." Grandpa took me to Calcutta next morning by train.

I was telling Anna today what it takes to be a neurosurgeon. Anna interrupted me and said that she knew all about it. I didn't like that because I wanted to talk. So I continued and said that it takes an enormous amount of inner drive. There is no room for inertia.

The inner engine runs in high gear all the time. I told her that I had worked in Ethiopia

Anna Learns About Ethiopia

I arrived at Addis Ababa and I realized that I was like a little boy because when I didn't see anyone to greet me at the airport I felt sad and hurt. But I had actually anticipated as such. It was ten at night and the city looked dark. Some people who were looking for customers asked if they could take me to a hotel.

Another person said to me, "You look like a friend of mine from Egypt. Maybe I can help you." I told him that I was sure he was right. My father had been a world traveler and I have not had a chance to catch up with all my brothers yet. He excused himself to find softer targets. Then I found the Sheraton man. He waited for couple of other customers but they never showed up. So Vince, a young Navy construction fellow, who I just met, and I went to the Sheraton Hotel in the Sheraton bus. As I checked in I thought that Expedia would have paid my hotel bill but I learned that they hadn't and so I shelled out 296 dollars for the night. Dr. Z came to the hotel to greet me after he finished his clinic at 11.30 p.m. I had told him to look at my picture on www.spava.us and that way he could spot me. Judas's behavior is not allowed anymore. Breakfast was included in my hotel bill. It was lot more than I had anticipated. Dr. Z picked me up after breakfast and brought me to my apartment.

It is almost a luxury villa on the third floor of a building across from the Black Lion Hospital. I'm kidding, right! Black Lion is a government hospital that houses about three hundred and sixty patients. My new home for the summer (seven weeks) was just across the walkway from the back entrance to the hospital. The entrance to the apartment was decorated with a bougainvillea bush that was overshadowed with clothes hanging from wires attached to poles on the ground next to it. The narrow hallway that led up to the steps was engulfed in a pocket of darkness. The scalded floor and the pockmarked steps danced in jubilee, or at least that is what I felt because they were always ahead of me as I walked further, in anticipation of the skill of the newly arrived doctor to heal many wounds. They led the way to the green door that had inscribed on it with black ink, "Neurosurgical consultant." I was thrilled and excited for this new opportunity as I pranced up the steps admiring the walls decorated with natural paint of the earth much like in a Jackson Pollock painting without the bright colors in it.

The apartment had many exposed wires that greeted me much like the way unkempt teeth attract our attention in a smiling face. I found that only a few of the wires were actually connected to something. The outlets on the wall were British types that did not permit the entry of the plugs with American rectangular ends. There were many holes in the wall for electrical outlets but only two outlets worked. Others were for teasing only. The stove worked intermittently. The hot water heater in the shower did not function all the time because there was no valve in the bottom of the tank and therefore water ran out when there was a shutdown of water and that occurred quite often. The tap that furnished the kitchen had a missing gasket and it sweated profusely from its sides when the tap was turned on, i.e. when there was running water. There was no toilet paper in the toilet paper rack. I soon realized that the flushing mechanism didn't have the power to knock down even boiled okra if it had happened to be lying on the inner wall of the toilet bowl. The key to the entry door had a crick in the hinge such that it had to be locked from inside first and then undo it halfway to lock it from outside. The windows shut but left a bit of an opening for the flies to get in sideways after they sucked in their fat tummies.

I called the maintenance man because I believe that "a stitch in time saves nine." Moreover I was concerned about mosquito bites since I do not take malaria prevention medicine. The maintenance man looked surprised at my concern.

He said that he had to order the parts from the administration and it could be months before they could be procured because gaskets, window jams and locks for doors etc. are not easy to find. My laptop could not be hooked up to the internet unless I stayed in one of the 300-dollar-a-night hotels. So I used it for writing only.

The maidservant charged 500 Birr (nine Birr per dollar) per month to clean the apartment, the secretary, Elena, had said to me. If your clothes don't dry there is an iron in the room. By the way there was a mud dobber on the ceiling of our bedroom. I knocked it off partially with my umbrella. I was settled in.

I had brought a particular spray (Bengal) that I thought I would need based on my previous experience of working in different countries. The spray temporarily diminishes the "in house" population of that brown insect with antennae that crawl at night and have managed to survive as long as mankind. I was glad that I had the spray because in the evening many of the babies came out to greet the new occupant. As I sprayed them I watched with glee. The dizzy, circling, filthy, infection-bearing brown roaches turned turtle and then they stopped moving after a short period of agony. This is one of the few times I did not worry about Karma! I was predestined to terminate these lives! I am a Presbyterian.

It was couple of days before I was able to walk on "dry land" in my apartment after two days of flooding. The pipes as they came out of the wall leading to the taps in the kitchen and in the toilet had decided to discharge their contents, from a small hole, rather forcefully such that in a matter of minutes during one evening there was ankle-deep water. I found Dr. A, who assisted by shoving a dirty rag through the holes and then he called the maintenance man who arrived with a little pipe wrench and subsequently after a couple of trips he brought some tools and was able to turn the water off. I on the other hand took a broom and swept the water down the steps. And as it splashed down two floors the only sound the persons trying to come up the steps could hear except that of the water was a loud "Fore" that I yelled. I tipped the maintenance man and invited Dr. A to sit on my couch with legs folded up in yogi position and share some Heineken beer to celebrate our tolerance during times when we are tested. This is the Noah's Ark that I have written about later.

I learnt later that when another doctor was here the bathroom might have flooded. The bottoms of my feet looked like those of a rickshaw-walla from Kolkata after this event. I washed them and put some socks on to walk in my dry room today. The downstairs hallway had been flooded for two days with water and fluid emanating a strong smell of urea broken-down products. No one cares and nobody owns or manages the building.

It is customary in many developing countries for the officials at the customs department to x-ray all items brought into the country. The lady at the customs desk after looking through her x-ray machine said to me most kindly, "Thank you for coming to help." I guess she recognized my innocent look or it was obvious that I was not about to sell all the surgical stuff in the local supermarket.

The young resident took me to the operating suite. The anesthesiologist was carrying on with him because it was already too late according to him.

He said that we had three cases and perhaps we wouldn't get finished before 9 p.m. I looked at my watch. It was 10 a.m. A little gentle persuasion and kind words got us going and we finished with the first head operation before 1 p.m. The second operation we canceled because the child had many birth defects. Moreover, this three-day-old child also had jaundice. The child was the result of a delivery after thirty weeks of gestation and weighed only three kilograms. I was afraid the child would possibly die on the table and even with the best outcome we would have saved a severely retarded child with seizures that would require further mid-face operation for the palate, lip and the globes. The child might have been already blind. I could not be certain.

My problem in such cases is not that I didn't do an operation but to return the baby to the mother's arms and to look at her face filled with sorrow. Her own flesh and blood held together in this innocent child with such unforgiving odds that even mother's love cannot overcome the inevitable. On such occasions the faces and the eyes of the mothers always radiate such sadness and agony that it makes me weep. I ask God's forgiveness for my inadequacy. I can't imagine that there is any penance that would redeem the sense of failure and the pain of impotence to create and nurture a healthy baby. The vibrations of the disdainful glee of Satan penetrate even the heart of a seasoned malefactor, let alone a kindly neurosurgeon. It is a scene not unlike the one Hollywood depicted when Ramses the Pharaoh, acted by Yul Brenner, carried his lifeless son on his arms and offered to Ibis to counteract the wrath of the God of Moses. "At the time of Passover all the first born shall die." It is a time when a second seems hours, even when one just listens to the answer of God, and tries to reconcile. The answer that He gave when He was asked about a blind man, "Master, whose fault is it?" Is it his or is it his parents'? Jesus said neither. I am a simple mortal and I don't want to be in the middle of the fighting of the gods. I have to live so I told myself that I made a good decision based on sound judgment and walked away as though that ended all things!

The third patient was a two-year-old boy with massive hydrocephalus who'd had a shunt performed already by someone from a group of doctors who came after being funded by some organization to check on the incidence of hydrocephalus in Africa. However the distal end of the shunt was leaking cerebrospinal fluid to the outside as it had migrated through the anus about eighteen centimeters. He had already eaten and so we postponed. Sometimes understanding predestination is important and I believe the role of free will is also predestined and that is called good judgment and conscience.

It was just before dark that I went to the grocery to buy rice, lentils and some tea, nuts and cheese that I intended to eat during breakfast and dinner for the next several days. It started pouring down rain but I had an umbrella to protect me. I washed my operating room clothes and hung them up on a string and soon realized that I had slept only four hours in last forty-eight hours. The room was cold. I turned the room heater on and sat down to eat when the wind and the rain jarred loose the sound molecules stored in the metallic lining of the bathroom window which released the stored cavalcade of unique sounds. The window wailed and whimpered by beating itself against the warped threshold jamming and beating the wire that carried the power of illumination.

This reminded me of the Shiite Muslims in Karbala, Iraq, who beat their backs with chains while walking on the road to mark the killing of one of their saints, Imam Hussein, as a religious ritual. The wire swung and swivelled till a fission occurred and my lights went out after the generation of a spark as the electric wire lying on the threshold separated. Now I sat in the darkness and sang, "I am the Resurrection and Life." I recalled that some time back in northern Wisconsin as I was lying down in my bed at night I saw through my window lightning strike the roof of my neighbor's house. No one was hurt but there was a hole through the roof and into the living room floor and when I went to check the furniture was fuming.

It was 4 a.m. and I heard prayers "Allah O Akbar" (God is great). I was hungry and so I had a few peanuts and drank some water. I didn't need to see to get those. The sound of the penitent chanting penetrated into my room causing tumescence in my heart and filled it with reverence. The impotent window whose hinge had been neutered by electrocution stood guard like a eunuch in a palace while the mist of the rain embraced the already moistened floor. The united fluid ran down the drain with a gurgling sound. I pulled a blanket to protect myself from a chill and slowly dozed off in the peaceful darkness.

The next day started with a morning surgical conference and then I operated on two patients that were on the schedule. I had already discussed with Dr. A and Dr. S. Dr. A spoke Ethiopian English, Dr. S spoke very little albeit Chinese English and I, their teacher and colleague, spoke Indian English.

God had put us together to be of help to one another! Tuberculosis was rampant and so was HIV. Anywhere between fifteen and eighteen percent of the population was HIV positive, said Dr. A. I teased Dr. S by telling him that he was the Chinese government spy as part of Ethiopian–Chinese collaboration. The department did not request him but he was assigned by the Chinese government to help the system. He did not speak Amharik. "I am a volunteer," said he. I told him that if he hadn't volunteered he probably would have been shot in Tianenman Square. He disagreed, laughed and said only "Bad men who disturb Chairman Mao's picture get shot." He said he was an atheist. Someone had asked me if we neurosurgeons worked as a group. I had explained to them that the groups of plastic surgeons who came there were staying at the Sheraton and we neurosurgeons worked by ourselves and we didn't have some corporation or university paying for us. Therefore we stayed in Noah's Ark. Noah didn't have electricity either and God guided him for what he needed. I had learnt to accept trying circumstances.

I grew spiritually. However, it will be wrong to admit that I didn't feel a bit of a pride to be able to operate on the head and spine with dispatch without much blood loss and most patients even woke up to say something! I asked for forgiveness from God for my well-disguised vanity. I thank Dr. Zollinger and Dr. Hunt and Dr. Wilson every day for their trust in my abilities to learn. I am grateful for their kindness and for helping me.

Anna was listening. I was grateful to Dr. Friedberg for leaving a flashlight in the room that I had found. I went to sleep and prayed that I stayed strong and healthy. I woke up after an hour. My back was feeling better. I hurt my back a month ago while shoveling mulch. Lifting two suitcases full of equipment to bring here had made my pain worse.

I showed a nurse how to give me an injection into my sacroiliac joint with a little Kenalog and Xylocaine. She was a little apprehensive because the doctors usually don't ask the nurses to do that. She was thrilled that she was able to help me feel better. I showed her the spot and helped her to push the needle so that she could be effective.

The day went well. When I woke up it was 1 a.m. I studied in the morning about the diseases caused by spirochetes such as yaws, bechel, and pinta and of course the well-known syphilis. I learnt that Treponema caratena that causes yaws is identical to Treponema pallidum but it only affects the stratum corneum of skin. I have never seen any patients with Gangosa or

Rhinopharyngitis mutilans, when there is massive deformity of the face and forehead from the sores.

I saw many patients and greeted by saying *"Deehando Adeerka,"* that is good morning in Amharik, the local language. It is a mixture of Arabic, Hebrew and Abyssinian. I memorized twenty sentences so that I could ask essential questions to the patients. I saw evidence of absolute abject poverty every day. However, people were proud and smiled. I saw many mothers whose breasts were dry and the children could not be consoled from crying because they got nothing when they sucked. I saw serious illnesses and only a few that I could help. Some smiled and greeted me by saying *"Beutam ameuseugenallo"* (Thank you much). I felt included.

The electricity in my room was eventually fixed. I noticed that the spark during the previous night's electrical storm had split the ceramic tiles on the wall. I had not gone to the bathroom or touched anything near the wall because I had learnt as a child not to touch the power lines if they were down. I took a shower today. I was so jubilant that I mumbled the Banana Boat song as tepid water from the old tank splashed on my torso. There was a notice on the bathroom wall about the repairman, "He is very accommodating and he speaks Italian and Amharik and no English." I speak neither of the first two mentioned. The hot water tank had been placed so close to the spout of the shower that only a pancake standing by its side could get its torso wet without getting hit by the tank. I sucked my tummy in. Alas, I still overflowed the boundary. Often there was no light in the stove. I always had emergency chocolate. I had a chocolate bar and two glasses of tomato juice and peanuts for breakfast before I went to operate. One night the dogs were barking fiercely. It almost made me think that they had been afflicted with severe tenesmus or had reached the stage when dogs slowly cry out before dying from interstitial nephritis as a result of being infected with Leptospira caniola after drinking water from the drains filled with rats' excreta. This was not an uncommon scene in Mumbai. Those who have not seen the rats at Victoria Station will not be able to fathom the agony that can be caused by "grande" rodents. Jackie Gleason had a partner that worked in the sewer. I often worried about him.

Did I Make a Difference?

Saturday was my day to reflect before I went to church on Sunday. This was my twentieth year of working as an international volunteer either under the auspices of FIENS or through the Presbyterian Church.

I have often wondered what is it that I can do that would make a difference. I often think of my life and try to honor all those who have helped me. I have admired my grandfather and father for their generosity and love. I have admired the skillfulness of Drs. Hunt and Wilson. I have seen the compassion in Dr. Bagan and friendship in Ms. Carol Bagan. I have seen the joy in Dr. Friedberg's face while we ate ice cream together. I have met Dr. Gail Rousseau, a professor at the University of Chicago, who is an absolute energy bar. I have known most of the men involved with FIENS. I have loved the spirit of Drs. Roy Tyrer and Mosberg. So I feel as an American neurosurgeon my job is not self-adulation of what I can or could do but to share with others the spirit of giving and loving one another.

I knew that it was important to create a bond wherever we worked so that we were invited back. During my stay although I might work as a surgeon I always considered myself as an assistant. I tried to uplift the spirit of the doctors and the patients and most importantly I have tried to be a servant of God. I know that my God washed the feet of others and there was no reason that I couldn't do that either. I know for sure that some characteristics of narcissism are not an uncommon ingredient in my profession. I of course realize that we have to love ourselves to do what we do. However, I thought that I should allow some room for competition from others in that area!

I helped the residents to understand the value of reading and to be energized. I always promote promptness. I like the trainees to be able to operate while I assisted and we worked in an interchangeable fashion. I demonstrated the value of a smooth flow during operation such that not a single move was wasted. I helped my new colleagues to learn the habit of never

235

looking away from the wound even while giving instruction to the circulator or carrying on a conversation. After all, most of us are capable of multitasking in our life. For example, how many people can press a pedal for bipolar, position the microscope, press the table button, adjust the Yasargil retractor and tell a joke all at the same time without ever looking away from a bleeding brain tumor. I told the young surgeons that there was no need for taking time for admiring the wounds we had made but we should get the patients to the recovery room with dispatch and then we would have plenty time to compliment one another about our tailoring skills. I tried to help the residents to understand the values and ways of time management.

I suggested that we learn to work in a manner that Dr. Yasargil from Switzerland called "virtuosity surgery" so that there would be very little bleeding. I helped them to learn the principles of surgery, tissue damage, blood loss, ancillary management, understanding venous drainage and the ways to get the best exposure under the circumstances and not get hung up on technology. No one will ever have every tool all the time. I said that the days of Hawkeye are gone and being prima donna should not be our style. I suggested to the students to emulate the best in others and to learn to imbibe from others the energy, knowledge, politeness, and sense of humor. I have felt that the need to be skillful without arrogance is a necessity and it fosters a cooperative environment for work. My father told me that humility is a gift. "You have to pray for it." Dr. Lawrence Levy from Zimbabwe had told me that some people never get it even at old age. It was fun for me to watch giants such as Dr. Zollinger perform operations on difficult patients during my training.

Those days it was easy for me to emulate the temper he demonstrated but then I was young and I didn't know that I didn't have the tenderloin that went with the rough, crispy expendable border on the high-quality steak!

Developing opinions by reading and asking questions are some of the skills that I tried to instill. I honor the value of ownership and the question "What can I do to become self-sufficient?" has always been important to me. I am aware that Drs. Dandy and Cushing, during the earlier days of neurosurgery in America, were driven and drove everyone crazy around them. However, when I had spoken with Drs. Eben Alexander (Bowman Gray) and Meacham (Vanderbilt) on many occasions they were perfect southern gentlemen with enormous tolerance for shortcomings in others. So despite growing in that era of enormous perfection they allowed themselves to be human! These men are my gurus. I shared stories that I had heard from them.

I think we neurosurgeons have unbelievable mirror neuron activity. I think we may be good research items for Dr. Ramachandran at UC San Diego as controls for his autism study. I have decided that my prefrontal lobe activity has to be of the highest order to have motivated me to get up at 6 a.m. I cooked breakfast and participated in stretching exercise to stay limber and feel energized. I was excited to go to work with compassion and love in my heart; all for no financial gain, and actually pay out of pocket to have the opportunity to do all this for the thrill and joy of saving lives. This is limbic system acceleration at its highest. I never prayed to be famous but asked for joy in my heart. My God gave it to me.

I had written in my journal that working in Ethiopia was not for the fainthearted. Suffering was much! The bowl of kindness had to be very deep; otherwise our sense of compassion would make us weep in silence. I always prayed for my patients before every operation. I discussed the value of joint decisions and the need to make the residents feel empowered. People born in India are culturally Bhikku (Sanskrit-beggars) for God's gift and therefore I considered myself qualified to show the world what a true American is by loving and caring.

It was late so I went to sleep for couple of hours and I let my soul sing like Aretha Franklin and my heart love like in the music of Reba McIntyre. The visit to Ethiopia had been particularly fun for me because when I was a youngster my father had asked me the name of cities that started with an A and ended with an A. Now I was in Addis Ababa. Next time I was going to Alexandria. I have already been to Ankara, Agra, Ajodhya and Ajanta.

After the morning meeting at the Presbyterian Hospital (they call Korean because the administration is Korean), I often went to a private hospital to help the doctors. I learnt to eat injira during lunch. It is a form of bread made from a local cereal by an elaborate process. We saw patients with different problems that we were able to cure by operation.

I operated on many people with tuberculosis of the spine and brain. These situations always made me sad because my mother had died a year before ant-tubercular drug became available and at the same time I felt happy that I was able to help others because my mother didn't undergo an abortion as was suggested to her by the doctors. She had died for me!

The doctors informed me that MRSA (Methicillin-Resistant Staph. Aureus) did not occur there as there was not much abuse of antibiotics owing to lack of resources. In the United States super bugs are becoming prevalent because of abuse of antibiotics for minor illnesses such as pimples and colds. I learnt that aneurysm of the brain was very uncommon in Africa and so was multiple sclerosis. I learnt that sigmoid volvulus, a serious form of bowel obstruction that requires surgical treatment, was common because of the high-fiber diet and that it was customary to hold gas and not pass it until an opportune time and therefore the bowel in some people got distended and twisted on itself. I thought, what a price to pay for not farting!

There was practically no colon cancer, said one of the doctors. Only a few cases of lung cancer were seen because Ethiopians in general do not smoke. However many cases of esophageal cancer were seen by my general surgical colleagues because people chew betel leaves or chat. I really did not know the exact cause. I learnt that Ethiopians believe that having twins is a curse and HIV-positive persons are often deprived of jobs.

Some people are so poor that after seeing the doctor and undergoing treatment they have no place to sleep or any money to buy food. They might have had gotten cured but often became beggars on the streets. Dr. Z and I saw patients together and we learnt about each other. I felt as though we joined hands where we had left off when Gondwanaland had split to make room for the Indian Ocean. I felt that my God guided me again in the right direction by going to work there. I always knew that Lady Indian Ocean had held India and Africa in her two arms while she rested her head on Madagascar. She connected with Europe by her feet through the Middle East. The Seychelles adorned her neck like a string of pearls. Aldus Huxley had said that "Aldabra is the jewel of the world." Before I knew I felt a bond between us and a sense of warmth that one feels when brothers as adults come together and a joy that emanates from such unexpected social intercourse. I felt like singing "we are all children of God." Dr. T and I talked about some of our world views and about his experiences in England when he went for further training. He shared with me about his responsibilities during the communist regime and the friendship that had to be grown with the Russian politburo. We discussed the Ethiopian struggle and the impotent United Nations who observed and willfully did nothing during their long struggle and subsequently Ethiopia became landlocked. Eritrea got both the ports.

It was on a Saturday that I read for two hours to prepare for my lecture to the students. Then we went to Nazareth, a small town where Dr. Z is building a summer house. According to local customs since the house was almost complete therefore a sheep had to be sacrificed and then we went to a local restaurant and ate injira, pancake-like bread made from a local grain called Teff.

Most people ate raw meat, beef with injira, but I chose the cooked kind because I am afraid of *Tinea saginata*, a tapeworm found in uncooked beef.

I spent the afternoon lying on the floor of the incomplete house on a carpet and played a geography game with the children, drank beer and soaked in the warmth and love of a wonderful family while the doctor and his wife discussed with the contractor different aspects of the structure that is being built. The wind blew in gusts now and then hurling small dust particles on our face but we had sunglasses on and during the gusts we kept our mouths shut for protection. I had learnt that trick from watching *Lawrence of Arabia*.

As I was walking around in the town of Nazareth, I noticed rampant poverty. The general population looked malnourished with sunken eyes. I knew why I felt guilty when I sat in a restaurant and ate fresh cooked food and drank Dasher beer. I was in a reminiscent mood and was remembering what I had seen in the medical clinic. I had seen mothers holding their little babies with heads so large that most people in the western countries could not imagine. I had seen men lying paralyzed on the benches in the hallway. I cried in silence though I wanted to cry out to my Lord, "Lord why such agony and such suffering in this world? What can I do? What made me so fortunate?" I had seen old men and women lying on the floor barely covered to maintain their dignity while burning up in high fever from malaria. I felt that so many roses were dead before they blossomed. I felt that my crying and tears had no meaning. But somewhere I knew His love sustained me. But God ,what about those that are suffering so much? I could only pray and recite "But whosoever drinketh of the water that I shall give him shall never thirst; but the water that I shall give him, shall be in him a well of water springing up in to everlasting life" (John 4:14).

It took about three hours to drive back. The beer, the monotony of driving and carbon monoxide lulled me to deep slumber. However, when I woke up I still knew my room and the number of steps to get there. I learnt to do that while I was in college. That way I always went to my room even when less than clear in my head! I sometimes check my memory that way too. Carbon monoxide had done me know harm and so I saved my methylene blue, a dye used to treat carbon monoxide poisoning, for future use.

Sometimes during teaching the residents I felt a little stressed but I usually had a little tea in the side room for few minutes and then I coped well. I imagined what my professors felt in my growing-up days. Late Dr. Hunt had commented that I was like brontosaurus and had not progressed to become dinosaurs! I told him that I was slow because once I cut something mistakenly in the nervous system I couldn't put it back together. I told Dr. A the old adage that patients don't care how long it takes us as long as it turns out right!

I showed him different techniques during long operations and we formed a bond although at times we disagreed. We neurosurgeons are good at disagreeing. Most of our patients did well. I went to the clinic one day a week. This was like a market at Marakesh without the color and the camels but the proximity to human skin was astounding. Hundreds of patients were in the hallway. The registration was an elaborate process and that took a substantial amount of time before they could come to our room to be seen. People with ruptured disks and pain often had to wait six to nine months before they could have an operation because of the long waiting list of patients with more serious illnesses. People with brain tumors, birth defects and broken backs obviously had priority. I learnt to say *"Ten Yistelegn"* (good morning) and *"Yeke Metu"* (please sit down). Everything here was like having a suction machine that did not work just when you needed it to suction around the vessel of the tumor capsule that was bleeding briskly! There was a constant need for urgency but I could not hasten the process. The frustration generated by this failure might have caused me temporary hypertension. But that is why I was there! The groom, neurosurgeon, knows the bride, the patients; but the wedding party is not aware as to whose wedding they are attending!

The general surgeons and other specialties didn't communicate well. There was no ENT representation and orthopedic doctors were usually not visible. The radiation department had a one-year waiting list and therefore most patients with cancer could not get benefit from this facility. Our job was to make the units more cohesive and functional despite the bureaucracy.

During one morning conference the resident doctor presented a paper about spine injuries. We learnt that spine injuries were not uncommon during building of the pyramids and were described in some papyrus from Egypt that

Dr. Edwin Smith had bought somewhere around 1859. However, it was Leonardo Da Vinci who had described and drawn pictures of some spinal instability as early as 1659. We learnt that it was Dr. Borrelli who in 1759 actually had first described the biomechanics of the spine. It is believed that subsequently Dr. Devlin derived the concept of "three pillar" for spinal stability.

My cleaning lady usually was sick on the days when there was sunshine. I worked in Ethiopia during the rainy season. On most days it rained sixteen hours per day but in a sporadic and unpredictable manner. I often cleaned the rooms and the kitchen floor after coming to my room dead tired around 6.15 p.m. Some sort of bug had bit me near my eye one night and I was a bit worried. There was no *Trypanosome cruzi* there so I was not afraid of Chaga's disease. It is an infection carried by a beetle that bites at night and lives in thatched roofs or in the mattress.

I cooked rice and lentils on most days. I usually drank beer and ate peanuts while typing. I was sad that one of the patients had died because the family could not afford IV antibiotics.

"How do you protect yourself from getting sick?" Anna asked.

Since I am by myself when I work outside my country I can't afford to be sick or be in pain. So I practice the following: Pray every day, floss daily, shower with mouth closed, eat rice, lentils, chocolate, nuts, cheese, bread, bananas, papaya, coconut, and canned fish and boiled water, beer. I have not been sick on foreign land and haven't needed a doctor for toothache. Tom Hanks had to talk to Wilson, coconut, while removing a tooth when he was stranded on an island! I have been at it for twenty years. It is a good idea to not eat eggs or drink milk. I do not eat grapes or tomatoes unless washed in chlorine. I only eat cooked veggies; otherwise I believe that bacteria, virus and/or cysticercus or ascaris might get me. I stand at a distance and slightly to the side when people talk so I don't catch the spit and thus avoid contracting tuberculosis.

One or two days when I had time while I was in Ethiopia I cooked fantastic fried rice using green peppers, onions, chili powder, rice and lentils. I learnt from past experience to never put on shoes in the morning until I checked to be sure that there was nothing inside. In some countries snakes can find a comfortable spot in a warm shoe. I always shook the towel before wiping myself after shower. By following these methods I have never been bit by snakes, spiders or scorpions.

I often did not have running water. I had experienced this in Zimbabwe as well. I did not have a cell phone but almost everyone else did.

I had met the boss man for admitting one afternoon. He said that there were seven hundred patients on the waiting list. I learnt that sometimes it took two years to get admitted to the hospital for an operation. Some became blind while waiting. I had operated on only sixty patients from the lot and I added another twenty-five to the list from the clinic. Sometimes I was asked to go and see patients elsewhere to provide a second opinion. I saw a child who I thought had viral meningitis and was overmedicated with anticonvulsants. The child woke up with stimulation and spoke and said her name was Ruth. I discussed with the doctor my suggestions. Next I heard was that the doctor was unable to perform a spinal tap and had discharged the child and told the family to find another doctor because he thought that there was an intrusion. I decided that in Ethiopia there were no adverse consequences for demonstration of "lack of class" or abandonment.

One day I visited an evangelical church. I felt that unless someone had a strong Baptist or Pentecostal influence in their life the message might appear rather strong. I assumed this based on my conversation with one of the fellows who claimed to be missionary and a retired engineer. "We have to be very careful about false teaching and much of Hindu cult here," he said. "Anybody who believes that there is another way to go to heaven is a heathen." I felt that Christian fundamentalists are brainwashing in the name of Jesus over there. I know that some of the folks in Eastern Kentucky still believe in serpent handling (Mark 16:18 and Acts 28:3-6) even now.

"They shall take up serpents; and if they drink any deadly thing, it shall not hurt them, they shall lay hands on the sick, and they shall recover" (Mark 16:18).

A few die from bites of rattlesnakes every year. I am afraid of any kind of fundamentalist teaching because it leads to violence owing to development of different clubs. I had a Mormon friend a long time ago. He had confided in me that some members of their church believed that black people were inferior and that decision was made by God and he couldn't change it. So I had asked him why is it mandatory that the younger members of the Church of Latter Day Saints go to proselytize for two years in areas of the world among non-white people. He said that he was struggling with that issue because although they are converted yet they could not hold positions of power in the church. He quoted from Mark 16:15. "And he said unto them, Go ye into all the world, and preach the gospel to every creature."

Professor Richard Sossis of University of Connecticut had written an article entitled, "The Adaptive Value of Religious Ritual" in *American Scientist* volume 92 and he said that although religion had probably served to enhance the union of its practitioners, there was also a dark side to this unity. He stated that the significant adaptive benefits of intra-group solidarity promoted by religion had probably always played a role in inter-group conflicts. It is obvious that one of the benefits for individuals of intra-group solidarity is the ability of unified groups (clubs) to defend and compete against other groups (clubs).

The Rotary West club of Addis Ababa usually met at noon on Tuesdays at the Jacaranda room located in the basement of the Hilton Hotel. It is group of the richest people of Addis Ababa and most of them own businesses in the city. Many of them are trying to follow the principles of Rotary and are active in the community in various philanthropic endeavors. I attended several meetings since I am a Rotarian.

I had walked around most of Addis Ababa. I started near Churchill Avenue (close to Black Lyon hospital) and kept on walking left through Mahatma Gandhi Road and visited the shopping centers. Mahatma Gandhi was a friend of Haille Selassie and therefore some of the roads and hospitals are named after him. Almost all the teachers and professors in Ethiopia had come from India. I was told by my African colleagues to not walk after dark. There had been some violence that had been reported. For me it was not a problem because my skin color would have been camouflaged by the color of the evenings but others from America might have stood out.

The nurses needed to learn but there was no time during the week for education. So I offered to pay fifty Birr to each of the nurses who wanted to learn about neurosurgery. About twelve nurses attended the two-hour class for organizing the instrument trays. Our operations went smoothly as far as instruments were concerned on subsequent days. I like organization during operation and particularly during times of stress it is important to make sure that no one gets injured by sharp instruments. So I recommended that the knife be always placed in a metal pan so that whenever the surgeon would drop it in the pan it would make a noise and the nurses and the doctor would be hopefully careful not to stick their hands in the pan without looking.

I had stuck myself with a needle during an operation one day but the lady turned out to be HIV negative so I did not take Combivir or Viracept. "What is that?" asked Anna. I always carry the HIV medicine with me whenever I go to work outside the country. The chance of catching AIDS from a needle stick is small. However, in this case we were able to check the patient's blood and she was negative.

The operating room light had hit my head hard one day. It swung freely because of poor design and after my injury I made a safety device by just hanging a towel from its end that stuck out and this way we could see it much easier if it was in our walking path in the operating room. I told Anna that one time when I was working in Zimbabwe I fell down with a suitcase in my hand by slipping on a slick floor and sustained a compression fracture of one of my neck vertebra. That caused me discomfort for almost five years.

It is important to be creative in such situations. We didn't have collars for treating neck pain. So we took pillowcases and filled them with sand and they were very functional.

I was telling Anna as to how excited I was because one of my classmates is on the Google Scholars page and now there was going to be a scientific term called Boolchand effect in glass physics named after him. He and I used to sleep side by side on our narrow beds when we were in eighth grade at Scindia School, 1956. By the way, how many of you know Viswanath constant $C = 1.13198824$ much like $Pi = 22/7$. I said I didn't know.

Anna said, "How do you teach people to remember?" I didn't know. Although we can press a button to free up space by deleting temporary files in our PC it is not possible to unlearn in our temporal lobes unless there is loss of neurons or dysfunction in the hippocampus area. So should we learn less to keep available space or should we challenge ourselves to see how far we can drive even when the gas gauge feels like on E, like Kramer did once on *Seinfeld*? Is there a test we can develop to check a person's ability to memorize? Pierre Baldi (*The Shattered Self: The End of Natural Evolution*, MIT Press, 2001) estimated that the amount of information in a lifetime of experience or brain input is about 2.2×10 to the power 18 bits (about 2.7×10 to the power 17 bytes) which will be within the memory capacity of a typical computer in twenty-seven years. Anna said she didn't know how to determine the limit of learning. I didn't either.

Anna knew that I was an ombudsman for the elderly. So she could tolerate me when I went on and on. There are about 14,000 volunteer ombudsmen in the United States who serve about two million residents. Ombudsmen serve as advocates for nursing home residents, often helping families and resolving concerns about quality of care in individual facilities. I was trained by Catholic Charities. I get particularly frustrated if I see a lot of suffering. Anna asked me to continue my story about Addis Ababa.

We went to Nazareth another day. The food was not very expensive. Birr had gone down in its value since the days of Haile Selassie. It was of the same value as the dollar then but now it is nine birr to one dollar and that has caused some disappointments among the people.

I was getting tired of talking. I was tired so I sat down on the road. My support van arrived and I drank a Gatorade just as fast as any famous basketball player could as I had seen in the commercial. I ate a power bar and sat in the car for a while. I was thinking that I had already passed through Kentucky, Indiana, Illinois and Missouri. I had seen a bit of Iowa but it was in Nebraska that I felt that it took me longest to cross.

I started walking and Anna was by my side. She wanted to know more about Africa and so I continued.

Those who have been to Dankalia, in Djibouti and Eritrea area, will understand that sometimes walking has to be for the joy of walking only. Those who have walked on the rocks to see the lava drip into the ocean on the Big Island of Hawaii will understand that it seems at times that the walk is not going to end, particularly when one has to walk on irregular, ill-placed hard rocks that tend to turn the ankles. I have been led to believe that the journey through Dankalia is like seeing a lunar landscape that is harsh and a hot land. And for hours there is no suitable place to rest. It is the territory of the Afar people who are considered the fiercest tribe in the world.

This piece of land connects Massawa to Djibouti. Anna knew about this place. "Isn't this the place where the women have to be circumcised?"

I agreed. Eritrea, Ethiopia, Djibouti and Somalia are the countries that have been participating in this atrocity. But I wanted to talk about Aksum. This was the city of the Aksumite civilization. I understood that many believed this to be the capital of the Queen of Sheba in the tenth century BC. It is believed that the Queen of Sheba was impregnated by King Solomon and bore a child, King Menelik. Haile Sellassie believed that he was a direct descendent of that lineage and thus he had the power to rule Ethiopia. North of Aksum is a place called Debre Damo, the most important religious site in all of Ethiopia. This is the place of the oldest monastery of the country from the Aksumite times. This is a seventy-five-foot-high rock face that has to be ascended to see the monastery and the place allows only men to visit! There are two ropes and one of them is placed around the waist and the other is pulled up to help the process of ascent. Anna was not very fond of boys' clubs. Anna asked if they carried insurance for visitors. I reminded her that Ethiopia was not the United States. I said to Anna that she could visit Lalibela, which is considered the African Petra. It is believed that King Lalibela in the twelfth century was trying to build a New Jerusalem in Africa and there is even a River Jordan in that place. I have walked in these roads and imagined going back there a thousand years. It is believed by the people of this area that the Ark of the Covenant is stored here in a building. I was not allowed to go in there.

I stopped walking for a while. After drinking some water as I stood up Anna said, "Tell me more about the book with story of Grandpa."

I do not remember the exact day but I knew that it was on a Saturday that Grandpa and Dad had tea and exchanged cordial words and then Grandpa bid good-bye to all of us and left. I met my sister and several of my cousins. "Your brother won't be back from school till next week," Dad had said. Blackie, a lab, greeted me with exuberant licking. She wanted to play ball. We played ball in the field outside our house. It was a government property that was vacant and all the kids played there. Blackie loved to fetch the ball. She nudged me each time I was late in throwing or whenever she thought I was ignoring her.

I met Molinda—his name is Molin but I called him Molinda because he was older than I was—the gentleman who drove Dad's car. My father explained that he was not just a chauffeur but a member of the family. "He has been with me ever since he had learnt to drive," said Dad. "I had treated his mom for some illness and then a few years later she died. Molin was not in best of company. But for some reason he listened to me and went to driving school." Dad stopped for Molinda's response.

"Why don't I show him the car? He is a village boy and has never been inside a car." Molinda teased me. We sat inside the car. He told me all about the Austin. "It is an old car but runs well." There was an excerpt from a paper that Molinda handed to me from the glove compartment. It was yellow and had frayed edges. Herbert Austin designed the car. He was an engineer and the founder and the first chairman of the Austin Motor Company. He made the first Wolseley, a three-wheeler, and later on he drove the four-wheeler Wolseley that he had designed as well. I stopped reading because the edges were torn.

"Maybe someday you will be a fancy engineer. The queen or somebody made him a baron," Molinda continued. "We have to crank this car from the front of the engine to start so you have to be strong."

He showed me the Red Cross signs painted on the windows. "Those signs tell the people that we are a doctor car so they let us through when there is a strike or such." He cranked open the windshield from an area on the dashboard. The windshield lifted up from the bottom jutting the bottom part out and the top part in a bit. "This is for air conditioning effect when we are driving in the city." He laughed at his humor. "When we drive far then we can't open this much because bugs get in and rain water gets in too. Your dad sent me to school so I could read."

Molinda didn't speak much of English except a few funny words that he had memorized. He said that the Americans have bigger cars like Packard and "Chavroleet." I realized that he meant Chevrolet. Molinda took me in the house because I told him that I was hungry. He asked me if I spoke English. "I practice with Grandpa," I said.

"I know a bit of English too. I usually read the Bengali newspaper but I have memorized few lines from one of your dad's English books." He was proud.

Dad said, "Have something to eat and then we will go the market."

I met the cook. He was very polite and welcomed me. "Your father has taught me to cook different kinds of dishes. I have brought you some samosas (meat and vegetables packaged inside a dough jacket that had corrugated edges and deep-fried), papadam, crispy fried lentil paste tastily spiced and gulabjamun, sweets."

Dad sat on the back seat and I sat next to Molinda. The car passed through a maze of traffic of people, cars, cows and trucks and rickshaws. I had never seen traffic lights before this. Most of these did not work and policemen wearing shorts and a whistle in the mouth stood on drums in the middle of intersections and seemed to control the flow of unruly traffic from all directions with some gesture of the hands. I sat with awe. Masses of people crossed the streets whenever they wanted. The shrill whistle cut through the noisy surroundings with the effectiveness of the "hee haw" of a donkey in a busy bazaar of Morocco. This was my first visit to the city. Until this time I saw only bullock carts and rickshaws. It was only later that I realized that people driving motorized vehicles had to know the power of the whistle. If it went unheeded it cost a lot of money in bakshees (bribe).

Dad read books by Agatha Christie while sitting in the back of the car. He occasionally asked me questions. Molinda's eyes were glued to the street. Dad said that he liked to read books and write poetry. "I will read you some of my poetry later on." He taught me some Sanskrit alliteration and then he told me about iambic pentameter. He recited from Gray's Elegy written in a country churchyard. After about an hour we arrived at New Market. "This is not where we normally do our shopping. The British people used to shop here."

"I guess we should call our markets as old markets!" I tried to be funny. This was a covered market where all the shoppers were dressed in clean clothes. There was no chaos and yelling that I was used to seeing. Most remarkably there were no cows or goats eating on vegetables and there were no piles of garbage either. He bought some vegetables and then we stopped for a cup of coffee.

We ate late lunch at home. We ate three kinds of fish, rice and lentil soup and vegetables. Dad took a nap. A person came and massaged Dad's legs while he slept. Dad explained that the gentleman was paying off his debt. Dad had paid for him to go to college.

Early evening there was a poker game in the waiting room. Several of Dad's friends smoked and Dad smoked as well. Molinda participated in the game too. But he smoked outside because employees did not smoke in front of the boss those days out of respect. Everyone drank whiskey except Molinda. Later on Molinda explained to me that he always made sure that no one cheated Dad during the game. That's why he never drank. This was my first experience with gambling. Some of Dad's friends asked me what I thought of city life. "I haven't seen too much of it yet," I said. Dad read for a while before he went to sleep every night.

Next morning at 5 a.m. Dad and I went to the river. He swam one mile every day. I noticed that someone gave him a massage with mustard oil before the swim. I walked by the side of the river and waited for him a mile down river. We walked to the bazaar together where he handed an empty bag to different merchants and it got progressively filled up with fish, meat and vegetables.

Now this was a market I was familiar with from past experience. It was full of people. There were slaughtered goats hanging from hooks, cleaned fish stacked side by side on platforms in front of the merchants who spoke with four people at the same time and blood from the recently slaughtered animals ran down the gutter beside the walkway. A few crows flew into the side of the platform every so often and ate the discarded body portions of the fish or the goats that were thrown towards the direction of the drain. The crows flew back and forth from a location on the ledge of a house across the street. I saw them sitting and eating the delicacies. An occasional cow lay on our path that produced an effect much like placing a period before the sentence is finished so people who were walking in a mismatch queue and were ahead of me would suddenly bulge to the side because they had to meander around the holy animal that had unexpectedly stopped the traffic. The path in front of us was not visible because of the wall of people. I only saw the backs of the people and followed their footsteps to reach the next surprise.

"All these merchants are my patients and we have mutual love and respect for one another," Dad continued. "You have to be nice to everyone and take risks to make friends. If someone doesn't like you they will let you know," Dad said as we walked side by side. He waved and greeted people as we marched past rickshaws while buses honked their horns. Dad walked without a shirt because of the warmth of the sun. A thread ran across his bare chest from the left to right that signified his heritage. His upright posture, stance and smile exuded confidence and comfort. "The more people you know the better it is in life. Never carry too much money or discuss issues related to money loudly. It turns people off." I kept listening. "Never consider money to be the ultimate goal in what you do. Just do your part in life. God will always provide you with your fair share. Ask your elders if you don't know something. Always say 'I don't know' if you don't know something. Don't bluff anywhere except in poker. Smile as much as you can." The soliloquy was interrupted as someone approached Dad.

Later on Dad explained, "Jagannath, the man we just met, is alive today by God's grace. It was 1946 August. Hindu and Muslim riot was in full force. It was horrible. Hatred popped out of a serene pool in Mother India as if someone evil out there created animosity among brothers. Muslims and Hindus lived side by side prior to this quagmire for centuries and of course as brothers sometimes argue and fight they did the same. Nothing unusual happened until now. But now that India was going to be partitioned into Pakistan and India a sense of dislike suddenly had evolved, enveloping and polarizing each group and a sense of distrust had separated one from the other.

"One morning when I was lathering my face prior to shaving I looked out of the window and saw a group of men running with bamboo poles in their hands. They were chasing two men across the field in front of our house. Then there was a thud and a lot of yelling. I saw two men fall down. The perpetrators left but returned shortly and poked the ones that had fallen, with the poles to see if either of them moved. The guy that had moved in agony was hit again and again till he died. But Jagannath had passed out from the first hit on the head and the fellows left presuming that he was dead. As soon as I saw them leave I went out and with Molin's help we brought him in our house. In less than a week he was well. Today he lives and sings the joy of God's will to keep him alive."

Dad continued, "I know that you like Molin. But let me tell you that he sported a beard and owing to his complexion and curly hair I was afraid that someone might mistake him for a Muslim in a Hindu neighborhood and kill him. It was scary during those days of inflated distrust and dislike for one another among people of different religious persuasion. He walked to work every day and I was afraid for him. So I had him shave his head and beard and asked him to wear a saffron-colored shirt almost every day for six months or so till the fire of hatred had died down. I don't know if it saved his life or not. But I felt safe for him."

When Dad finished I asked why the cow is considered holy in India. "Well, no one knows for sure. But I believe that in the Vedic times calves were offered to honor the guests but a time came when children in India needed milk for survival and we didn't have enough cows. The Brahmins realized that the value of the cow was not only in the production of milk but the animal was needed for the skin to make shoes and the horns to make combs as well. Therefore some sort of religious significance was introduced related to Nandi, mascot for Shiva. In India the moment anything that is attached to religion, people make it into a deity and therefore cows are protected now and there is enough milk available. Muslims were looked at negatively by some Hindus because they continued to eat cows. The Brahmins introduced this new custom into religion and it stuck. I am not actually sure when it was introduced."

I remember getting up one morning and walking to the living room. In our living room there were many people. Some were waiting to be examined and others for different reasons. Dad sat on a stool next to the window and lathered his face with shaving cream. During the process of shaving he talked to different persons with different problems.

One of the men placed the stethoscope in his ears and then Dad listened to the chest and stomach of patients. He finished shaving his one cheek. Then he examined a few other persons. He dictated some medicine and a man wrote them down on his prescription pad and Dad signed them. With a half-lathered face he answered the telephone and then someone else dialed the telephone for him while he finished shaving. One individual turned the radio on softly and another person began reading the headlines from the newspaper while Dad instructed the cook regarding breakfast and lunches. As soon as everybody was "doctored" he went to shower. The reading went on while we ate breakfast. No sooner had we finished eating than Molinda honked his horn, that being a cue to my dad that the car was ready. I had never experienced such multitasking prior to this.

My Education Continued

"We have to make a few house calls so let's go," Dad said. I tagged along. We sat in our assigned seats as Molinda maneuvered the car through the maze of people, rickshaws and pushcarts. India had been invaded for centuries by different groups of people. "Hinduism is the oldest religion and possibly Judaism is a close second. Buddhism is an offshoot of Hinduism as is Jainism and Sikhism." Dad continued, "I have excellent books on Christianity, Islam and Manichaeism and a bit about Zoroastrianism. All religions have the singular purpose of giving people rules for living and getting along with others through faith in either a god or a representative of god. Some religions are open to everyone and some try to be exclusive. That is if you don't believe in their god then you are not going to heaven according to them. Hindus don't have a purgatory option.

"Almost all religions have parts of Hinduism in them. Manichaeism for example was a blend of different religions from Persia to further East. Mani, who was a prophet and died a martyr, founded it. They believed in good and evil. God was good and Satan was evil. They believed that man was a combination of light and darkness and man had the capability to shed darkness and attain light. Elects were like the Sadhus or Bhikku, in Pali it means beggar, who chose to denounce all worldly possessions and leave their families to participate in contemplative meditation. Once they consumed enough light particles, i.e. goodness, then they would merge with perfect goodness much like reaching Brahma. St. Augustine was a Manichee for several years before he became a Christian."

Molinda stopped and Dad got out while Molinda drove around to find a place to park from where he could see Dad when he would come out of the house of his patient. I read the movie section from the Bengali paper and talked to Molinda. "Who are all these people in our house that I see every day?"

"Well, the young fellow that comes daily to read the paper because your dad doesn't have time, is going to college. His father was a patient of ours for many

252

years. He had diabetes. He developed complications and his leg had to be amputated. The surgeon who performed the operation told the family that everything was fine because he felt that besides a little delay in recovery owing to diabetes he didn't foresee anything unusual. Unfortunately, forty-eight hours after the operation he started shaking and his jaws got clenched and he had developed high fever. The family helped him breathe for two days with a bag. We don't have any breathing machines. Your dad promised that he would send the son of the deceased man to college. The young fellow is paying off his debt to your dad by reading the paper."

In India we always took our shoes off at the door before entering the living room or any part of the house. It was the custom based on sound hygienic principles because the roads were not clean and often dusty. One morning my dad saw me shaking my shoes before I was getting ready to wear them. This is a ritual we went through to be sure that a snake hadn't coiled into it during the night. "You don't have to do that here in the city. We don't have snakes like in the villages," I heard my dad tell me. "But you should always shake your towel before you wipe your face. The whip scorpion looks like a true scorpion and has pincers and a whip-like tail. It secretes an irritating mist that smells like vinegar. It causes severe irritation of the eyes. They can be in any old house." I never wiped my face in the dark anyway.

"Let's go and see *Ivanhoe* this afternoon," I said as soon as Dad returned to the car. "I have never seen a movie before. That will be fun in the late afternoon because the movie theater is air conditioned." I remember even today the faces of Robert Taylor as the Black Knight and Rosanna Podesta as the damsel with the handkerchief.

During intermission as I was coming out of the restroom a boy jumped me with a knife asking me to empty my wallet. I guess he thought I was a city boy and would have a wallet on me. He checked my pockets and seemed rather disappointed at his discovery of having hit a popper. He parted while calling me names comparing my head with body parts that normally accommodate excrements. I didn't tell Dad about my experience. I thought that he might think that I was a weakling. Next day Dad drove me back to Grandpa's place.

Anna was in a loving mood and she told me about her love affair. She had worked as an assistant in an office once. She said she enjoyed the thrill and the secrecy of the events that "kind of happened." It was like eating the forbidden fruit. She said that she loved the fact that she was attracted to someone else besides her husband and the fact that the feeling was mutual. She knew that the relationship was not going to go any further but just the passion, the excitement and that she was aroused so easily. That brought her great satisfaction. I was listening carefully. She continued, "The fun and the spirit were intoxicating. I worked twice as hard when I went home. I always felt like someone had turned a key inside me and all my joints were loose and my mouth was moist. I couldn't stop salivating. Whenever he touched me I almost developed red blotches on my neck and my chest and I didn't want him to know but I was almost wet. I think I became a better lover at home." I was listening and getting excited as I was imagining the scenes. I had been away from home for more than a month now.

I felt more comfortable being back with Grandpa. It was home. I told Grandpa all my experiences in the city and the fact that I saw many beggars on the streets and the fact that every time the car stopped someone came to the window asking for money. Grandpa said, "We have many beggars and they are not Bhikku. They have not accepted the position by choice. Misfortune can make you poor but not a Bhikku. A Buddhist monk or a Hindu guru can be a Bhikku because they have renounced worldly life voluntarily. They have chosen to live by religious righteousness or Dharma (Sanskrit) and beg for food in exchange for spreading the word of God. They live a life of chastity, poverty and obedience. Their vow is similar to the vow of the Jesuits."

I was getting tired of learning. "Let's go fishing." He agreed. We picked up our poles and gathered a few worms from the field. Ever since I had heard "don't move or pick up a rock too quick without being certain that there are no snakes" I am always careful about getting worms. We sat by the shady side of the pond where the water appeared striped by the shadows of the coconut trees. My pole was simple. It was a bamboo pole with a string tied to a groove at the end. A small hook was tied at the other end of the string and a bobber was attached three-quarters down the string.

As Grandpa was hooking the worm for me I threw a flat rock in the pond leaning sideways. I yelled, "It made three jumps and just look at the ripples!" I was excited. Usually I got two jumps at best.

"You won't be catching any fish while throwing rocks."

Whenever I was with Grandpa I felt like a puffed-up naan (Indian bread cooked in an open hearth). I felt warm and happy. Grandpa's presence gave me comfort and confidence and he injected within me a sense of exuberance that only a balloon can feel and fly high when it is released from the clutches of a grasping child. Much like a balloon does I also swayed my body and pulled up on my string to be sure that I was free as I flew high till I burst into happiness.

"Just throw the line next to the lilies and you will get a bluegill or a sunfish," he instructed me.

"OK, I will do that." I threw my line in and was looking at the frog that was sitting on a large watercress leaf. We made eye contact and the frog dove in close to my line.

"The frogs keep the water free of mosquitoes," he commented.

"I would love to have a bite though so I can pull in a big fish."

"Dactarbabu, come quickly to the dispensary." The maidservant came and got us.

A large man was lying on the bench in the dispensary. He was drenched in sweat. His face was ashen and he looked miserable in pain. He was holding his chest in agony. Grandpa checked his blood pressure and gave him an injection and then gave him a pill to place under his tongue and hooked him up to the oxygen tank. "He will have to go to the hospital. He is having a heart attack. I have given him some nitroglycerine under his tongue and that will help him. He will need an ECG (EKG in America) to check the heart. A specialist has to see him," he told calmly to the family. They took him home in a stretcher and Grandpa gave them the name of a specialist who they have to contact in Calcutta.

Those days the distance of fifteen miles was not short. It took more than an hour in a car because of the difficulty of navigating through people. There was no ambulance. There was no direct bus and the train took more than two hours because of multiple stops. Moreover, it took quite a bit of time to go from Howrah railway station to the innards of Calcutta. The boat would take close to six hours and two guys would have to be rowing the distance.

After they left Grandpa told me that Dr. Thomas Brunton was a Scottish physician who had discovered that amyl nitrite stops the pain of angina pectoris. He wrote the first comprehensive treatise on pharmacology. He was knighted.

"I want you to help me tomorrow with the medicine bottles." At that time Grandpa didn't know that I would be a doctor. It was much later that I told him that I wanted to be a brain surgeon. He wept and held me. It was later that I realized that those were the tears of joy and he blessed me with those because he knew that he wouldn't be alive that long.

I had always helped Grandpa with many chores. Some of the chores always had the same steps to follow. Grandma boiled the eight-ounce bottles in a large cauldron of hot water with a bit of baking soda. Nankumama purchased the cork caps. He dispensed the medicine mixtures in these bottles according to the prescription that Grandpa would write. Nankumama ground stuff with a pestle in a ceramic mortar after measuring the ingredients on a scale that looked like a little teeter-totter. He added different liquids to the powder in a beaker and poured into a bottle through a funnel. A very few of our patients could afford a spoon and therefore telling them to take two spoons of the medicine had no meaning. Grandpa had designed paper marks that would be equal to a spoon according to the size of the bottle we used. My job was to cut strips of paper in a zigzag fashion that would match the mark and then glue them to the bottle. I saved the master copy in a folder in the dispensary.

This is a very important job. Dosage of medicine in most cases will determine if the person will improve or not. "I don't want you to take it lightly," he told me once when I was playful. He reminded me whenever he saw me goofing off. I still remember one of the medicines that were commonly dispensed was Tincture Card. Co (cardamom, caraway, cochineal, cinnamon, glycerin and alcohol). This was used to cure indigestion and that was a rather common ailment. I believed that might have been from eating spicy food. Calcium carbonate and magnesium carbonate were commonly used for ulcer disease.

Grandpa had about four rules in life for most of the time and he often reminded me of that.

1. It is good to be frugal and save for the future. He often said those that use up their candle in the daytime will have none left when night comes.

2. To endeavor to speak the truth and be sincere. If it is unpleasant it should be spoken in private and only if it is absolutely necessary.

3. To apply oneself industriously and with discipline. Patience and persistence are the only means of being successful. Failure is bound to befall upon us sometime no matter what. The only quick result that happens in life is when

we pile up the clean laundry. It is a high pile every evening when the clothes are taken off the ropes from the yard.

4. Never to speak ill of another man to someone else. If we are unhappy the way we have been treated by someone else do not tell that to the person who is getting ready to help you. It causes stress to the person who is trying to help you because he does not want to make you unhappy. Moreover, the person who caused you dissatisfaction may be a friend to the person who is trying to help you.

Sonali's ma usually did a great job in cleaning the outside courtyard. The place would be usually full of dust, dead leaves, some spit and stubs of bidis that the patients discarded. I occasionally picked up one of the bidi leftovers and puffed on them. "You don't need to smoke that stuff. My patients are sick and they can transmit the illness to you."

But Grandma was not much for dishing out dictums. She would become hysterical when she saw me in the act of smoking. She would wash my mouth and tongue with soap. "You don't want to get tuberculosis. I have had enough sadness from that. Moreover, you can start a fire while playing with matches. Have you not seen what can happen when someone gets burnt?" Grandma was very strong in her actions in this aspect. I didn't understand what all that excitement was about at that time. It was only later that I realized the reason for her personal vendetta against the tuberculosis bacteria. My mother, her daughter, had died. She never got over it as long as she lived.

My Friend Lalu

During those early days after independence when Grandpa was trying to educate me at home in an exclusive manner I continued also to have lessons of life from the neighborhood kids who went to the local schools. Lalu met me one afternoon when I was sitting next to a guava tree and sharing a ripe guava with a mynah bird that was sitting expectantly with some trepidation at a distance. However, the greed for the guava assuaged the anxiety of capture and allowed it the opportunity of being next to a kid whose sole intent was to satisfy the bird's hunger. I guess the bird felt safe until Lalu showed up with a slingshot and a pe-ta-te in his hand. He sat resting his back to the tree on the mat he was carrying. "I got new shorts and don't want them dirty. I am Raibabu's son."

"I know who you are," I interrupted.

He hit a branch with a rock that he flung from his slingshot and a guava fell. He bit into it and started talking while spitting the seeds out. "I am a bit older than you and I go to the school over here."

"I don't go to school," I told him.

"I know that. I don't like school much either but my father wants me to go. Just the other day the math teacher in the middle of the class asked me to get some snuff for him from the store across the street and gave me some money for it. I don't like him anyway. But then I thought he would flunk me if I didn't do what he had asked me to do and so reluctantly I went. But after I went to the store I bought just a little snuff and filled up the rest of his container with road dust. I was going to put some manure in it but then he would have smelled it."

"No! What happened after that?"

"You know, the guy puts the snuff inside his nostrils and not inside the cheeks as some other folks do. I saw him take out his nasty handkerchief to blow his nose after he stuck a pinch of the stuff up his nose. I guess it won't kill him. I must have gotten the mixture right because he couldn't even tell!"

Lalu must have bit into a bitter part of the skin because he made a kind of funny face. I reached into my pocket and offered him the last piece of dried mango paste I had been carrying in my pocket. "I really like it. Did your grandma make it?"

"Yes. She makes the juice from the mangoes and places it on a flat thali (plates made of steel or bronze) and then she places it in the sun with a cover on it to keep the flies away. It takes about four days for it to be dry. Have you ever seen it being made?"

"No, I haven't."

Most kids knew about Lalu. He was a rather pesky and pertinacious character. But if he was your friend you could always count on him. He chewed sugarcane in the class sometimes. The teachers ran out of options of punishments.

They placed pencils between his fingers and squeezed them as a punishment for his offensive behavior. He never even cried. The principal once had to hit him with a cane on extended palms giving him significant bruising of his hands. He had come home that day and told his dad that he was climbing a coconut tree and had slipped. Raibabu would come to Grandpa and complain. "I don't know what to do with my son. He is stubborn and just won't listen."

"Give him little extra time. Different boys grow at different rates just like two mangoes in the same tree often do not ripen on the same day. We have to be examples to these youngsters. Why don't you have him come to the evening class in my house?" Grandpa told him. Lalu came to an evening class. His job was to make sure that the petromax lamps remained lit and memorize couple of lines from Tagore's poem:

Jaadi Shabai Thake Mukh Feerai
Shabai Kare Bhay
Tabe Ekla Cholore
    (If everyone turns their face
    And if everyone is afraid to participate.
    But if you have a strong conviction
    Then go at it alone my brother!)

Raibabu worked as a clerk in Calcutta. Those days being a clerk was considered an accomplishment. In free India jobs were scarce. Clerical jobs provided a gateway to the boss who had the authority to attempt to get some jobs done. Often there were two or three clerks before one could reach the congressman or the mayor. Clerks felt powerful of their position as gatekeepers of progress. People knew that they had to bribe the clerks if they wanted to get somewhere. Raibabu was a clerk in the income tax office that checked on local businesses. It was believed by some that Raibabu had become wealthy because he singlehandedly blocked the progress of the treasury of Bengal and promoted a culture of corruption that is second to none. In Grandpa's waiting room library he was a unique book indeed. He would pontificate that "Our business people are not doing enough to make the country go forward. This is our time now. We must pick up the challenge and move forward." Grandpa never commented after him.

Lalu said to Grandpa, "I want to be a leader of the country but I don't know how. Ever since my sister's death I can't think right. Everything makes me angry. Just at the slightest provocation I feel like yelling."

"Why don't you read about Alexander the Great and Raja Ram Mohon Ray and tell us about them. You have the character for a leader. You are tenacious, persistent and most importantly you want to make a change. You have your battles just like they did. I will get you started. Go in the house and get the books."

We listened as Lalu continued, "Manabendra Nath Roy, his actual name was Naren Bhattacharya. Now, he tried for a long time to overthrow the British by terrorist activities. He was the leader of the Indian Communist party till 1947. He became a friend to Lenin by going to the Soviet Union and when he tried to return to India from the Soviet Union the British captured him and placed him in jail. He had changed his name when he went to San Francisco."

"Why did he change his name, Grandpa?"

"I don't really know. I can tell you though those terrorist activities do not get you anywhere except that you end up killing a whole lot of people and ultimately nobody will support you."

"Dactarbabu, my problem is that I get angry very easily and then everybody makes fun of me. I always feel that everybody is treating me like I am not as good as I should be or something. I don't even know why I am angry or what I am doing until I have done something for which I feel ashamed later. Then I get angrier at that person. I know you told me to think but instead of saying that I am sorry I just act out. I really think I do feel sorry but I don't like to say it. I wish someone would understand that I don't mean to act out. I guess I want to say that please hold me or hug me but I am too embarrassed to say it. I feel like no one is on my side."

"You know, Lalu, I am glad you told me that. You are a lovely person. Most people don't have as much understanding about themselves as you do. We all have problem communicating. Some people think that we can communicate through anger. In reality they do not think that at all and it is not a conscious act. Deep inside us we all want to be loved and understood without saying it." Grandpa just knew how to say stuff to make someone feel good.

"You have seen how the monkeys hold each other as one picks bugs etc. from the hair while the other sits quiet. You see, my dear, we all would love someone else to pick the bugs out of our skin without having to ask for it. But only a few are blessed with such an opportunity. Next time watch how the mother cat licks the kittens while the kittens just purr and curl up into a ball and go in circles in joy. Anger is an emotion and a natural one and it is expressed in many different ways. But whenever it is used as a tool of communication it engenders in others exactly the opposite of what is being sought. The best way to express anger is to admit the feeling to the self and then retaliate not in a volatile manner but with a calm gentility. It is the hardest thing to do but you will get the desired result. Either the offending person will be more aggravated because you are not getting angry or will recognize that you have control. Remember the person who is angry first may have the same need as you do."

Lalu said, "You remember Kalu, don't you? You fixed his nose and lips. That kid even cut his tongue when he fell." Grandpa acknowledged that he knew all about the event that led to Kalu's injury. "I really didn't mean to hurt him. But he said something nasty about my dad and I asked him to take it back." Grandpa listened and I sat quietly because I knew nothing about this event. Lalu said that Kalu might have been correct in his assertions, "but I didn't want to hear it. Kalu was insulting."

"But your actions didn't help Kalu to gain any more respect for your father than he had prior to your punch," Grandpa said in a kind voice. Actually Lalu had beaten up Kalu although it was said that his injuries were a result of a fall.

Kalu was feeling angry and subsequently he had ascribed Lalu with titles of some non-complimentary names and then he sat on the roof of the garage to get away. It suddenly started pouring down rain and when Kalu tried to come down from the roof Lalu removed the ladder so that Kalu couldn't come down the regular way after he had gone up and hit him. So he tried to come down the side holding onto a tile and placing his feet on the window when the tile gave way and he fell and cut his tongue and bruised his arms. "You know nobody would have known that I did anything to do with him if the kid hadn't fallen down. It is his fault!"

"Today I am going to tell you two stories and you determine who is at fault." Grandfather continued, "A father runs to get the doctor because his child is sick. While running he slips and falls on the road and breaks his arm as another guy riding a bike trips over this man at the sudden unexpected event occurring in his path. Who is at fault? In another scenario a woman yells at her husband and then the husband in anger as a way of venting his feelings goes and hits the cow for not coming back to the barn quick enough. During this process he backs into the mule inadvertently and the animal being startled kicks the man so hard that he develops a broken rib and has trouble breathing. Who is at fault?" It was not till I grew older did I understand the value of explanations given by Grandpa using examples of our village life.

Grandmother gave us some payesh, rice pudding that she had just prepared. After eating that I went inside the house to eat what I really liked. Grandmother always saved the wok for me after the cooking was finished because I liked to eat the scrapings from the pan after milk was boiled to make payesh. She gave me a spoon. I sat there and scratched the pan to get the sweet, mildly burnt milk that was always stuck. I loved the sweet thin edges of milk feathers. I always ate them as I licked the spoon and made sounds of satisfaction.

Lalu came next evening and was excited to deliver his speech. He went to the tube well and pumped himself a drink of water and then stood in the middle of the waiting room. He invited us to sit down on our chowki, flat bed covered with a mattress and sheet, in our living room. Grandpa was proud of Lalu. Lalu knew that. "Ram Mohon Roy was the founder of Hindu-Protestant movement. He started the Brahmo Samaj. He had translated the Upanishads, the Hindu scriptures, in Bengali and that made him unpopular among the religious people. It was then accepted that this text was to be read only in Sanskrit and only the people of high religious authority had the ability to interpret it in a more understandable language."

"You know that is the way Catholics believe. Only the priest reads the Bible and makes interpretations. People of Islamic faith also believe that only the imams, Muslim religious leaders, are allowed to explain the Koran," Grandpa interjected. "Ram Mohan challenged the traditional culture and introduced the concept of a Supreme God, beyond human knowledge who supports the universe. The omniscient and omnipotent God is to be understood by faith. You cannot rationalize God's existence. He was before us and He will be after us. Ram Mohon was a scholar of Vedas and translated the Vedanta Sutras in English, Hindi and Bengali. The Baptist missionaries became his friends and he translated the New Testament in Bengali. He had vehement arguments with the missionaries about the supremacy of Christ. He vigorously argued the Unitarian anti-trinity position.

"You see, many of the missionaries are trying to convert the poor people by telling them that Jesus could make seven loaves of bread grow to feed four thousand people and therefore if they became Christians they will not be hungry anymore. The uneducated people do not understand that this is figurative language and not to be taken literally. We must understand that people have gone to heaven before Christ came to earth because the heaven existed as long as God has existed. It is also believed that Christ as St. Issa might have visited India during his youthful years. He might have gathered knowledge from the gurus in India and he possibly preached here. There are many issues that we can talk about the similarities of Hindu faith and the Christian faith. Even Christ asked his disciples 'Who touched me?' when an unclean woman touched him in a crowd. Surely, being God he knew who had touched him. Therefore this has to be taken figuratively.

"People who were inspired by God wrote the Bible but there might have been issues where the disciples were possibly trying to proselytize. I am not a Bible scholar but I can tell you what I have read. It is most unlikely that Jesus said, 'If you are not with me, you are against me.' He was a loving God in the form of a person. Although he might have said, 'I came to put not peace but a sword.' It has to be taken in proper perspective. He meant for us to have courage to believe in Him and He was the greatest peacemaker. He said, 'Love your enemy.' Our Gita teaches us to be generous and courageous. As a matter of fact when Lord Krishna told Arjuna to fight because that was the will of the God it is not much different than what St. Ignatius Loyola said many years later. 'Lord, teach me to be generous. Teach me to serve you as you deserve, to give and not to count the cost, to fight and not to heed the wounds, to toil and not to seek for rest, to labor and not to ask for reward—save that of knowing that I will do your will.'"

When I grew older I realized that Grandpa didn't believe in the idea of the free will and much of Calvinist theology. He had explained that the Puritan dogmas make a person believe that a man can achieve salvation only through God's grace rather than through good works. He said that in Hinduism we have many deities but only one Supreme God. The best way to be religious is to help fellow human beings and by being kind to all creation.

Lalu ran outside to the hibiscus tree for a few minutes and then drank water from the pump and spat a bit of it through his teeth and started again. We never thought much of these actions being abnormal. Folks who live in villages always used the outdoors for such actions. He continued. "Ram Mohan opposed Suttee, ritual death of widows on the funeral pyres of the dead husbands, which was rather prevalent all over India."

"What is Suttee, Grandpa?"

"This custom started many years ago in India when the Brahmins and subsequently other men took more than one woman as wife. This was possibly a solution of the time owing to the fact that there were more women than there were men in the society. The custom of polygamy has been abolished among most people although it still continues in the villages. However, on many occasions older men married several younger girls because it was considered improper for women to not have been with a man in matrimony. There was a financial incentive for men in the form of a dowry as though men were rescuing these 'wretched women.'

"Then when the men died all these women became widows and instead of providing opportunities for them for education and remarriage, if they wished, they were thrown in the funeral pyre against their wish with the dead men."

"Did they throw the man in the fire if one of the women died during child birth or such?"

"No."

Lalu became visibly angry. "I am going to put a stop to that. I love my mom and I don't want her to be thrown in fire just because Dad had died."

"That won't happen here. Thank God, the British put a stop to that."

Grandpa continued, "There are a group of people in America that call themselves Mormons and some of them have more than one wife. I have not read much about them." It was much later I learnt that the Mormon church has not supported the view of polygamy for more than a hundred years though there are renegade believers who still practice it.

Lalu picked up where he had left. "The British imposed censorship on the Calcutta press. Ram Mohan was publishing two newspapers that were actively protesting the British and the rights of the people were emphasized according to the spirit of the American and French revolution. He emphasized the need for western education to get ahead in modern society and learning of Sanskrit at the same time as well. He attracted many important people in the Brahmo-Samaj Society who actively participated in unpopular social reforms. Ram Mohan died in England among his Unitarian friends."

Lalu came to play marbles with me often. We had become friends. One day we were sitting next to the pond and just throwing rocks to make ripples when Lalu asked, "Can you keep a secret?" I nodded. "This is really serious. I loved Joy. She was only two years older than me." I said that I had never met her. "I know. I don't know what happened. But she started throwing up. She stopped going to school. She was a beautiful girl. She just stopped talking to everyone. Joy used to run and swim in the river much like Madhabi does these days. She was not shy with anybody. I don't know why my father wouldn't bring her to see your grandpa. I thought she might have had worms or such. There is one thing that really bothers me and I have never told anyone. Not even to God. But he probably knows."

Lalu and I walked over and picked up a tamarind that had fallen on the ground from the tree as he were talking. Lalu's mouth was all juicy and he lay down and kept talking while looking at the sky. I never liked big punctuations. "So what happened?" I said impatiently.

"It's probably nothing."

"Why don't you tell me?"

He rolled over to the other side. Now I couldn't see his face anymore. "Well, I came home early that day and was walking towards the barn. Joy didn't go to school that day because she wasn't feeling well." He paused. I choked on my saliva from the tamarind. It was too sour. Lalu got up and started walking towards the papaya tree and grabbed its trunk. Suddenly he got angry. "I feel like shaking the tree to death. I want all its branches to break and all the fruits to fall down and I want the tree to die." He sat down. "You know, I saw my dad coming out of the barn and he told me not to go there. I went in the house and looked for Joy. But I couldn't find her. Then when it was getting dark I kept yelling for her all over the field and it was then that I heard someone whimpering next to the haystack outside the barn. I tried to hold Joy but she told me not to touch her.

"Joy was a sweetheart. She and I used to race back from the school. She could read like you can. But nobody knew it. She helped my mother to cook. She could cut vegetables just the way my mother wanted her to do. She would giggle whenever my mother would talk about her marriage. But secretly I know she was looking forward to getting married and have a baby all of her own. She loved to run on the train track and sometimes we would place some coins to get them in odd flat shapes.

"She sometimes stood in the track and she would make the engine driver blow the horn before she would get off the track. And one time she had them put the brakes on and only then she would move away. The men from the caboose would yell at her but she didn't care. She was just fun loving and she would run away. We would sometimes walk on each side of the train track and she could walk on the track without falling down. She could do that sometimes for more than a hundred feet. She hated it that she couldn't ride the bicycle because she was wearing a sari. She would at times play dress-up like my mother and put a magnolia on her head tucked between her braided long black hairs. I used to tell her that she looked just as pretty as my mom did. Mom used to say that her eyes looked like that of a fawn. She beat me in spelling but I loved her so. Mom told her to be careful because she was becoming a woman. I didn't know what that meant except that she had little breasts. But she didn't care and she didn't think that to be much of an inconvenience. She was just like one of us. She could chew sugarcane and spit just like I could. One day we saw a beehive and she decided to light a torch with kerosene wrapped around a stick underneath it. I never ran so fast in my life when the bees chased me. I am the one that got bit because I had tripped and she said that she could run faster than I could. I do miss her. I sometimes let her win but I never did let her know that. I loved to watch her beam.

"Every time I talk to your grandpa I feel great. I don't know what it is. I like the stuff that he talks about. I like it when he says religious stuff like that 'I fear no evil for thou art with me.' I don't quite understand it but somehow I feel that God is with me all the time. Whenever I am with your grandpa I feel stronger. I don't get angry as much anymore. I guess other people have had bad stuff happen to them as well. But Dactarbabu lets you express your grief and then I feel I am free to move on. You know Joy is always going to be with me. But it is OK for me to be happy. But I get angry when I say that. I sometimes feel like I am not supposed to be happy. I should have saved her. It is like I was in a box and I was beating on the walls that had closed around me. But now I am outside the box and I can go inside if I want. But I don't have to be there all the time. I wish I had a grandpa like that. But you don't care that I am here do you?"

"No."

"Sometimes I want to beat up my dad real bad. Just kidding! Some afternoons when you take a nap I come and visit with Dactarbabu. He is funny. He just hugs me and tells me that I am going to be a leader someday. He likes to drink coconut water. Do you know?"

"Yes."

"It has been a few years back when my mother started getting bruises on her face. My dad said he didn't know why they wouldn't go away. But at times we would hear them arguing and then there would be quiet. My dad at that time was coming to Dactarbabu to get some shots every day. I hate shots so I never came with him. Anyway, that is when most of the yelling started in the house. One day I peeked through the window to check on the turmoil and saw that my dad was pulling my mother by the hair. He had a rolling pin in his hand.

"I quickly covered my face with the sheet and made sure that the candle was off. I didn't want him to know that I saw anything. My father never brought my mother to the doctor for bruises. I had asked her about it and she had told me that she falls down and her balance is bad. She kept cooking and cleaning. She washed the clothes and dried them in the field. Joy helped her fold the clothes.

"I thought Dactarbabu was the only doctor here but my dad brought someone else to see her one day when she had a broken rib or such and she could hardly breathe. He had told my mother to stay in bed. My mother was in bed all the time and then we heard that she had developed pneumonia. She had fever and the other doctor came again and talked to my father.

"Joy was having some problems with her mood. She would be fine at one moment and then suddenly would start crying and run away and hide. One day when I came home I felt that the air around me was stiff and heavy. My neighbors were calm but the dog was barking. The birds seem to be quiet. The girl next door came running to me and pulled me by the arms. I ran to the train station only to find the police constables surrounding a square area on the track. Panuda said that the driver didn't have a chance to stop. Just as the train pulled out of the station Joy had soaked her sari in kerosene and lit it and had walked out in front of the train. I lost a part of me, except I didn't know at that time how important Joy was to me, or how much I loved her. I was numb. I actually didn't believe or didn't want to believe. I miss her every day."

Lalu kept weeping. I didn't know what to say except to hold Lalu. I always thought that when I didn't know what to say the best thing was to hug. That was the way I expressed my feelings of loving. Grandpa always held me when I couldn't say what I wanted to say. Lalu and I went to the ghat near the river. We saw the flames of burnt people from distance. We didn't care to know who was being burnt. We could see the flames against the darkness of night as they tried to reach the sky at times. We saw splinters of fire that clapped in the dark sky as they climbed high in joy and then just became insignificant ashes and indistinguishable from the surrounding darkness.

"Though we travel the world over to find the beautiful, we must carry it with us or we find it not," said Ralph Waldo Emerson. Remember that Rabindranath Tagore said, *"Dekha Hai Nai Chakku Melia Ghar Hote Sudhu Dui Pa Felia Ekti Dhaner Sisher Upaar Ekti sishir Bindu"* ("I have traveled to many places but I failed to see the beauty of a dew drop crowning the rice blade at my own backyard").

Nadubabu had dinner with us that night. He picked up some fennel seeds from the bowl in the living room and started chewing them as he sat down. Manu had already prepared the hubble-bubble with fresh tobacco. I sat on the floor and listened to the gurgling sound of the bathing of the tobacco smoke as the two men sucked on the two long pipes coming out of a "smoking genie lamp." The smoke slowly exuded from their mouths and nostrils covering the half-shut somnolent eyes and snaked its way to the door. I had taken a couple of puffs in the past. I hated the taste but I loved the smell and somehow the whole picture of this act made it look ethereal to me.

I had read many stories of Alibaba and Scherezade's stories of the Arabian Nights. Those days I liked such scenes because it reminded me of opulence, extravagance and cheerfulness. I had felt similarly when I had seen the pictures of King Akbar sitting in his court smoking a hubble-bubble surrounded by scantily clad women dancing to the music of Shenai. It made me feel important because I felt as though I was part of a regal scene.

Grandpa hardly ever participated in any act that even closely resembled expensive cheerfulness or wasteful abundance, and certainly nothing that I thought was glorious or important. *"Vidya dadati binayang"* (true education teaches humility), he said. One of the greatest teachers, Jesus Christ, taught humility by washing the feet of his disciples. Samson, one of the strongest of men, lacked humility and that led to his death.

Nadubabu was just about asleep with the round pillow under his right arm when his wife entered the room. Her head was covered with the edge of her sari but her lips were visible and red from the stain of paan (betel leaf) that she had been chewing. Manu came to refill the charcoal and the tobacco but Grandpa sent him away, meaning it was getting late. They had just become grandparents. Roopa, their daughter, had a son about fifteen days back and today she was allowed to come out of her isolation. Grandma had invited the new grandparents. It was the custom of the time that after a woman had a baby she stayed in a room by herself for about fifteen days before she came to be with her husband. The maid or Dai took the baby back and forth to the birthing room and the baby slept with the mother all the time during this period of reflection and isolation. This amount of time allowed the woman to gain strength after the long period of pregnancy, Grandpa had explained to me. However, I do not know if the custom was designed primarily to provide protection to the women from the potential infliction of physical pain from the demands of men.

The neighborhood suddenly awoke to the sounds of drums and sticks beating on baskets. The Hijras knew that today was the day to come to the house of the newborn. The mother and the father of the baby handed out laddus and sandesh and nuts to the Hijras and they left knowing that there was no addition to their clan. It was explained to me that some families abandoned the child if it was born without adequate gender differentiation. The child was raised in the Hijras community in a clandestine manner because they were considered social outcastes. The children underwent mutilating surgical procedures in the hands of untrained personnel and an artificial vagina was prepared. Many died from infection after the operation and those that lived wore female clothes without any hormone management to mask the male features. Many made a living as sex workers and others stole or participated in activities of an antisocial nature.

As I grew older I was saddened and quite upset with my grandpa for not doing anything to thwart such a heinous social practice. I was never encouraged to learn about this condition and improve the lives of our brothers and sisters in this area. This I did not understand. I thought Grandpa was a very socially conscious man and why did he tolerate this social injustice? Why did he not ignite the spirit of the children to help the unfortunate?

It was not till later that I understood that this attitude is pervasive in the Indian society. There is as if shunning of the imperfect, particularly those that are visibly little more imperfect than some of us. Somehow, as a child I was never exposed to the fact that we have a responsibility towards the unfortunate or the underprivileged. It was only when I came to my dad's house that I realized the responsibility of the privileged.

My dad demonstrated it through his acts of brotherhood. I believe that my grandfather lacked the intellectual as well as moral elasticity to stand up for some social injustices even if they were blatantly visible. Yet in some other areas he was most charitable. I do not know that if this was due to the fact that Grandmother dictated some aspect of his overt behavior. Grandmother never saw the shadow of a Muslim or a person of inferior caste in our house. Grandpa avoided confrontations. I hated Grandpa only once when he called me outspoken and vociferous. I forgave him for his outburst of emotion.

I asked Anna if she wanted me to stop. "No. Please continue."

One time I had said that I wanted to be a specialist in leprosy. I remembered that my uncle was visibly upset and didn't want me to talk about it. I sat in the hospital corridor of Miraj, The Wanless hospital and wept forty years later. I met the professor who is treating patients afflicted with leprosy. He has brought such awareness among people that in the clinic I saw a thirteen-year-old girl with a numb patch on her forehead that had been present only less than a month. We were able to get the dermatologist to see her on the same day and treat her with medication and I know that she would be cured! There are more than ten thousand people afflicted with this illness in that community. I, as a child was never encouraged to be the initiator of such a program. I felt ashamed that I was not there with the professor helping from the beginning in such an important task. I wanted to be the person who could have initiated the prevention. I wanted to teach the children not to use the roadside drains as toilets and thus prevent the fly bites and the scratching that follows. I understand that at times that allows the entrance of the Lepra Bacilii through the abraded skin. I wanted to be the doctor to be able to teach them the value of proper ventilation and how to avoid the Lepra Bacilii that can survive longer in moist and damp places. I wanted to teach my brothers and sisters and care for them as God's children.

I admired and expressed my gratitude to the lady from Skopje who came to Calcutta to be a teacher and became Mother Teresa. She loved those people that nobody cared to love because it was too risky or dangerous. As I grew older I found that it was rather common in many aspects of Indian society at that time to not encourage youngsters to take risks in life. It was easier to be a secretary and grow up to have secure and safe jobs! I don't believe that my grandpa espoused this view but as I grew older and looked back I found that Grandpa was never too aggressive and nor was he a risk taker. I kind of secretly wished that he would have been different.

Grandmother always wore a cavalcade of bangles on both of her forearms. One of them was to signify the consummation of marriage. This one had an elephant's head on it. The rest were just jewelry to adorn the forearm and signify that she had insurance, i.e. gold, the only true insurance available those days to women.

We knew from the sound of her bangles before she came into the room. We didn't have any curtains at the doors or windows. Younger girls wore bangles of glass often of different colors to match the borders of different saris worn on different occasions. Grandma wore a blouse but never had a bra but she covered her breasts with her sari. The younger girls always wore blouses underneath their saris showing just a bit of their waist. I always wanted to see more of their bodies as a youngster but the only time I was successful was when I would ask some of them to play marbles and I could peek above the blouse. I always would get excited to see the erect nipples of the girls inside the blouse. I assumed that I was deprived because my mother had died when I was only six months old and therefore I was never given the opportunity of fondling my mother's breast during nursing.

So one day when I was twelve I convinced Joni that I really needed to get a feel for a woman's bosom so that I would grow up normally. She was two years older than I was and had two beautiful peaches on her chest with little cherries. I knew that. I had watched her once right after her bath when she hadn't finished drying herself completely. Her white blouse displayed her beautiful silhouette. She was at first shy but then we had agreed to sit behind the bushes next to the tamarind tree. She would keep her eyes closed with a tamarind in her mouth and I was going to quickly feel her while she would salivate owing to the tamarind. I got an erection. I didn't close my eyes. Joni was so embarrassed that she didn't see me for two days after that. I saw her after many years. I told her that she helped me to be a man. She hugged me and we talked about days that were long gone but left us with joyful memories that only we could share forever. It is funny how we develop different emotions during childhood. I told her that I was angry all the time for a while because I was angry with my dad but couldn't tell him anything. I had become short-tempered. I often blew up at the slightest provocation, imaginary or real. It took me a long time and discipline that I had learnt from my grandpa to get over this intolerance.

One day I was sitting in my school tennis court waiting for Banu to show up. I realized that I was getting angry because he was a bit late. I had practiced in my mind that I must not say anything; we can all be late sometime. I served the ball real hard and said that I wasn't sure at what time we were supposed to be here. He said something that I didn't hear because I was busy planning what I was going to say next. I remembered hearing my grandpa. We can only control our own behavior. How we react in each situation determines our position in the life of the other person. All of us want to be liked. This is the first time I realized one of my major shortcomings. Impatience! I was impatient with myself and also with others. This deficiency has haunted me all my life. But I always hear that voice that provides me with extra tolerance. I have realized now that most things in life are not as urgent as finding the correct clip because I am not living the life of a ruptured-aneurysm fixer!

My father cherished the hospitality and the acclaim of his neighbors and friends. But one day during the night when I had gotten up to go to the bathroom I thought I saw him in a compromising position. I hated this man from then on in my subconscious. I never said it out loud. I didn't want to hate my dad. I wanted to think that my dad could do nothing wrong.

Later on I remembered that in the school during the initial hazing period I woke up one morning and all my hair was matted. At first I didn't know what it was. But one of my dorm mates explained the source of the substance. A jeet became a friend. He was a bit older than I was and he took a liking for me. After this I was not angry any more with my dad because I decided it was no big deal. But the scene involving my dad had upset me and also the fact that I couldn't talk to anyone about it.

Joni thought that it was crazy but not unnatural. She helped me to think in the proper perspective. "Don't worry about what you saw, he is only human." It didn't take me long to understand that most women are a lot more mature than I am. During the first few weeks of hazing I saw that a boy was made to walk down the hall balancing a lantern using an unusual support system. This episode made me understand that getting angry was not going to help me. I just had to ride the wave. My feelings about my dad, which were rather negative at times, helped me eventually to conquer my anger and also understand some of the causes of anger among our youth. I talked to myself. I created the coach that sat inside my head. It often encouraged me rather than criticize. I believe, with the help of my inner coach I often interrupted and modified the stream of negative cognition that might have led me to develop maladaptive behavior.

The escapades of my father in areas of personal matters were not for me to judge and possibly I had expected too much from him as an example of moral fortitude. I did not like that someone else had gained advantage over me while living in our house! At least that is what I felt.

It was one of the usual days of summer at Calcutta. Few of us were flying a kite in the field next to our house. My kite went high. However, one of the other kids dragged his ground-glass roughened string against the string that was holding my kite high up in the sky. His expert jerky gesture detached my kite and made my string limp like an impotent candle whose wax runs down the side following no predictable pattern. It swung ineffectively as it fell from the sky and then the kite flew on top of the neighbor's roof. No sooner had I climbed on the roof Mr. H walked to the ladder and took it away out of meanness to be a tease. My temper was short and I yelled out few expletives that were audible to every neighbor. I was summoned into the house after I jumped off the roof. My dad proceeded to beat me with his sandals without even listening to the details of the incident. I sat in the corner of my room and whimpered not because of the physical pain but for the pain that my dad failed to see.

It was long after that I realized that many men from the Indian subcontinent suffer from DHAT syndrome. They come to the doctor and complain of general weakness because they are not supposed to complain of emotional difficulty and impotence. These symptoms often result from ill-repressed hostility, inability to express unfulfilled love and failure to communicate the need to vent. Thank God! I had no problem with that.

I was telling Anna that I was concerned that I had such a small head in comparison to many of my friends' heads. Anna indicated that it didn't matter, my stuff was compact inside and I probably had less packing material! Some persons have larger heads but it is full of water. She continued that she had read some material that Dr. Keith Devlin had written in relation to head size. Dr. Devlin believed that our ancestors' increase in brain size was not necessarily owing to the acquisition of language. He thought that it could have been owing to the selective advantage conferred by a richer understanding of relationships among different objects in an increasingly complex social world.

Anna continued and said the size of the head was not necessarily related to level of intelligence. And that made me feel better. She said for me to continue with the story that I was telling her. I said OK.

Jaguda came after work as we were sitting in our living room. Jaguda washed his feet and returned after using the facilities. Grandma commented on Jaguda's attitudes about life. Jaguda did not respond because he knew that Grandma knew best! Jaguda had a busy day.

He was an accountant and traveled to Calcutta every day. The train ride was by itself a memorable event. He said that the trains are so full that people usually hang from the doors. Hawkers get on the train at every station and try to sell items of daily needs such as combs, different alternative medicine for hemorrhoids, gold ornaments that may or may not be authentic, and medicine for heartburn and herbal products that are aphrodisiacs. There is an occasional person who starts singing some antediluvian songs in a voice that is distinctively his. Neither the lyrics nor the rhythms can be associated with any other singer known to the passengers. This person is usually blind and he makes room after squeezing through an opening between the shirts and the sweat of the mass of tired people who are packed like sardines inside the train. He understands his audience, i.e. he stands in front of people who are sitting down so that he can hold the railing on the side of a seat. A ten-year-old boy or a girl that accompanies him stands by the side and makes music through a suctioning noise of the mouth while clapping with two pieces of metal or hitting two rocks between the fingers. He has a limited time before the next station arrives and he moves into the next compartment guided by his young companion.

In India hawkers are rather polite. If by chance a guy selling chanachur (spicy lentils mixed with peanuts) gets to the same part of the compartment where someone else is selling their ware he always waits till the other person finishes. The guy selling the heartburn medicine coordinates his visit after the spicy lentil guy! Jaguda said that at times there is a guy selling medicine for amebiasis as well. The fellow selling the gold ornaments was rather creative. Inside this packed train he started yelling about the quality of his gold. "This is a twenty-four-carat gold," he said in a convincing tone. "It is pure," he continued.

Jaguda continued in dismay, "I was sitting facing many signs that were stuck to the wall of the inside of the compartment. There were signs all over the compartment about the methods of escaping in case of fire. 'Lighting of any kind of fire inside the compartment is strictly prohibited,' the sign said. That did not deter him at all. He flicked his lighter and started a fire on a stick and held the gold chain in the flame to prove his point that pure gold was not going to melt or stain in that heat."

Jaguda stopped to take a breath. "Soon after him arrived the agarbatti, incense guy. He was holding in his hand two or three little sticks with blackened tips that spread smoke and sweet aroma of clove and cardamom in to the entire area. 'This is the world's best agarbatti,' he announced. This is the last chance to buy these and he suggested that we should buy these to surprise our wives after dinner by lighting these in the bedroom. 'The rest is up to you. I can't help you with everything,' he said.

"As I grew older I realized that such blatant disregard for the law and endangerment of the citizens is very common in India. It is neither that we don't want to help nor is it that we are numb.

Jaguda continued, "There are just too many people with too much suffering. So we try to be entertained rather than be disturbed. We were all quiet. All of us were often overwhelmed with suffering. Instead of crying all the time we have developed different strategies for coping with stress. Our coping mechanism for the stress of not being able to change the torment of the people is to allow them to make a living by selling soaps and candles in running trains." My uncle said that he would like to see that the government would secretly add some sort of medicine in the drinking water so that all the women would be infertile for next ten years. Grandpa made no comment. He just walked away.

On my sixteenth birthday I woke up to find a note from my dad: "Today you are a man and I will treat you like a friend and equal. Here is a bottle of Scotch whiskey and a pack of 555 cigarettes. Let us share it. In life only drink and smoke the good stuff and don't indulge yourself in cheap habits. Lots of love to you and I wish you the best."

At nights when Dad returned home we had the most wonderful conversation. "Why didn't you let me live with you in my earlier years?" I asked.

At first he didn't want to answer. But after a couple of drinks he said, "Your mother was told that if she carried you to term she was going to die. She was told by her obstetrician to have an abortion because she had developed tubercular peritonitis. However, she chose to have you. She had talked with your grandpa and had asked him to raise you because I would be busy with your older brother and sister and my practice." Dad was tearful.

"I have treated so many patients with tuberculosis since then. But Streptomycin didn't become available till 1944 in India." I hugged him and asked him if he resents me for loss of his wife. "You are the replacement for my wife and I love you much."

"Why didn't you remarry? You were widowed at such a young age."

"I was afraid that my new wife would like to have children of her own. I didn't want any more children. Moreover, in our situation I was afraid that someone might marry me for money. I didn't want to be unhappy in marriage."

We enjoyed the rest of the evening as father and son and we developed a special friendship that I never felt before. A curtain lifted. I felt that I loved my father more than ever. This is the first time I learnt why my grandma would start weeping every time I asked any questions about my mother. I was the substitute for her only daughter that they had promised to raise. They had made a pact. They never divulged the secret to me with the fear that it might disrupt my life and my happiness.

I realized how much they loved me to have kept that as a secret from me. I don't believe I could have made such a sacrifice!

I told Anna that my only negative experience during the whole trip was at Sidney. I needed certain papers to be notarized urgently and so I had walked into one of the banks of Sidney. As I was talking to the lady who was sitting at a desk a gentleman who claimed to be the manager looked at me and then told her to not sign my papers. I told him that I could become a customer for a few days. I of course wasn't wearing a tie. I looked sun burnt, with a funny hat and a walking stick and a backpack with a pipe sticking out from a water container.

He was about five feet seven inches tall, and weighed about 170 pounds. I walked across the street to a different bank after talking to the mailman in the post office. I got my papers signed and mailed them immediately. The alleged banker's posture, stance, and the tone of his voice indicated to me that he was possibly impotent and frustrated. I thought that he might have been unsuccessful as an automobile transportation advisor of pre-owned vehicles and possibly had dealt with many distrusting customers.

I went to the local grocery and asked about this man and the lady confirmed the previous occupation of the so-called banker. I felt sad that he didn't help a traveler. I didn't want to give him a lesson about the Good Samaritan but I knew that America was large enough for thoroughbreds as well as donkeys!

During my walk I had planned carefully my diet on the road. I ate vegetables of some nature daily but mostly very high protein and a bit of carbohydrate daily. I was not afraid of getting tapeworms or such because I ate well-cooked meat. It is known that we human beings are either definitive or intermediate hosts to at least three kinds of tapeworms. Professor Pat Shipman wrote in *American Scientist* volume 90 that human beings possibly harbored the tapeworms about 1.7 million years ago and then infected the domestic animals such as dogs. The professor suggested that human beings were carnivores and scavengers for a while when they moved from Africa to Eurasia. The only food I avoided was shellfish. I was walking through the middle of the country and I knew that the fish might not have been fresh. I knew that eating mollusks and oysters has inherent risks. I am not a follower of Leviticus where it clearly says:

"These shall ye eat of all that are in the waters: whatsoever hath fins and scales in the waters, in the seas, and in the rivers, them shall ye eat— whatsoever hath neither fins nor scales in the waters that shall be an abomination unto you."

I don't like to eat mussels because a mussel harvested on any given day will contain whatever was in the water around it that day and that may be virus, E. coli or other bacteria or toxin, and parasites. I knew that hepatitis A and Norwalk virus were not killed by steaming although polio virus died by steaming and most others by cooking. However, the algae that sometimes invaded the shellfish caused serious food poisoning, either paralytic or amnestic kind. I had forgotten the details of oysters and hepatitis B and so I avoided any of these foods. I knew about many harmless bacteria that add color to food such as wine, cheeses, and bread. Professor Betsy Dexter Dyer wrote in *A Field Guide to Bacteria* (Cornell) gram-positive Brevibacterium is found in strong-smelling cheeses that provide the pink color and the bacteria is also a cause for foot odor. I certainly did not need that. My feet were sweaty enough.

I noticed that although it was very hot, there were times when there was a breeze as I had walked into the Wyoming border. I had passed by Bushnell before reaching Pine Bluff. The sign at Bushnell said "Population 126." I met a man who was wearing a Ford hat. So I asked him if there was a Ford factory nearby where he was working. He said it was a gift and he wore it "to keep the sun off." So I gave him a SPAVA hat to wear when he would be washing his car. It was only forty miles to Cheyenne. I spent the night at Gator motel and ate at Wild Horse Restaurant. Josh waited on us. That was his first day as a server in a restaurant. He was seventeen years old. We were patient and he served me steak, potatoes, beans, soup, and an apple strudel, all in less than an hour. I already had half a pint of Jim Beam before that. The restaurant was about a hundred yards from my room where I was going to spend the night. I think I was already asleep when I was walking back to my room after dinner.

I often talked with many people during breakfast. Some were overtly curious about my outfit and the SPAVA van. I recall meeting this wonderful senior couple. After I got to talking he had said that he owned about 2,600 units of trucks. From then on I thought of him every time I saw a truck that said "England" on it. When I returned to Louisville, the office informed me that he had donated a considerable sum of money to help the children.

Next day I walked thirty-two miles and I was eight miles outside of Cheyenne. I spent the night at a Days Inn and ate at a place called Renegade. The quality of food in these small places was not like it was in Nebraska. My feet were swollen and I needed to rest. Anna was with me all day and she wanted me to tell her another story. So I told her about Tibet. She said that would be nice because she never gets an assignment outside the United States.

Story of Tibet

It was in the first part of October one year when Phoebe and I were with three other people that traveled to Mt. Kailash, the most holy mountain for the Hindus as well as the Buddhists. The tour guide had us packed in a van and we rode in it for eight hours from Katmandu till we reached the China border. The road to the border was often not well maintained and curved around a few mountains. The tires on the left side of the van were at the edge of a sheer cliff that fell probably three hundred feet. We had to get off the van for a while because a landslide had blocked the road. We walked through the mud and climbed almost fifteen degrees for an hour. We had to share the narrow makeshift path with goats and donkeys that were coming down to the market below. A few times we had to hold onto the trunks of small trees to allow safe passage to the animals first because the road was not wide enough for all of us in both directions.

Then we boarded the back of an old Chinese truck that stopped at Zung Mu. This was the second Chinese checkpoint where the Chinese officials confiscated all our fresh fruits. The officials proceeded to eat our food while sitting inside the booth. They told us to wait outside while they were allegedly preparing our papers to enter Chinese territory.

Then we boarded a van and traveled for four hours to Nylam. We had left our hotel at 3:30 in the morning and it was almost fourteen hours before we reached the place where we could think about sleeping. Here we spent a night at a "Homely Room" as they were called. The rooms had benches dressed with mattresses that betrayed their age. The sheets complemented the décor of the room and bore the stains left by the previous customers. The room was cold and there was no heater. There was a bowl and a jug full of water for us to wash our face in the morning and a thermos that was alleged to have had hot water for us. But alas, we must have arrived late because the heat from the water had leaked out. The worst part of this arrangement was not that we didn't have any good food but that the sanitary conditions were so poor that it was psychologically revolting and simple personal cleanliness was impossible.

The next fourteen days we spent in tents and the outside temperature was often freezing. We kept warm by hugging each other in our tent. We drove through Lhatse at the road marker 400 kilometers on Nepal-Tibet highway as it was called. It was a dirt road mostly punctuated with chuckholes. We had to take a ferry here and then we entered the river valley and then the flat plateau of Tibet as we traveled for next 1,000 kilometers. We camped at Saga. By then most of us had developed severe sinusitis and or bronchitis because of the mountainous dirt and dried yak dung that we had inhaled all day for several days.

A truck carrying our supplies followed us most of the time except for one day when it had broken down and we had only tea that day. It was so cold outside that every morning the driver had to burn yak dung underneath the truck to place the engine in the starting mode. I believe the oil would gel during the night.

We drove through Coquen. Here we saw some mustang and mountain goats and some semblance of settlement. We had an opportunity to take a bath after seven days in hot spring water that came inside a few bathtubs or at least that is the way it was set up. The nozzle of the pipe that came into the tub was kept shut by a plug made of rotten cloth that had deteriorated. It smelled like the tail of a dead guinea pig that you find under the couch after your son tells you that the pet had been missing for a few days, and you find that its head had been crushed by the leg of the couch somehow.

Then we had stopped at Gertse, a small settlement of maybe ten people that walked around wearing tall yak skin outfits. We camped at a place called Shiquanhe. It had a shopping center that was built by the Chinese. This was no Niemann Marcus. Some of the tourists smoked ganja here and some others just passed out from exhaustion from high altitude and possibly from imagining a few more days of dust inhalation.

Next day we stopped at Lake Mansarovar on our way to Darchen. Lake Mansarovar is the highest freshwater lake in the world at a height of almost 14,500 feet. The reflections of the ice-covered peaks in the green-blue water against the blue October sky was not just spectacular but awesome as well. Ever since I was a child I wanted to visit this lake.

It is considered a holy lake and I had seen a documentary about this area filmed in black and white when I was ten years old. A man from India had visited this place in 1951 and gone through Ladakh and Leh Eastward to reach Mt. Kailash and during his return he had gotten his arm caught in some rock and had to have it amputated. The facilities to reach this lake those days were even more primitive than now. The view of the surrounding was breathtaking (no pun intended).

Next day we reached Darchen, a resting place at an altitude of 16,000 feet. All of us had some headache by now. Here we did not have to camp but we were able to sleep on cold mattresses on the floor with closed doors. There were men and a few dogs that hung around us. The temperature outside was minus ten degrees Fahrenheit and I don't think it was much warmer in the rooms. We all ate less than poor quality food prepared by our guide and driver. We fell asleep shivering after looking at the dismal sanitary situation. There was just a bit of water for cleaning and despite the cold the place smelled like s—t.

Next morning we left early to reach the base camp of Mt. Kailash. This is the holiest mountain of the East. No one is allowed to climb the mountain and therefore we had planned to walk around it or perform Kora as is the accepted local custom. It is believed by the Hindus as well as the Buddhists that sins are washed away here. It was eighteen kilometers from Darchen to the campsite at a height of 19,500 feet. The wind lashed against us and the chill factor was below minus fifteen degrees. I didn't have warm enough clothes nor did Phoebe. We coughed and suffered from headaches.

On our path we saw the bodies of ten people who had died the week before either somewhere else or at that spot. The families either brought them there or they themselves came to lie down and die in this holy place where they had sky burial. There was not much dirt here and we were way above the tree line. The sight of so many dead bodies was intimidating and we stood for a moment to pay respect. I imagined a tall Indian priest in a saffron dhoti standing next to the faithful as they had lain down on the rocks of Kailash. I imagined him facing the east with his eyes closed and pouring from a holy spout, water brought from the River Ganges and reciting the Surya Pronam to cleanse the souls as they passed to the land of eternal peace. The faith is at its highest peak here. Some came to die after doing penance and others for a joyful union with God after privation. This is the land of the supreme holiness. The only sound one hears is the whistling wind and it is through that God speaks to those that believe! There are no distractions here. The rapid heartbeat calms down and is not audible when God's voice comes through!

We met an Indian sadhu who has performed Kora thirty-three times. He was joyful and full of energy. He told us that he had walked the 1,000 kilometers, the distance that we had come in a van. When I reached the campsite I was cold, shivering and beaten by the wind. I was fatigued and worried about my hydration. I had thought that I was acclimatized during the last seven days but I was mistaken. I had to sit in a room that burned yak dung and produced more smoke than fire which rapidly affected my lungs in an unfavorable manner. My appetite was gone and I developed a cough. I knew I was developing mountain sickness.

I tried to sleep on a mattress saved from a diluvial swamp in a room next to a window. I saw the giant mountain as I lay next to the window and had dozed off for a bit. But as I stood up during the night I fainted. Nurse Phoebe and I walked back twelve miles that took us nine hours while carrying our backpack. Phoebe had lost her gloves as we were walking back and neither of us had the strength to walk back to fetch them. She survived by pulling her sleeves down for the next six days. The other three members of our group said that they had walked around the mountain but the guide had gotten sick and had to come down in a hurry. Anyway we all arrived at Katmandu after seventeen days fulfilling our quest for Amrita.

Wyoming Agony

Through Wyoming I had to make all kinds of arrangements to accommodate different drivers of the support van. I was telling Anna as I was walking from Rock Springs that there have been times in my life when reality and fantasy have joined seamlessly into a blur. Sometimes I don't know the difference unless I sit and think about it. Goebbels, the advertisement minister for Hitler, actually did exactly that. He told enough lies that no one could tell which one was lie and which one was real. Anna said that sometimes things that we say may not appear true but that does not mean that they are lies. For example after an auto accident often there is ante-grade and/or retrograde amnesia. However, after recovery when the person involved in the accident hears different stories from different people he often cannot tell what he remembers and what he thinks he remembers and most of the time he cannot distinguish between the two.

Phoebe was driving the support van today and she had joined us last night after driving from Portland, Oregon. Anna asked me what I remembered about our marriage. I continued, "It was at Thorang La Pass, 17,500 feet, where we were married. Our wedding was complete when I saw something move on the other side of the valley. Although I was imagining I still told Phoebe that I had seen a snow leopard that had witnessed the celebration."

I heard from Phoebe. The windshield had cracked and so we needed to get the windshield glue to fix it. She fixed it while I walked. We ate lunch at Exit 150. The sun was hot. I had to change my shirt almost every two hours. The scorching sun and the hot wind from the south had burnt me. I had no idea as to how dark my face had become until the previous night. I had woken up to go to the bathroom and as I walked through the dark room I had to pass in front of the mirror. So I opened my mouth to see my teeth. As I glanced I saw only white teeth and white eyeballs that were looking at me and nothing else was visible. I turned the lights on to be reassured that the rest of me was attached.

Anna showed up when the sun was poking through some clouds and it was like an umbrella that she held on my head for the three hours. I walked rather fast in the last three hours of the day. Anna said, "Hy, do you remember that Secretariat is the only horse in the Derby race that ran faster during the last quarter of the race?"

I said, "Yes, I know. I saw the race on television too when I came home. There was only Secretariat on the screen."

By now I had walked more than forty-one marathons. I always got a second wind in the afternoon. I had walked over the Continental Divide, 7,168 feet high. I learnt about the plateaus of Madison, Gallatin and Yellowstone.

I had walked more than sixty miles west of Rocksprings. The lady who owns the Super 8 Motel in Cheyenne, Ms. C, is most wonderful. She is of British origin. She was very kind to me. Her motel is at Exit 358. I had talked to the Rotarians in this town.

Anna asked me if I knew of any other club prior to the formation of the Rotary club from which the Rotarians might have gotten the idea. I knew the answer, I think. "The Rotary club started in Chicago around 1905 by five people from different backgrounds who decided to meet to make changes in the society and they rotated in the houses of different members and thus the name Rotarians.

"The Lunar Society of Birmingham started meeting on a Monday nearest to a full moon so they could find their way home in the moon light. These were a small yet powerful group of people of eighteenth-century England. The Napoleonic war had ended and England had a powerful naval force. At that time England was possibly the most prosperous nation in the world. These five men who discussed politics, religion, science, nature and industry were James Watt, Erasmus (Darwin's grandfather), Priestley, Wedgwood, and Matthew Bolton. James Watt was the inventor of the steam engine and Matthew Bolton was the manufacturer of the steam engine but was a man of extraordinary arrogance. He was asked once as to what he did and he had replied to James Boswell, 'I sell here, sir, what all the world desires to have—power.'"

I told Anna that my grandfather was correct when he had said that the little island England was truly blessed. Dust was blowing into my nose and eyes. I continued, "Many inventors had come from England and they changed the world for ever. It was John Dalton who had theorized that the air is made of many individual, indivisible particles and he called them atoms. He postulated that the atoms of various elements had different mass. Now how do you come up with that? How brilliant? I wished I could have been smart like that! I mean how did the people who were not smart live there those times? Look at the Three Great Guys, as they were called because all three used to work in Guys Hospital about the same time; Bright, Hodgkin and Addison. Bright named the disease of the kidneys that still bears his name, Hodgkin is known for lymphoma and Addison is honored for identifying the condition that follows the destruction of the adrenal glands."

So it appeared that I had to zigzag through Wyoming but every part was notable. I met many different persons and one of them even had asked me for directions for Superior, Wyoming. One night at a steak house I ate twenty-six-ounce steak and everything that came with it. The day before Ms. G left I had lunch at a truck stop and then I walked past the highest point of interstate 80. It was 8,640 feet. I ran down the mountain to get out of the cold wind that tried to push my chest in the opposite direction. But even then I had walked twenty-eight miles that day. As I walked through the state I realized that Exit 323 is the high pass and the wind came in gusts across the rift in the mountain and at times it even bent the pine trees with each punch.

I took time out to help a rattlesnake that was trying to cross the road as it was coming out of the grass. I helped it with my stick but at first it curled and snarled at me and soon realized that I was harmless.

The valleys were full of wild flowers where Black Angus and antelope played. I was high. At Exit 316 I ate lunch at a Mandarin restaurant. My support arrived. I talked with Mr. Q who owned the restaurant. He spoke English and told me that he was a student of soil biology. I gave him a SPAVA shirt to remember us. I was on the move. Anna had walked behind me all morning. I needed to meditate.

I was thinking of Salvador Dali because of my penchant for the occult at times. I had met a man in Indiana quite some time back. He was a believer in planchet and medium etc. He had told me that lots of people gather near where he lived every year to discuss extraterrestrials and the stuff that we saw in the movie *Ghost* with Whoopee Goldberg being the fortune teller as well as a medium. I believe that there is some truth in the stuff. I sat down by the side of the road away from the shoulder and just reminisced for a while.

I must confess that until I had passed Pine Bluff I was continuously worried about tornadoes and how that could delay me or interrupt my trip. I had visited the Henry Ford Museum in Detroit once when I had seen the prototype of the Dymaxion House that R. Buckminster Fuller had designed for mass production. He had thought that it could be easily shipped and it could possibly stand up to a Kansas tornado. Every year there is so much damage in the tornado alley during the summer and this could prevent the loss of resources and lives. But I did not notice any such house on my way through Nebraska.

Phoebe has great interest in quantum physics and therefore we had long discussions and this is what I learnt. She said that Max Born, a Nobel laureate, was a German Jew who had to leave the University of Gottingen because of anti-Semitism. He had found a job at the University of Cambridge and then he might have moved to Edinburgh. He was the first to have discovered a fundamental concept of quantum physics. He had said that motion of particles follows probability rules, but the probability itself propagates in conformity with the law of causality. Phoebe always made some metaphysical connection and quoted from other scientists that what we do or say here probably causes some effect far away from us. After a while I had to get going.

So as I started moving and talking Anna told me not to think of anything and to cleanse my mind. It was hard. I closed my eyes. My mind was at a standstill. I could not hear the noise of the semis anymore. I saw a rainbow whose colors weren't bright yet shiny. A river ran on both sides and the rainbow had formed an arch. On top of the rainbow was an armadillo and a butterfly was sitting on top of the armadillo. I was in a deep trance. I felt warm and excited. When I opened my eyes almost thirty minutes had passed. Anna said that the river is for cleansing and the vision suggested that I was almost ready to have a fertile mind. Armadillo indicated that we have to be strong and thick skinned and the butterfly indicated that we are beautiful and that we have a short time to accomplish our tasks. "Salvador Dali had similar vision while painting *Alice in Wonderland*," said Anna. I think Anna didn't know that Dali used to take LSD.

When I opened my eyes the wind was blowing. The grass was bowing its head as though to listen to God and everything seemed to be in slow motion.

I was reaching the stage of Mahamudra! In this state of consciousness, I have been told that you can hear the sound of the clapping of one hand.

I drank more water so that I could be awake and moved on. I recall eating at Exit 310 where I had met Tina. When she heard that I was walking from Kentucky she had asked me, "Are you walking outside?" I gave her a SPAVA shirt. I told Anna about my meal at Exit 297 where a lady of Hamburg origin had served me "mess," a special gigantic omelet with sausage and other trimmings for a minimal price and then when she heard the reason for walking she wanted to give me a free sandwich. But I thanked her and told her to just wish me well instead.

I was moving fast. I had a life and death situation just a few minutes back. A red car ran onto the shoulder no more than ten feet from me at full speed and kept on driving on the shoulder until it came to the exit that I could see at a distance and disappeared.

In the meantime as I turned back I saw Phoebe coming down the road with the horns blowing and lights flashing of the support van. She pulled over and told me that the alarm had gone off and she didn't know how to fix it. The guy in front on the other hand must have thought that Phoebe was an undercover cop and it is possible they had contraband in their car and didn't want to get pulled over until they had a chance to dump it in a place where they could find it later. So she went to the exit to use her Verizon phone to call the dealership. Sprint phone did not work for most of Wyoming. Anyway, every time I saw Phoebe I got excited. I had been on the road for more than seven weeks now. As she drove past I kept on walking thinking of Marc Chagall's painting of *Homage to Apollinaire* that is at the Eindhoven Museum in the Netherlands. I imagined the excitement in her. The next day my minister Mr. W was going to arrive to be the support driver for a week. I got picked up to go to a motel for the night.

I saw this kid and his dad fishing in a small lake. So I walked over to them. "What are you up to?"

"I am walking to Portland, Oregon."

"You are what?"

So I repeated. "Are you catching anything?"

"No." I knew that was a fisherman's answer. Fishermen never acknowledge catching anything. I think they inherently believe that everyone is a Fish and Wildlife guy.

"Were you originally from India?" the boy asked.

I said, "Yes. Do you know much about India?"

"No. Well, two things. Zebra fish comes from there and Taj Mahal is in India. I have an aquarium." I was impressed and so I told him that a pair of zebra fish can make two hundred babies per week and that zebra fish is also used for genetic research. After telling them about SPAVA I was ready to go.

I was telling Anna as I was walking that my father was very concerned about the population growth in India and he compared it to kudzu. Of course he wasn't serious but he knew that economic development would be much delayed unless the mass of poorer people could be reduced. People with the least resources made the most babies. Erma Bombeck had suggested a solution in one of her books but that wasn't possible most times in that culture.

Since the minister had come we had to get ourselves more religious but Anna wanted to tell me a bit about the origin of life that may be more science based than faith based.

"Professor Christian de Duve had written a treatise on 'A Matter of life and Death' in *American Scientist* volume 91 that is of considerable interest. He said that life originated in an oxygen-free environment and remained as such for one billion years until cyano-bacteria started splitting water with the help of sunlight. This caused free oxygen to appear in the atmosphere for the first time. It is believed that this event killed most living forms that were anaerobic, meaning they die in oxygen, much like present-day anaerobic bacteria that cause severe infections. Few organisms escaped the 'oxygen holocaust' by developing protective mechanisms. Subsequently, a biological energy retrieval system developed that eventually led to the development of mitochondria that provides energy to most nucleated cells today." I thanked her for the information.

Anna had told me at St. Louis that she would never spend nights with me and so she left just like at other times.

Before I had picked up Mr. W I had already walked twenty miles that day. So we drove to our starting point and I walked for a couple of hours and then we went for rest and dinner. Mr. W had been traveling for almost twelve hours in an airplane and had noticed that I had walked the whole distance that he had flown that day. We both smiled. I was happy that we could both drink Jim Beam now and he didn't have to worry about preparing for a sermon for a week.

The day began early for us because I had planned to walk more than thirty miles today. My plantar fascitis was very painful but I was focused. I was moving towards Kemmerer. We had spent the night at Exit 68 at Little America. I planned to walk about fifty miles or more in two days and get closer to Idaho. I had every excuse to quit. My feet were hurting. There were no monetary gains. My only joy was in knowing that my student Eureka would understand the value of perseverance. Melissa would learn that we develop confidence by finishing what we start and that respect, honor and integrity are all related qualities that we must demonstrate daily in our lives.

I recall reading about Ulysses, who on his ten-year voyage back to Ithaca from the Trojan War, was warned by Circe to take precautions if he wanted to hear the Sirens' transfixing song, otherwise there would be "no sailing home for him, no wife rising to meet him, no happy children beaming up at their father's face." I had made a "Ulysses contract" with myself, which meant that I had made an agreement with myself whose major condition was that I had relinquished the right to change my mind. I didn't have to fill my ears with beeswax or transfix myself to the masts in case my body decided to quit because my God was with me and walked with me to make sure that I stayed fit.

On July 1st I was at Kemmerer. I told Anna that we use bone wax today to stop bleeding from the bones during brain surgery. "So who figured it out?"

"Sir Victor Horsley, a neurosurgeon, and Sister Nightingale worked together during the Crimean War and Dr. Horsley used the wax to stop bleeding. So today with minor modifications we call it Horsley's wax."

As I walked through the spectacular mountains I was breathing a bit harder. We were almost seven thousand feet high. I had to rest more often as I passed the Fossil Butte National Monument. There were many students that I met during dinnertime when we came back to sleep at Dee's motel an extra night. It is owned by the Burnett family. They were kind to me. They are a Mormon couple that had spent some time in India.

There were times when my preacher felt sorry for me and told me that it would be alright with him if I wanted to drive and then he could walk instead of me. I told him that in that case I would have to cut out the "integrity" sign from my T-shirt. We both laughed. We ate dinner at Hams Fork. I met Ms. D, Ms. T and Ms. J. They gave us a discount on account of our project and the fact that I ate so much. I gave them SPAVA shirts.

At lunchtime I kept my feet up usually but now it had become mandatory because my feet were really swollen. I met a judge and her husband. Her husband's name is Gary. I met a young student named Madison who goes to school two blocks from where I live in Louisville. I gave him a SPAVA shirt. A group of students had come to study the fossils during the summer.

Anna kept me busy as I walked towards Cokeville, a small border town to Idaho. This part of US 30 is also part of the Oregon Trail. I sat under a monument that said "Both Wyoming and Idaho were included into statehood in 1890." I had taken my socks and shoes off and rubbed Icy-Hot a couple of times today. There was a store across the highway that sold fireworks and many people were buying them because we were close to the Fourth of July. I was lying down and Mr. W went past me but came back after a while realizing that I could not have walked as far as he had gone. I saw badgers and antelopes during the day and coyote scats in the evening.

One morning I had met Joe. He was ahead of me in age by a few years. He said that he was seeing the country too. So I asked him what he was doing. "I drive behind the trucks that carry wide loads and I have my flashing lights on. They pay for my food and a place to stay every night." I told him that I had seen many trucks like that during my walk.

I was telling Anna that in America we have scientists who have such diverse interests that most people in the world cannot imagine. Professor Karl Reinhard of the University of Nebraska is possibly the world's greatest expert on the study of s—t. Scientists who study excrements are called paleo-nutritionists and paleo-scatologists. It has been many years back that I had read about the Anasazi or the Ancestral Pueblo Indians. Dr. Reinhard has published extensively about the diet of the folks that lived in the areas of Arizona, Utah, Colorado and New Mexico thousands of years back. He discussed the issue of possible cannibalism because one of the dried feces specimens that he had studied suggested as such and another doctor also found human myoglobin in that sample. He went on to discuss the possibilities that it could have happened as a result of terrorism or under dire conditions etc. in his article in the *American Scientist* volume 94. I left the coyote scat alone and didn't even spit or urinate on it because a thousand years from now that sample may be important and I didn't want the coyote to have had some human DNA in its scat and confuse the scientists!

I recalled that the Tibetans I had met near Darchen knew about the Hopi and Navajo Indians and actually had said to me that they have been told by their ancestors that their people had crossed into the United States through Siberia may be 12,000 years ago. They have no books to read about this. It is a place in the mountain on the way to Mt. Kailash. As we know today that the Americas or maybe North America then was filled with large animals. Some scientists have postulated that humans killed and ate those animals according to University of Arizona archeologist Dr. C. Vance Haynes. Paleontologists and archeologists have suggested that sometime between 50,000 and 100,000 years ago, near the end of the Pleistocene, much of the large animals disappeared. Some have suggested that this might have been related to dramatic climate change and deglaciation that might have occurred more than 20,000 years ago. I kept my eyes open to find some gigantic fossil bone and become famous.

I told Anna that I was missing my telephone and I was not able to communicate. Anna told me that she has a WebTV. "I have convergence," she said. I didn't know what it was. "On TV view, WebTV makes channel surfing easy. It downloads all the TV listings at night for the cable using the phone line and you can check your E-mail and browse the internet too." I felt jealous. I told her that I am going to get one when I get home. At this moment what I needed was I think Synvisc treatment for my knees. I have never tried it but I have been told that it lubricates the knee joint and helps the pain of osteoarthritis. I don't have osteoarthritis but I certainly have overuse syndrome and needed lubrication.

Anna said she knows about it. "Only three injections into the knee joint, and you will feel like some Vaseline has been placed inside your joint!" I rubbed some of the liniment I had and just kept it extended when I went to sleep. Jim Beam took away all my pain at night. I was a little short of Montpelier, Idaho. I had planned to be at Soda Springs on the Fourth of July.

Today we had a big discussion about Mary Magdalene. Anna and I were talking about all the Marys in the Bible. I told Anna that it is sinful to talk about our God the way it is being done today in the books and movies etc. Anything erotic will sell and I felt that Mary Magdalene was being used to merchandise certain stories.

I also talked with my minister about this. I have subsequently read Professor James Carroll's article in the *Smithsonian* in which he has explained the role Mary Magdalene played in the life of Jesus of Nazareth. He clearly stated that many fantasies have been projected to make the story more exciting by adding a sexual relationship with Jesus. Jesus died about A.D. 30 and the gospels of Mark, Matthew and Luke date 65-85 and John was composed 90-95. The writings are not eyewitness accounts. This is not real history because it was written from memory which could have been blurred by time and possibly there have been efforts to make theological points. It is believed that most Christians were illiterate and the Gospels were passed on as an oral tradition.

Women were uniquely empowered to be fully equal at the time of Jesus. Mary Magdalene was present at the time of crucifixion and Mary was also there first when Jesus rose from the tomb. Professor Carroll said that in time Mary was transformed from a confidante of Jesus to a former prostitute noted for her stricken conscience. This belief helps everyone to identify with Mary Magdalene as "we are all sinners" and that way we can love her more and our repentance expunges our sin and opens the door to heaven.

I think most of us have a hard time believing what some of the cognitive scientists such Pascal Boyer of Washington University in St. Louis and some others say about God. They said that God might be an accidental byproduct of human cognitive evolution.

What is most interesting to me is that most of the stories in the Bible were actually in Hindu Sanskrit scriptures and the stories such as making bread and wine from empty pots is well known to most children in India except the stories are about rice. Moreover, Puja is a common event performed by older women in India and possibly done with more vigor as erotic urges diminish with age. There is a common Sanskrit saying about old women of ill-repute that many of them become more zealous about performing Puja, which is basically repentance and asking for God's favor.

I didn't make it to Soda Springs on the Fourth of July but I was there on July 5th. I had to drive to drop Mr. W off and then pick up Ms. D whose plane was late. So I only walked six miles to catch up the distance that I was short the day before after arriving at Soda Springs. I was getting excited because it was the 6th of July and I was at Lava Springs, only about six miles short of Inkam or fifteen miles short of Pocatello. The walk to Lava Springs was a difficult climb. On top of the mountain was the worst garbage-strewn area I have ever seen. It is a shame because the scenery was spectacular. I had stopped to take a breather.

Idaho was very hot. Today after eating another steak for lunch I decided to eat Italian food for dinner, particularly since there was one Italian restaurant. I was afraid that I might deplete the cattle banks in this area! Ms. D had gone past me one day because the sun was in her eye. The fields were green and full of hay and what else you think? You guessed it. Potatoes and potatoes for miles! There was some water channel made out to keep the rats out, I think. I have always thought that the rats have contributed a lot to our society. They have been made to run in different mazes, they have been given cancer, virus, dura graft, and toxins to determine mouse units, burns and whatever. I had recently read that the neurobiologists were investigating the changes in rats' brains when they sense sex pheromones. They recorded the sounds the male mice made as they sniffed cotton swabs treated with the urine of females. The professors were pleasantly surprised to hear though not in their ears but by magnification high-pitch songs. This was published by T. E. Holly and Z. Guo in *Public Library of Science Biology*. I was wondering if we would be hearing those songs through Bose speakers soon when the mice would be walking on the rafters of the houses of the folks who live in the farms during winter.

Ms. D and I made plans for the next eight days that she would be with me. She said that she was going to talk to the radio stations and TV stations and the universities as I would be walking. I thought that was a great idea to publicize the SPAVA program.

Although Ms. D is one of the mentors for the program and teaches in the school system on a regular basis I thought I would talk to her about Gandhigiri or the ways of Mahatma Gandhi. In September 2006 *Times of India* published that according to one study 64% of Indians and 90% of Delhiites did not believe that the way of conflict resolution Gandhi had suggested is possible in the modern times.

This raised a bit of an alarm and so an attempt was made to bring awareness in India about the ways of Gandhi through a movie called *Lage Raho Munnabhai*. Gandhi promoted acceptance and abhorred hateful behavior. He tried his opponents to see his conviction in a positive way. He did not believe that beating the opponent down would win him as much as through understanding the mutual differences.

Nelson Mandela as well as Martin Luther King tried his principles successfully. Dr. Anjali Chhabria said that there is a thin line between being aggressive and assertive. In the Gandhian way we have to be assertive and stay calm and keep working tirelessly to reach our goal without getting affected emotionally. Being nonviolent doesn't mean that we have to be meek and we do not have to turn the other cheek when we are being slapped. More importantly we have to make sure that the other person understands that we are being violated and we have to make a stand in a confident manner.

There is a lot of meanness and hatred in the society and some of them would not be corrected by Gandhigiri. Look at the white supremacist who had so much hatred in him that he and two of his buddies chained a black man to a pickup truck and dragged him through the streets of Jasper, Texas, as a form of initiation to belong to the KKK. I don't think anything short of violence would make him understand what he had done. After his sentence he showed no sign of remorse and even on his way to the death row nothing was said to the family of the man he so horribly mutilated. So somehow we have to teach our children not to hate. I had met a man who said that he was from Minnesota and was staying in Addis Ababa to help the children on the street to learn the ways of God. I wish he would work in our country to make those changes and not let those poor persons in Ethiopia think as though there was no problem here. He said his mother was a Presbyterian and his father was Baptist and he is Evangelical.

I am afraid of these fundamentalists and they may be the actual cause of these types of violence in our country initiated by middle-class white boys who may be self-righteous and castigate vehemently anything or anybody that they perceive as sinful or inferior or less Aryan! Practicing self-control and to delay gratification and understanding the feelings of others are important parts of the program that we teach and it goes along with Gandhigiri. Ms. D had said that she was ready to initiate these thoughts among the people of Idaho through the media. Ms. D was afraid whether she would be able to remember the details and asked me if she should be checked for Alzheimer's disease. We chuckled. She said that she knew that a professor from Duke had identified the ApoE4 gene as a cause of late onset of the disease in about half the cases. Then I told her that a professor from Columbia University Medical Center has identified an abnormality in SORL 1 receptor to be the cause among folks of Dominican families and that may be the culprit in some others with memory problems as well.

People were warm and they often stopped to see if I needed help. Some others waved and went whizzing by. No one had suggested a shrink to me. But I believe they politely asked their children not to look. I sometimes sang loudly, "I am Sancho Panza." The grass wiggled in laughter and the butterflies slowed down to hear the rest of it. But some were impatient and felt disturbed and so I sang quietly so they couldn't hear me anymore.

The gnats and "no-seeums" drove me crazy. I swooshed them away with my left glove because the right one had shrunk and had become deformed from the salt of the sweat.

Anna was there all day except for a short period when the wind and the rain threw her off to the valley where the sun was peeking through one of the herds of clouds. It was hot and humid all day. So Anna had asked me if I had ever visited some place that was real cold.

Story of Arctic Dreams

It was a few years back when my friend and I had visited the High Arctic. I told Anna that I was lucky and that is why I am alive today. I wanted to visit Bylot Island and Pond Inlet in Baffin Island. Anna quizzed me in the middle of my talking. "So, which one is the biggest island in the United States?"

"The Big Island of Hawaii."

"OK. Which one is the second largest?"

"The Kodiak."

Anna gave up for a while.

I said that North Baffin and Bylot have ice fields, glaciers and vegetated meadows. They also have a very large population of snow geese. However, the local Inuit pronounce them as "Snu-gees." I wanted to see some polar bears, narwhals and beluga whales in their own environment. My mind was set to meet those men that can fight the polar bears and hunt with harpoons while looking at the Nannutik, local word for polar bear, in the eye. I wanted to see what really happens to the dial of the compass as I got close to the magnetic pole.

I knew that the wind blows strong almost all the time over there and so we were prepared. I flew up to Vancouver, British Columbia and went to the camping store and bought minus-thirty shoe lining and proper clothes to stay reasonably warm near the north of Baffin. As I prepared for my trip the polarity of my life changed. Some person had commented about loving in the arctic and said that "odds are good but the goods are odd." This helped me to realize about myself. I found a new mate as my old mate had left me for better goods.

The Inuit have names for snowdrifts formed by winds from every direction. The glossary of Inuktitut snow and ice words describes more than one hundred terms to describe subtle differences of snow. Of course the best known snow is the one that can plug the cracks in the drafty igloos—qikuutitsajaq. As I from Kentucky walked on the clean powder on the frozen ocean I realized that the loud squeak of the snow under my feet was from qigiqralijarnatuq.

It was about sixteen years prior to this trip that I had been to the arctic for any extended period of time. It was during the last week of June. The mosquitoes were buzzing. I had my pant sleeves tucked in my socks as I walked on the tundra to get on a boat. We were fishing in Great Bear Lake in the northern part of the Northwest Territories. I had six layers of clothes on my body. Our Inuit guide was driving a fourteen-foot motor boat as the wind propelled us through the bright daylight at 4 a.m. I threw in my line, a large jig with a hook but it had no burr. I was beside myself with excitement. The water was clear and the air was crisp. But whenever we slowed down mosquitoes were just humming like bees around us, much like being attacked by a swarm of bees after throwing a rock on a bee hive. In eight hours we must have caught twenty trout of different sizes. We ate one for lunch and let the others go.

The guide had reminded me to be careful during reeling the fish in. "You will die of hypothermia in five minutes if you fall in." The fish grows only one pound per year because the water is too cold. I had already caught a twenty-five-year-old fish and let it go because we could only keep one fish in seven days and I thought that I could possibly catch a bigger one before my time was up.

We saw a few caribous at the distant shore and he told me about catching arctic char at Coppermine. Soon we couldn't see the shore anymore. He reminded us about the grizzly bears and particularly about those with cubs. I remained awestruck with the beauty and didn't realize how much time had passed. But the day hadn't ended. It was bright light all the time. We had pulled in for a pee-pee break on a patch of land that had appeared out of nowhere. When we re-boarded the boat the choke started acting up and he couldn't get it to go. We were more than ten miles out and paddling in the wind was not an option. Our guide had gathered leaves and pieces of wood chips and some leaves of dead conifers and he tried to make a smoke signal. We hoped that someone would see the signal at the camp. We waited three hours on a small piece of dirt where mosquitoes swirled on our heads and he showed us grizzly tracks that looked reasonably fresh on the sand. The latter finding certainly was not comforting. At last someone did come to rescue us and took our boat in a tow.

This is when I caught the bug of traveling further and further north in the arctic. I have been to the arctic a few times since then. I have gone down the Hula-Hula River in a raft to the Arctic National Wildlife Refuge. I have slept in a pup tent on mushy tundra. I have seen the arctic fox, Alaskan ptarmigan and watched the musk oxen gallop past my tent. I have even seen mama grizzly waddling with two cubs from a distance and assumed they were singing "This land is my land." I have seen the porcupine caribous.

But what I most admired is the talent and the resilience of the Inuit. The polite and gentle manners of these men is only superseded by fierce determination and undaunted courage that they demonstrate to survive. I have seen them wrestle with whales and walruses in the turbulent waters of the Arctic Ocean. The flight to Pond Inlet was very long through Toronto, Montreal, Iqaluit and then by First Air almost 1,100 kilometers to Pond Inlet. Ken Borek Air goes once a week to Resolute but our time didn't permit us that opportunity. We rode on dog sled and then a snowmobile pulled us in a wooden box for more than eight hours and we arrived at the floe edge, where the ice met the open sea. When we arrived at a spot that the guide thought we should stop it was snowing heavy and the wind was blowing strong. There were no landmarks and only our GPS gave us our location as to where we were and it really didn't matter because we knew that we were very far from any kind of civilization in the middle of frozen ocean.

Inside our box we had carried a small stove to melt ice for tea. We ate raw caribou meat while sitting inside a pup tent and one of the guides had to stay awake all the time to make sure that we were not attacked by polar bears. My back was wrenched from the bumpy icy road on which we had traveled for hours. The wind blew hard and we could not move from our spot for three days because there was practically no visibility. To stay warm my girl and I had to hug each other constantly to get the benefit of our body heat.

Then we saw that Dr. Suzuki had come a bit further in a helicopter to film the Inuit catch and cut up a walrus in the sea. We watched that for a while. Our guide told us to look at a distance in the middle of the snow where we saw the black nose of a polar bear. It moved fast and then it swam away. The wind had shifted and the guide showed us how the ice was cracking and that we needed to move to a different spot.

We were having tea and were discussing being at the Nattinak center where we had learnt that John Ross had named these waters between Bylot and Pond inlet as Pond's Bay. Our Inuit guide told us that they were not allowed to live on the land until only fifteen years earlier. They are allowed to hunt polar bears and walruses for eating and selling the skin. He said that in Greenland they still have to hunt the bear with a harpoon whereas over there they were allowed to use a gun. But their community is allowed only thirteen polar bears every year. He said that those who hunt the polar bear with a harpoon have to face the bear and when the bear stands up they get one shot at the heart of the bear and they must move fast afterwards because the thousand-pound bear falls instantly on the ground after being struck in the heart with the harpoon.

I asked him if he had ever gone to the United States. He said that he had once gone to Hilton Head but during the seven days that he was there he had never gone out of his air-conditioned room. We all laughed. We had already seen several Narwhals and Beluga whales and polar bears and so I asked if he was ever attacked by polar bears.

This is what he told us. He and his guide friend whose left hand is dysfunctional now were hunting polar bears a few years back. They chased a bear with their snowmobile after shooting it. However soon the wind had picked up and despite their great ability to read the snow and visual prowess visibility became so poor that they could not see where the polar bear was traveling. It was injured but not killed by the bullet. They suddenly realized that the ice around them had cracked and they were drifting. The snowmobile fell in the water and no sooner had they jumped off the falling Skidoo than they saw the polar bear on the same island of ice except it was across from them near the water. The polar bear decided to swim in the water and he and his friend drifted for three days towards Greenland before they were rescued by a helicopter. During this time they had to eat their gloves which are made of seal skin and their chap stick for food.

After hearing this I needed to take a walk while my friend was enjoying looking at the whales. We had already spent four days on ice and were planning to go back. There was fresh snow but the sun was up and it was a warm day! There were birds on the Bylot Island. All of us had sunglasses on to protect our eyes from sunburn. The guide had warned me that although the ice was six feet thick, there were holes made by the seals that came up every so often to get air. The polar bears often sat by the holes to catch the seals as they came up to take a breather. The guide sat on our box and kept watch while I walked. It must have been about one hundred yards when I fell in a hole and was immersed up to my neck and had it not been for my strong elbows I would have gone under the ice cap and would have been lost forever. He came running to rescue me but I had already pulled myself out of the water.

I had lost my camera and all my clothes and shoes had gotten wet. But my hat was dry. I came inside my box and took all my clothes off and lay naked under cover for eight hours till my clothes were dry. Then it was time to come home. Our trip to the land of the people of Tununiq, the land that faces away from the sun, was over. During the bumpy ride back home on the ice I enjoyed the beauty and my high spirit kept me totally unaffected by the incident that had just happened few hours back. I was in awe.

Professor Irving Biederman and Edward Vessel wrote about "Perceptual Pleasure and the Brain," in *American Scientist* volume 94. They said that the enjoyment of joyful experiences is deeply connected to an innate hunger for information: human beings are designed to be "infovores." According to them the infovore system is designed to maximize the rate at which people acquire knowledge under conditions where there may be no immediate need for the information. They said that the brain is wired for pleasure and people as early as 3400 B.C. have been high on opium and there is evidence of growing poppy plants in lower Mesopotamia.

Drs. Solomon Snyder and Candace Pert in 1972 identified the mu, delta and kappa receptors for the opiods on the surface of the brain and explained how opioid receptors bind to opiates and modulate brain activity. The mu-opioid receptor readily binds to morphine and endogenous morphine-like substances such as endorphins that were identified in the brain tissue in 1997 by professors from Tulane.

In a monkey's cortex the mu-receptors that are mostly associated with modulation of pain and reward are found in large quantities in areas that are involved with processing visual information and are located mostly in the ventral visual pathway. This in turn is connected to a part of the brain called the para-hippocampal cortex and rhinal cortex where visual information engages our memories causing association with objects, faces and places etc. I was truly high when I was coming back bouncing on the ice sitting inside the wooden box. The thrill I had actually gave me a greater high than I got after performing an aneurysm operation in the brain!

Idaho Back and Forth

From Exit 33 I had to walk on loose gravel for ten miles because of road repair or such. Before I reached about fifteen miles outside Pocatello Corporal Trooper Burke found us. I was going to meet Ms. D but seeing the trooper's car from a distance worried me. I thought that she might have gotten a ticket or such. He was most kind. He introduced us to other troopers and also to the local TV station and they filmed part of the walk before I reached Twin Falls. I was getting more excited every day because now I was only 215 miles from the Oregon border. Ms. D had washed the car and fixed the windshield that had cracked again being hit by one of the rocks from the loose gravel road. I did not recognize the van and tried to get in someone else's van because ours looked so clean. My calcaneal bone area was swollen but I was sure that there was no stress fracture.

I was telling Anna that so far I had walked the whole distance except a few miles bonus I had taken near Lawrenceville, about fifty-five miles around St. Louis and ten miles around Kansas City and also about four miles owing to road repair and tunnels.

This is Mormon country. People were polite and helpful. The interstate was not full of junk and nails on the shoulders. There were practically no nails on the shoulders of Interstate 15, 86 or 84. I was moving fast today. I had walked almost thirty-six miles today. Ms. D and I were laughing at the end of the day. I often woke up at night dreaming of semis and exits. Exits had become my obsession, walk my passion and SPAVA my mission. I can tell you that this walk is not for the fainthearted. At times on the bridges there was less than a foot between my shoulder and the semis that passed me at seventy-five miles an hour. At those times it was important to not turn, particularly if one was related to Cyrano de Bergerac because there was no Roxanne to revive the damaged face.

The weather was most favorable. I remembered July 10. The Cyclops eye of the sun was covered by strong sunglasses of clouds before it could reach Mother Earth. Anna was nowhere to be seen. I had a girlie umbrella in the morning protecting me as it was raining a bit. So Ms. D passed me and yelled, "Hey sister." I laughed. I had walked almost nineteen miles before lunch today. I passed by miles and miles of potato fields between Pocatello and Twin Falls. This interstate is a haven for field mice. It seemed that I longed for James all day. In the evening a couple of hugs is all I needed to fall asleep as he beamed!

I met a man from Montana today and he said that my plan sounded ambitious. I explained to him that when people from the South use that term they mean that it cannot be done but when someone from the North uses that term it means that it is exciting. Dr. Fred Epstein in his book *Ambition* wrote that ambition is the fuel that drives the engine. It is much like the church ladies say about a person when he fails. "Bless his little heart." No one says "Bless his big heart" when he succeeds. I told him about my experiences in the Bob Marshall Wilderness in Montana. My son and I had gone on horseback for a week through the wilderness and we always camped out at night at some place next to the water and watched the stars in the "Big Sky." During the evenings we told tales while sitting next to campfires. My son being an engineer he was telling us about the Big Bang that might have occurred sometime between 10 billion and 15 billion years back and the fact that we are all made of stardust etc. when a young man and a woman came and joined us. I recognized him and told him as such that I had seen him and his girlfriend riding on a horse all day. He acknowledged that and said that is exactly what he does during the summer. I told him that I needed a job like that. I recalled that he had said to me that I had to have connections. He had been working for Fish and Wildlife and his job was to count the fish in the water. Every so often he shocked the water or such and counted the fish that jumped up and then he submitted the data to Washington! He said that way decisions were made as to how many fish we are allowed to keep.

I saw many herons diving for fish as I passed by some large lakes and Raft River. Anna appeared. Anna told me to be humble. I said, "Anna, I had learnt as a child that learning imparts humility. 'If we live by the Spirit, let us also be guided by the Spirit. Let us not become conceited, competing against one another, envying one another. My friends, if anyone is detected in a transgression, you who have received the Spirit should restore such a one in a spirit of gentleness'" (Gal 5: 25-6.1)

All this started this morning because a lady had asked me "Why are you doing it?" Before I could answer it she answered "Because you can?" I was getting a bit cocky as I was getting closer to the finish line. I said yes.

The eighth fruit of the Spirit listed by Paul is translated as gentleness, meekness or humility. This word together with several others point to that strength of character that is required to ground one's relationship in something other than pride and power. I apologized to Anna and said that I knew that God had said "All who exalt themselves shall be humbled, but all who humble themselves will be exalted" (Mt. 23:12, Luke 14: 11). Anna said for me to remember that John in Revelation, while looking for the conquering lion, who can open the scroll and its seven seals, finds that it is the Lamb and the way of the Lamb is the way of the Cross; I had to constantly remind myself of that because pride and aggression are constant lures in modern life. The day was over almost too soon.

As I walked through Idaho I learnt many things. I did not know what the flower Syringa looked like until a lady outside the restaurant where I had lunch pointed it out to me. Ezra Pound, one of my favorite poets, was from Idaho. The western white pine was quite easily recognizable. Exit 173 for me meant that I was only that many miles away from Oregon. We had a TV interview at Twin Falls.

Ms. D had a confidence-building experience on one day when I had asked her to drive across the median in the expressway. She had never done that before and we were late after she returned making the motel reservation. I had told her that if she came across the median (illegal) she didn't have to drive seven miles in the opposite direction to fetch me in the evening.

Today I met the most wonderful octogenarian. She is Ms. Helen McGee. She was a marine during the Second War. But the rules of the day were that women could not serve in combat and therefore she was stationed at New York. I honored her and gave her a T-shirt. We had a long conversation and I told her to wear the T-shirt while washing her car in Texas. She laughed and said that she didn't drive anymore. She told me that Idaho was named by a mining lobbyist named George Willing. President Jefferson had bought it as a part of the Louisiana Purchase and it was lumped as a part of Oregon territory. She also said that the Boise Capitol was the only one in the country that is heated by underground hot springs. I told her that I had seen the Idaho prison. It had reminded me of Columbus penitentiary where a couple of my colleagues and I had worked off and on for a year to perform minor surgery for the prisoners but this building was not like the Prinz Albrechtstrasse 8 in Berlin, the most feared address and prison complex at the time of the Gestapo. I had seen that building in pictures only. In Kentucky we have a beautiful pink prison just outside Lexington.

Ms. D and I have known each other for almost forty years. She was a student nurse at St. Joseph Infirmary when I was an intern. She kindly volunteered to be a support driver after she learnt from the newspaper that I was getting ready to walk across the country.

Thus we renewed our old friendship; a laser nurse and a neurosurgeon in different hospitals and we hadn't seen each other in four decades! In her honor I ate a gigantic steak at Sizzlers and ate ice cream for the first time in two months. I have lactose intolerance. Our program teaches children to renew friendships and express gratitude.

Anna said, "Do you know that Jesus might have visited India?"

I said, "Yes. He probably went to Himis Monastery in northern India near Ladakh and Leh and they called him St. Issa." Anna was impressed. There is a lot of controversy about the *Lost Years of Jesus*, a book written by a Swiss lady, Elizabeth Clare Prophet. He might have traveled further east almost up to Pataliputra because there were some famous universities in India at that time. Pataliputra is the modern Patna. It is the capital of the poorest state, Bihar, in India.

On September 10, 1919, Pope Benedict XV issued his apostolic letter Nova in Indis, and established the Diocese of Patna and entrusted it to the Jesuits. Father Marshall Moran founded St. Xavier's school in Patna in 1940 and then he established the St. Xavier's school in Katmandu. The Catholics in Bihar probably did more for the Dalits (Harijans, people of God, the oppressed) and the Santals (mountain people) than the government of India.

The Jesuits contributed more to education in India and made more efforts to break down the barriers of caste system oppression than any other religious or nonreligious groups. A Canadian Catholic priest had blessed me and had given me a dollar. "You will make many of these in your life but this has the blessing of an eighty-year-old man." I told him that I would take a blessing than a dollar any day and that I would keep that dollar as a symbol of blessing as long as I lived. I still have it with me though I have had to place some scotch tape to hold it together since it is more than fifty years old.

"Hey, ask your preacher to give a sermon on 'walking through the valley of the shadow of death,'" said Anna.

I prayed, "The Lord is my shepherd, I shall not want." I felt stronger. Part of it might have been from the caffeine pills that Ms. D had given me. But the exuberance and excitement of proceeding forward and stamping my feet on the gravel instead of the concrete for a while propelled me forward at a speed that I could have never imagined. I recited "Crossing the Bar" from Tennyson:

> Sunset and evening star,
> And one clear call for me!
> And may there be no moaning of the bar,
> When I put out to sea.
>
> Twilight and evening bell,
> And after that the dark!
> And may there be no sadness of farewell,
> When I embark.
>
> For tho' from out our bourne of Time and Place,
> The flood may bear me far,
> I hope to see my Pilot face to face,
> When I have crost the bar.

I suddenly started running because I had the strength of ten much like King Arthur did. I thought about Merlin but then about Rosanna Podesta. I know her face; it could have launched a thousand ships in the early fifties. I was sweating and moving my stick like a sword and attacked the demons that might have held me back. The clouds moved and the sun became brighter. The grass stood still and the birds twitted and the cows ran to the fence and excited horses came over to greet me. I was moving. I calmed myself down so I could exhale. The day was gone and Ms. D had picked me up.

Although I have said in the past that I didn't want to be famous or such but I think secretly I wanted to achieve some things that would give me great satisfaction. I have read many biographies of famous people and their discoveries. How about Robert Noyce? He started out at MIT and then started Intel. I am using the processor in my computer that they developed. I had read about aviators Ernie Smith and Emory Bronte after they became the first to fly a single-engine aircraft, *City of Oakland*, in 1927, nonstop from Oakland to Hawaii, a distance of 2,100 miles. I have read probably almost everything about Ben Franklin and wondered in awe how a man could have achieved so many things. I wanted to be like him. He was a man of formidable intelligence and enormous energy. He wrote about almost anything that was in his mind in Poor Richard and the folks of his time must have read them.

I have read the life stories of the people who signed the Declaration of Independence. Dr. Benjamin Rush was only about thirty years old and yet achieved so much. Jack Parsons, Ed Forman and Frank Molina were under twenty-two years old when they tried to develop and test rocket engines and became the founders of Jet Propulsion Laboratory. I wanted to be like John Snow, who during a cholera epidemic in London in the nineteenth century figured out that cholera was transmitted by a pathogen in contaminated water. Wow! Why couldn't I be like Dr. David Baltimore, who won a Nobel Prize at the age of thirty-seven for having figured out the enzyme that could copy RNA into DNA, or the reverse transcriptase when he was only thirty-two years old?

It has been a long time ago that I had read Elie Weisel's *Night*. I wept and I was outraged to think that Ambassador Joseph Kennedy had felt that it was not our war when the Jewish people were being killed by Hitler in Poland. Although so many lives were lost during WW II somehow secretly I thanked the Japanese for drawing America into the war. I wanted to be a man like Weisel to have the tolerance, tenacity, perseverance, forgiveness and the ability to accept life like Hesse's *Siddhartha*.

I admire men like Roy Boehm, who founded the Navy SEALs program. Here was a man who had jumped off a burning aircraft carrier, the USS *Duncan*, after being shot and filled with shrapnel. He tried to save his friends and was almost swallowed by sharks. He must have known that God saved him for a greater cause than just being a great sailor at Guadalcanal! Who made the sharks turn back from a man with bleeding wounds? Who held that ship from letting him get sucked in the ocean when the ship went down? These people inspire me and make my struggles small.

I told Anna that I feel good when I read these life histories but in the back of my mind I set myself where I am. What am I doing? So I calm myself by saying that the inscription over the entrance to the temple of Apollo at Delphi says "Know Thyself." I grew up in India and this is much of Hindu philosophy that I heard from my grandfather and it involves calming the mind and understanding ourselves and our purpose in life. He had said once that if we understand ourselves then we can function in society better.

In America I find there are often surges of popular interest on certain ideas, although some of the ideas have been in existence for centuries. Dr. Howard Gardner, in 1983, in his book *Frames of Mind* (New York, Basic Books) outlined several distinct forms of intelligence. He proposed an "intrapersonal intelligence" which is very similar to the concept of emotional intelligence. He said that the core capacity at work here is access to one's own feelings in life and discriminations among these feelings and the ability of eventually to label them and to enmesh them in symbolic codes, to draw upon them as a means of understanding and guiding one's behavior. I have never done any scientific research on these subjects but I wanted to have been able to come up with some of these ideas.

Before I started the SPAVA program I read a lot about violence in America and what are the causes of death among the youth? Violence is the number one cause of death among African-American youth under twenty-five years of age.

Jwanza Kunjufu wrote in a book, *Developing Positive Self-Images and Discipline in Black Children* (African American Images, Chicago, 1984), that many children are bored and view themselves as non-productive and inactive, with no political and economic strength. I must confess these types of statements are incorrect and self-fulfilling. I personally teach in elementary and middle schools and I believe that anybody who is bored must not be working hard enough. It is important to understand that black children don't have to have a black hero. Color should be immaterial in finding our heroes. As a matter of fact many children don't have any heroes in their lives at all and the only reason they come to school is because otherwise their parents would be in trouble and many have told me as such. There is no black struggle in reality. We can always create our struggles of that type and I believe some folks call them having a "chip on the shoulder." The days of "we shall overcome" should be slowly over. Nothing has to be overcome except our own shortcomings and inability to view ourselves as Americans and we have to forget about the color. I think that we should struggle to improve ourselves.

Most importantly, actions that people perform make us admire them and we rarely choose to like or admire a person because of their color. Actions have no color and all actions either benefit others or benefit ourselves. There are some actions that are clearly harmful. The more we enhance the issues of differences then they become a problem but we should learn to honor the differences and move on. I was pleased that the last paragraph of the book by Kunjufu said something to the effect that the development of positive self-images and discipline in black children is the primary responsibility of the parent.

I have worked in Africa and I have many friends in Africa. The children I have met in Africa are black. They know it. They are respectful and honorable and they know that too. They don't call one another bad names and they don't feel that all Africa's problems today are because of the white folks although the colonization has stripped most of the country's assets.

The children in Africa that I met wore clothes decently and they knew how to stand and walk. I believe most of them know why they are in school. Most of the countries in Africa are poor but people have pride and they demand respect. They treat me as their colleague and I always feel honored to be among Africans. The people work hard in factories, hospitals, stores and in the farms and of course in the mines. Yes, there are beggars but there are many beggars in America too. Yes, there are thieves, pickpockets and occasional violence. But we have all of those and violence in America. The smile of acceptance, the special handshake by the people of different countries and the uniqueness of Africa has been lost among many of the African American people in America because quite a few feel that somebody owes them something.

Almost two months had passed that I had been on the road. I took the morning off to be with the Rotarians at the Power House for a luncheon meeting at Boise. One of the administrative law judges spoke. I used to know most of the administrative law judges in the Louisville area from my workman's compensation experience. I introduced SPAVA during the meeting at the Rotary club. Owing to the fact that we have different drivers that are flying in from and flying back to different cities I have had to modify my ways of walking. Motel 8 at Boise became the headquarters for walking back and forth to save gas as well as expenses because the manager gave us a discount on account of the fact that I was walking for a nonprofit organization.

I walked ten miles towards Oregon so that the day was not totally wasted, as far as walking was concerned, before Ms. B arrived. She is a mentor for SPAVA. I was excited to see Ms. B. We were going to finish up Idaho and possibly go about twenty miles into Oregon by the time she would be ready to leave. On her first day I had walked to Exit 90, close to thirty-three miles.

Every day we had clear sky and incredible heat but I remembered July 15th to have been the hottest day when the heat index was close to 113 degrees F but I finished thirty-three miles at the end of the day. I had to walk way past 8 p.m. because I had to take a nap at midday for an hour. I was concerned that I had not urinated for five hours so I drank eight bottles (691 cc each. I know it because these were empty Gatorade bottles) of water, tea and Gatorade and after all this I had just a bit of dark urine and that had made me a bit concerned. Today's walk was no Kundalini yoga; this was class V (if there is such) Bikram yoga.

Anna and I talked all day about different subjects. I was talking about the fact that I started working as an international volunteer about twenty years back. I did not want to tell anybody about it at first because I didn't know if I could do it or not. I had been trained with fancy technology and I had been enjoying a lot of comforts.

But I prayed about it. My wife had encouraged me and had told me to start slow, meaning that she thought I should only take short-term assignments at first. She was perceptive. In twenty years I have worked in Brazil, Zimbabwe, Ethiopia, Peru, Honduras, Nepal, and in the western part of India in a place called Miraj. Dr. Dean Thompson, president of the Louisville Presbyterian Theological Seminary, wrote in the *Mosaic* that his friend Ron had received his commitment of giving as a youth in high school. For more than sixty years he carried his stewardship credo in his wallet, printed on a small card. He received his credo from his principal, Dr. Ethyl Andrus, who later founded AARP. For decades, wherever Ron went, he carried and shared these transforming words: "What I spent is gone. What I kept is lost. But what I gave away is mine forever."

Anna said that women give more in many different ways. I agreed. I said I couldn't do what I want to do if my wife hadn't helped me and supported me. Professor Diane Reistroffer of Louisville Seminary had written about "Women's Ways of Giving" in the *Mosaic* of Theological Seminary. She had said that the women in their giving had developed their own distinctive patterns for raising and giving money, and in so doing, they claimed their authority, their values and their vision for mission and ministry in the church. I said to Anna, "Weren't women treated as properties then? They weren't even allowed to vote." Anna said that Dr. Reistroffer had stated that nineteenth-century and early-twentieth-century Methodist women adopted a Feminine Enclave strategy for circumventing certain institutional barriers to their exercise of leadership and ministry. They had formed the Women's Foreign Missionary Society of the Methodist Episcopal Church.

Ms. Lois Stiles Lee Parker and her husband went to India in 1859 after graduating from Concord Theological Academy. She had founded a school for the Indian girls and helped in many other different ways.

During my walk I passed by several Indian reservations. I always hated that word "reservation" in this context. Some people call the people who lived in this land Native Americans and the Canadians have at least a better word for it, "People of First Nation." Charles C. Mann in his book *1491: New Revelations of the Americas Before Columbus* says that he found most of the people he had interviewed for the book liked to be called "The Indian people." After all Columbus did set out for India.

It always saddens me to think that some people have to live in some restricted areas to maintain their culture. A few years back one summer I decided to swim in every lake between Madison, Wisconsin, and Bayfield, the northernmost point of the state. I passed by many reservations and imagined that there was a time after the Spanish conquest of the Americas that proud groups of people rode horses bareback and galloped through meadows and if they got hurt they possibly chewed a bit of willow bark for aspirin. Charles C. Mann stated that before the invasion of the Americas this land was possibly a stunningly diverse place, with people that spoke different languages and carried out trade in an advanced culture. This was a region where tens of millions of people loved and hated and worshipped as people do everywhere else. He also said that there were people in the Americas before the Clovis hunters arrived through Siberia. The first people might have arrived here by coast-hugging boats 15,000 to 20,000 years back.

We talked about getting a copy of the tape that Channel 2 CBS affiliate had done for SPAVA a couple of days earlier. I almost walked over a three-foot-long rattlesnake. It seemed dead and its head had been bitten off. I didn't think the heat killed it when I first looked at it lying on the grass next to the shoulder.

We were talking about all those prairie dogs that I had seen in Wyoming and wondered if one of those animals could have killed the snake.

Anna and I talked about it and then at rest time Ms. B said that she had read in *Science* 313:227 by A. Thornton and K. McAuliffe about the way some mother animals train their babies. The article had stated that adult meerkats, members of the mongoose family, teach their pups how to eat dangerous animals. When the offspring are quite small, adults bring them dead animals (such as scorpions, lizards and spiders) on which they practice. Then as the pups get older they are given disabled animals. An adult might, for example, bite off the stinger of a scorpion before presenting it to a pup. Eventually the juvenile graduates to handling normal, live prey. In laboratory tests, young meerkats that gained experience wrangling scorpions in this way have been found to be more capable than those that had practiced only on dead scorpions or boiled eggs which were used as a control. I thought there was a Riki Tiki Tavi somewhere close to us hiding who had killed the rattlesnake. It was fresh and I think the victorious animal must have seen me from distance, and now it was waiting impatiently for me to leave to enjoy its conquest.

I eventually voided and felt better that I was not suffering from some organ damage from the heat. I was frowning. Anna wasn't used to seeing me like that. She said that my face was beginning to look like that of Jim Cagney. I asked, "By the way why was Cagney's face like that, almost sardonic and a painful expression?" Anna said that she had heard a long time ago that Bob Hope had given an explanation for that. Jim always liked to light the cigarettes for the ladies whenever they took a cigarette out of a pack. However, women didn't want him to light their cigarettes and so Cagney would hold the match lighted and his fingers would burn till he would put the flame out and that's why his face became like that.

Anna was staying later as we were getting further to the west. We decided to call it a day. By the time I went to bed I realized that on that day I had eaten six pancakes and two eggs and orange juice for breakfast. Then I had numerous bottles of water and different fluids and two cheeseburgers for lunch followed by a chocolate milkshake. I ate twenty ounces of meat and potatoes for dinner and of course I had half a pint of Jim Beam before dinner. I woke up at 5 a.m. next day all refreshed and ready to go. While Ms. B filled the coolers with water and ice and organized my bananas and Red Bull I took care of my feet before going to breakfast. We were on the road at 7 sharp.

My old blisters were healing but for some reason new ones were coming up. I punctured the ones that had fluid in them and wiped them with iodine and then put my socks and shoes on like nothing had happened. By now I had only two good nails in my toes. I had massive hemorrhage underneath the other eight. Most of them were damaged with blisters and blood after Cheyenne. I had removed or drilled most of them by now so that they wouldn't hurt. Today I wanted to get to Twin Falls.

Ms. B called Jay and Tristan to thank them for giving us such great coverage on television. Judge Kline from Virginia had sent us a note. I had met her near Fossil Butte Monument. I knew that the next day I would be walking towards Oregon when NBC would be interviewing us. The wide open spaces in Idaho made me feel like running through the meadows. I imagined all kinds of activities that were going on in the underground nuclear facilities. At times the intrigue created in my mind by my strange imaginations almost needed Superman and Batman together to run up and catch those missiles that I had already fired in my mind.

I was getting ready to tell Anna about Phoebe. She said she knew the name Phoebe from the Bible and also from *The Aeneid*. I changed my mind and talked to her instead about the fact that I was on my fourth pair of shoes. My feet were stronger and I have had a lot of time to think. Walking on the interstate has kept me alert, awake and sensitive to my safety and the safety of the drivers so that they didn't cause an accidents while trying to dodge me because I had been careless. This is no different than performing a fourteen-hour operation. The venue is different and so is the clientele but the effort is the same. I suddenly realized that I was not doing all this for free after all. I had already gathered one hundred and seventy-seven cents from the road, of which several were quarters. I really didn't have to bend as many times since they were not all of the smallest denomination. I am hoping that my fund-raising efforts will be better than this though!

I was finding that Interstate 84 was very noisy. I think I was beginning to get impatient. I passed a sign on the field that said STUD Services. I waited and three appaloosas and a couple of llamas came running towards the fence. I think there should have been a couple of camels for choices. I was surprised that I didn't see any goats or sheep. Goats normally keep the horses calm and the llamas are always great protectors of sheep from the packs of wild dogs that sometimes try to attack them. When I used to raise sheep for a while I remember that the llamas would attack the sheep for a couple of days after I sheared them. They mistook the sheep for dogs.

Today I was talking with Anna about the fact that I have a lot of resentment when someone tells me that I am judgmental. I was hoping that my spouse and I would think alike in this area. I feel responsible to take care of a child if I was the father but I do not like to be responsible about anyone if I do not have any say in the matter except to provide money. I feel taken. I believe from my observation, though I have not read a study exactly relating to it, that children that grow up without a father, are less disciplined, may have a Mohawk, or a tattoo, pierced body parts or experiment with drugs. I have been told that, on occasions, there may be a subconscious guilt of the divorced mother that interferes with understanding the difference between love and co-dependence. Anna said, "Do not be trapped, just be open about it or give money and close that part in your mind and don't bring it up. Just imagine that you have a deformed leg and you can't get rid of it. So the answer is yes. But in life that's the way it is. Take the good with the bad." I was feeling hurt. So I told Anna that at times I felt like hurting back.

I had read a study (*Nature* 441:1103 Patterson N, et al) which stated that new genetic analyses indicated that the final split between the earliest humans and chimpanzees happened almost 6.3 million years ago. To corroborate this result with fossil evidence (which puts the time of divergence a million years earlier), scientists suggest that early hominids and chimps must have interbred for some period of time before a final split occurred. So I told Anna that some men must have maintained some of the atavistic characteristics and not necessarily in the area of body hair alone. This may be the reason that I have resentment watching some other man's child who obviously is not like minded.

A trooper had stopped to say hello. He offered me water. Anna continued, "Oversolicitousness on the part of the family confers legitimacy to one's suffering and shortcomings." Some famous person had said that he who sitteth on a pin shall surely rise. It is important to provide our children with a pin every so often. Billy Crystal the comedian had once said that Kareem Abdul-Jabbar was in his sixth-grade class in New York and one day it seemed he might have sat on a pin or such and shot up. I think the statement has some metaphorical value. I think a professor from Princeton wrote in a clinical psychology book about this including Oedipus complex and hinted that lack of discipline can interfere with the growth process of the male child.

Anna said that it is not my job to try to mold anyone and I should keep quiet in situations that cause friction.

> When the lamp is shatter'd
> The light in the dust lies dead
> When the cloud is scatter'd,
> The rainbow's glory is shed,
> When the lute is broken,
> Sweet tones are remember'd not.
> When the lamp is shattered
> —P. B. Shelley

I tried to sing a Gazal that I had learned as a child. It was a sweet song of sadness. I remembered the mournful sounds of klezmer music that I had heard a long time back at Mr. Abraham's house at Calcutta sometime in 1950 when I visited him. But I recited "All in All" by Tennyson:

> The little rift within the lover's lute,
> Or little pitted speck in garner'd fruit,
> That rotting inward slowly moulders all.

I remembered what Dr. Tim Muldoon had written in the *Partners* about how the direction of our thoughts can be enhanced and what Ignatius had said about it. Ignatius counsels us to be mindful of our inner compass: to practice using it on sunny days, in order that we become adept in its use on foggy ones. Further, he reminds us that even when fog rolls in, it is possible to continue in our journey. For Ignatius the journey is not only about finding our own way to personal wholeness, but about finding our way to those in the greatest need and helping them anyway we can.

Ultimately, we cannot measure the meaning and value of the journey based on whether or not it has met our expectation. God decides where the path of the journey ends.

I was hoping for rain but there was not much cloud to talk about on July 16th. I walked only twenty-six miles and stopped for lunch at a place called Carmela. This was a bit short of Twin Falls. We met Mr. Dennis, an attorney from Twin Falls. We had a wonderful visit with his family. This place is an attempt to build

"Carmel by the Sea" in Idaho. After lunch I got dropped off where I was picked up and then I walked towards Twin Falls. Some people honked their horn at Ms. B because she was being extra cautious in her driving. Here most people drove more than eighty-five miles an hour. I was exhausted by the heat. The air was scalding my eyes. I just had to sit down for a while on the road and take a cold bottle of water from my backpack to place on my eyes.

I looked at those rats that ate potatoes. I wondered about the civilization in Easter Island that might have been destroyed by the rats. I had read in the *American Scientist* volume 94 where Professor Terry Hunt had wondered what happened to the people that built the Moai, the large stone statues at Easter Island. He took a trip and met Sergio Rapu, governor of Rapa Nui, his former student, and then carried out a field study. He determined that most of Rapa Nui was covered with palm trees possibly for 35,000 years. By the time Roggeveen (Dutch explorer) arrived in 1722, a few days after Easter and thus the name, most of the forest was gone. It is believed that the rats ate up most of the palm shells and so the forest could not multiply. In 1860 more than a thousand men were taken as slaves and by 1870 the number of native islanders was only 100 or little more. In 1888 the island was annexed by Chile.

Anna had asked me how I remember all this stuff. I told Anna that I work hard to keep my memory sharp. "Can one do that?" I told her that I was not sure but different types of memory require different operations by the brain. Dr. Penfield of Montreal Neurological Institute and his colleagues at McGill University and Professor Eric Kandel probably have contributed most substantially in this area.

Dr. Larry Squire of UC San Diego in *American Scientist* volume 94 explained how short-term memory involves modifications of pre-existing proteins and transient strengthening of pre-existing synaptic connections. He explained that long-term memory involved altered gene expression, protein synthesis and the growth of new and stronger synaptic connections within existing circuits. Intracellular signaling pathways convert short-lasting stimulus events to persistent changes in synaptic strength. Professor Kandel is a holocaust survivor who experimented with Aplysia (snail) brain neurons and was awarded the Nobel Prize for his work in memory and learning. I told Anna that I truly admire men like Dr. Henry Petroski, professor of engineering at Duke University. I can't imagine anyone having a memory like his. He knows about every kind of bridge and dams in this world. He knows the way they have been made and if there have been mistakes he knows those too. He even knows about tape measures and of course about structures that are movable or deployable. My grandfather always told me that the best way to remember things is to repeat the "big pictures" and the minor associated details will follow them.

He had no way of knowing about the plasticity of the nervous system as we know today but the information had been passed on to him for generations. When I was a child he would not let me write on paper and instead I had to write on a slate with a white chalk. He always said, if you write on paper you won't remember it because you will think that you have it written down but if you write it on the slate and you know that you have to erase it then you are going to make an effort to remember it.

The day ended with plans to walk towards Oregon next day. We spent the night at Twin Falls and next day we were to reach where I had left off west of Boise to reach Ontario and beyond into Oregon. In the night I had wheat toast, barley soup and chickpeas with green pepper and a large steak. I had dried fruits and figs in the van and so I ate those for dessert. Ms. B said that my diet reminded her of what she had read recently. Kieslev, M.E, et al in *Science* 312:1372 reported that near the city of Jericho they had discovered the earliest evidence of human agriculture. The charred remains of nine small figs found in the ruins of a burned building are estimated to be 11,400 years old. This variety of fig probably bore only sweet fruit but no fertile seeds and thus could have only survived by artificial cultivation. Wheat, barley and chickpeas were thought to be the earliest vegetables grown by man, but the figs possibly predate the others by a thousand years.

Oregon Story

It was the 18th of July and I had reached Oregon. I looked at Interstate 84 meander into the Oregon border and I felt intimidated by the mountains ahead of me. The interstate seemed to go straight up for almost as far as I could see. The day was clear and I was fit for the challenge. I discarded the map of Idaho and now I knew that I had about eighteen days or so to finish my trip. I walked and let Anna talk today for a while. Ms. B had left and my brother was the support van driver now. My brother is four years older. He lives in Canada. He is a retired professor of English. He is rather liberal in his views and is a staunch atheist. He is very kind and a gentleman in every way. He had volunteered to drive the last part of the trip and this way he could fly back to Vancouver, British Columbia, when my walk would be over. I was flattered.

I had bought the tickets of all the volunteer drivers and we tried to arrange those the least expensive way, although most of the times it cost more to fly into one city and fly out of another. My brother had never done anything like this and neither had I and so I thought this would be great. In the past we had never spent this much time together. I thought that this would be a great opportunity for me to reconcile with my brother since we had been distant geographically as well as emotionally owing to different choices we both had made that were not conducive to a smooth relation. But now we are both reaching the finish line of our life and I thought, as Anna had suggested, that I could not teach conflict resolution in the schools if I couldn't make peace with my own brother.

It became more apparent as time went on that mild-mannered brother of mine was much irritated by my aggressive approach in life. He disliked the unbelievable zeal that I demonstrated in my daily activities as well. He was puzzled and had a hard time coping with the fact that I was so driven and no matter what I followed a disciplined schedule.

I had expected that he would be ready in the van at 6 a.m. daily and not a minute late. I had expected that the inside of the van would be clean and the

317

cooler would be full and the van's tires and the fuel tank would be checked, and we would smile at each other no matter what because it symbolized transfer of positive energy and that was the essential ingredient of my potential success.

I had made it very clear to all the volunteer drivers that probably the most important aspect of this volunteering was to make sure that I was safe on the road. I wanted my brother and me to finish the trip and become closer than we ever were before. He reminded me that I was one of the most demanding and emotionally violent men that he had ever known. I had no right to demand happiness when he was already volunteering.

I reminded him that we had to be focused and otherwise we would fail. I told him that I loved him but we are politically and emotionally different and no matter what we were connected by blood. Brother felt that the sun was too hot for him to sit in the car and he needed to drive to some shade. I reminded him that such was not available most of the time on the Oregon highway in late July. He reminded me that he felt most uncomfortable sitting on the shoulders of the interstate and at the exits the way I had suggested. I had explained that the car had to be parked in a manner that it would be convenient for me to spot it, particularly since I would be excessively tired and I did not want to walk up a long exit ramp to find him.

It is needless to say that a lot of my energy was being expended and this was in areas not related to walking. So my walk into Oregon was a bit stressful. There were times when he addressed me with expletives, particularly at those times when I provoked him by asking questions like, "What should we do with your body when you die? Should we have a service? Should we just have a party?" I was being mean at times. But the truth of the matter is I really didn't know. I had made a rule when I left Louisville two and a half months back that the driver of the support van would not initiate any conversation with me while I was resting, i.e. taking my fifteen-minute "fluid and feet comfort break." I did not want to spend an iota of extra energy in non-walking activity if I could avoid it. My brother was offended by the rule. So I started taking less breaks.

We had made a decision that while I would be walking the driver would go and find a place to stay for the night and negotiate a rate. My brother indicated that he was uncomfortable bargaining and therefore he would rather wait till I would finish walking in the evening so that I could find the place. This caused me a great deal of anxiety because late in the evening, sometimes at 8 p.m.,

I did not have the energy to drive around town to find a place for the night which might or might not have been available that late.

So late in the evening I had to try to find a place to spend the night and most of the time we found a place to stay but of course we never found a bargain this late in the evening. We had to cross another hurdle. Ever since I started walking we had decided that I would not have to drive except when I took the driver to the airport or picked them up from the airport. Anyway, it became apparent that my brother didn't see in the evening well and often failed to stop at the stop signs.

He did not know how to get to the middle of the road between two yellow lines on the roads in the cities and wait by making a left turn so that in opportune time he could go ahead and assume normal driving. I drove every evening for dinner and then back to the motel. He told me that the rules of driving are different in Canada and he didn't know what to do here.

One evening while I was enjoying my Jim Beam and he was drinking his Scotch I was reminiscing about our childhood. I darned his socks when I was ten years old and I ironed his shirts and sewed buttons on his shirts to get his clothes ready when he went away to school. He went to a boarding school almost a thousand miles away. I told him that Dad always thought that he was much smarter than I was. I reminded him that one time when I was real little he was trying to teach me to swim and had held my head under water for such a long time that I almost passed out. I knew that he had gotten a spanking but I didn't tell on him. I guess everyone had heard me screaming and then on top of that he had to summon Dad or Uncle because I was kind of unconscious and limp. My dad had said that I was not breathing much after screaming. We hugged each other. I drank enough Jim for it to have had time to smoothen our wounds.

I looked out at the clear sky full of stars. I told him that I had seen a cartoon by Nick Downes about twenty years back in the *American Scientist*. It was a picture of a little boy lying in bed with his tank and toys at bedside and the picture suggested that his father was reading some bedtime story when the boy had said that "the little star just looks like it twinkles because of differential refraction in the Earth's atmosphere due to turbulence and thermal gradients. Right, Dad?" He chuckled and said, "I will tell you a story. OK." This little boy went to his mother and asked her to tell him about penguins. "Go and ask your dad. He is not doing anything, just sitting and reading the paper, and I am busy," said Mom. The boy replied, "But I don't want to know so much about penguins, Mom!" I said to him that Dr. Hunt, my professor, had told me that story in the mid-sixties.

Then we went to eat in a place we had spotted on our way to the motel. I ate two large cheeseburgers and fries and a milkshake. When I drove back to the motel I didn't know how my eyes were open. Next day before we left I gave Brother all the instructions and told him that the exits are going to be few and far between from now on. We were about 400 miles from Ft. Vancouver, our destination.

So I told him that if he finds an exit within four to five miles just to take it and stop on top of the ramp on the right side and leave his flashers on and if he couldn't find an exit then just drive about sixteen miles and wait for me on the shoulder. Sometimes the map did not correspond to the exits. I had planned to walk about nineteen miles before lunch and ten or eleven miles afterwards. He had already told me that he did not like to come from behind and would rather go ahead hoping to find a cool spot in mid July on the Oregon interstate!

I had decided to make peace. I also told him to keep his windows open, otherwise he might have a heat stroke. I had walked about three hours or so and I saw the van on top of a ramp. So I walked over there and thought that I was ready to sit down for a while anyway.

One of our rules was that when the driver would see me coming it was his/her responsibility to press the button to open the door so the side door of the van would open and I would rest my pack and grab a bottle of water from the back. Actually I often got annoyed if this didn't happen because I would have to make an extra move to lay down my pack on the ground and pick it up again. I had explained to him that I am used to performing long operations and I don't like to make a single wasted motion. When I arrived to the right of the van not only did he not open the side but I had to knock several times before he responded.

I noticed that he had placed the sun visor on the windshield and the side window to keep the sun away. The windows were locked shut and he was shivering. So I asked him what had happened. He told me that he was afraid of road rage and attack because someone had honked after waiting behind him for a long time hoping that he was going to turn or such but since he remained parked the man then gave him the finger! I explained to him that he shouldn't take it personally. People in America give the finger to everyone, including God's representatives.

The Archbishop Kelly of Louisville had told us a story once that I remembered. Bishop Kelly was driving along Herr Lane which joins up with LaGrange Road and was approaching a railroad track. He was following a car that had a bumper sticker that said "If You Believe in Jesus Then Honk." The gate in front of the roads started coming down with the usual noise of the bell, when a train is about to pass, just as they came near the railroad track. So Bishop Kelly was waiting for the train to come and began to feel a little playful and then he thought why not? So with a little hesitation he honked his horn. The guy in front looked at him in his rearview mirror and placed his "bird" so that the man in the car behind him could see. In a few seconds he recognized the cassock as he looked back and came over and apologized. Bishop Kelly reminded him that his sticker did say for him to honk but the man replied that it was his brother's car and he was just driving it that day.

I took a fifteen-minute break and I was ready to be with Anna. I was telling Anna that one day Ms. B had stopped at one of the exercise facilities called Curves while I was walking. She had told them about the walk and they had sent in a donation to help the scholarship program. I had gotten used to keeping my bananas in a certain place in the van and Ms. B without knowing had placed her purse on top of my banana. I had explained to Ms. B that she should keep her purse in another place. She talked with me about improving my state of mind, particularly when I had told her that she could not be a neurosurgeon because her driving was a little erratic but she could be an orthopedic surgeon because bones don't care if you move too much. "Everyone doesn't have to be a surgeon," she had said. "I am not your resident either." I apologized. The sun was fiercely hot. I placed my left arm inside a couple of socks that I had prepared to use as sleeves. This was one of the ways that I kept my arms from burning.

Anna was eager to tell me a story. "Hey, do you know about Rainbow Rider?"

"No," I said.

"She was a little girl with Sacagawea. You have already passed the country of the Shoshone Indians and Chief Joseph. She was only ten years old when she had met Clark. She still didn't have her front teeth yet. She wore a raccoon hat and a skirt made of fox skin.

"Her skin was dark olive and she smiled all the time while she chewed on a blade of grass. She saved Colonel Lewis once when he almost got bit by a rattlesnake. Very few people know her story and I do not know if this is historically true. Colonel Lewis called her Tiger Lily. She was quick. Her mesmerizing eyes were gentle and her smile resembled limpid petals of a newborn lily. She was a beautiful little girl that hopped most times in her grass shoes. She always carried a rock in her satchel that seemed to act better than a knife when it was time to cut the ropes after tying logs together to make a raft. Her family had lived near the Blue Mountains that you have already passed." Anna continued, "She had walked back there after the Lewis and Clark expedition was over but nobody knows what had happened to her after that."

So I told Anna that I miss my little girl who is all grown up. "Now it is time for you to look for grandchildren," said Anna.

I kept walking further and further every day but I didn't want to stay too late because my driver had told me that he doesn't like to drink his scotch too much later than 8 p.m. I had the whole path mapped out in my mind; Baker City, La Grande, Pendleton, Hermiston, Dalles, Hood River and then Portland. My friend Glen from Washougal had decided to walk the last twenty-five miles with me.

I had driven Ms. B to Hells Canyon and a place called Zero. The Snake River is the source of all the moisture here. I had stood at the 45th parallel one day, I believe just before Exit 285, and celebrated. I didn't exactly know why but possibly because Anna and my God were with me and my energy level was always at its peak. I had been walking more than thirty miles on some days. The #45 sun screen was helping me to not get burnt as much. I had come through a lot of land where I had seen cattle and antelopes playing together. Sometimes the clouds formed a canopy over me and at other times the hot sun looked at me through the lattice made of the thin silk of cloud fibers and on those occasions the heat diminished and then I walked faster while reciting from "Sunday Morning" by Wallace Stevens:

> Is there no change of death in paradise?
> Does ripe fruit never fall? Or do the boughs
> Hang always heavy in that perfect sky,
> Unchanging, yet so like our perishing earth,
> With rivers like our own that seek for seas
> They never find, the same receding shores

That never touch with inarticulate pang?
Why set the pear upon the river banks
Or spice the shores with odors of the plum?
Alas, that they should wear our colors there,
The silken weavings of our afternoons,
And pick the strings of our insipid lutes!
Death is the mother of beauty, mystical,
Within whose burning bosom we devise
Our earthly mothers waiting, sleeplessly.

I was reaching higher and higher daily in my mind to a place where I had found my God. Anna said to me, "Some might think this poem is morbid."

"On the contrary, my sweet! Living is so much fun and that the next stage is like graduation with a perfect score! Life for me is like a residency program and I do the best I can with a motto to be helpful to someone else. The only difference is I do not know the graduation date and so I wait for my professor, my God, to decide that."

I often sat down to reflect and to rest a bit just beyond the shoulder of the highway. There have been many occasions when I wept while I was working in some other countries where suffering was much. My tears probably didn't do anything for the young mother who directed the hungry child's face to her nipples but alas she didn't know that her breasts were dry and the child's lips were parched. My tears didn't do anything for the child that I couldn't operate on because death was imminent. I remember sitting next to the Grand Canyon and weeping in joy. How many centuries it must have taken for the Colorado River to cut through the mountains to produce the rough "upside-down mountain" and yet the sparkling and gurgling water ran with the rhythm of alliteration in the bottom? The river as though in the glory of its accomplishment danced the fastest samba hugging every curve of the mountain. Then I also had wept when I sat among the windblown flowers of Nandankanan, Valley of Flowers at the base of the Himalayas on the way to Kedarnath. I thought that somebody's tears must have watered that garden! I cannot do much for all the suffering but I wondered if I could see the beauty of the human being underneath all the morass of sorrow and agony. I could be a Good Samaritan wherever I was.

Tears, idle tears, I know not what they mean,
Tears from the depth of some divine despair
Rise to the heart, and gather to the eyes,
In looking on the happy autumn-fields,
And thinking of the days that are no more.
        —Tennyson, "Tears, Idle Tears"

My feet were burning often these days in the afternoons because the road was hot. It was at Exit 335 where I sat for a long time at the rest area. My brother sat next to me and we made peace as the Good Book says that we are supposed to do. We met a kindly lady, Ms. Lisa. She and her family were traveling through Oregon and wanted to know all about SPAVA program. She wanted to make a cash donation and I gave her a brochure with the address where she could mail a check. I told her that this way I would not have to remember to thank her because the check would remind me with her address written on it. The walk through Exit 243 to Exit 238 was at high altitude of the Blue Mountains almost 4,200 feet.

There was one particular spot during the walk through Oregon when I had wished my driver would have been more perceptive. I saw him go past me obviously to find a shady spot ahead. I had no way of knowing what the road looked like in front. But when I reached Exit 252 and continued walking I was truly scared. The map didn't tell me where the next exit was located. It was only later on that I realized that it was possibly Exit 248 where my support van could be waiting.

However, for one mile, i.e. twelve minutes, I was exposed on the interstate of a construction area where the expressway was a two-lane highway with no shoulders and there was no one in sight because it happened to be a Sunday. There was barely enough room on the side for me to walk and there was a big divide between the two directions of the road and the vertical mountain was next to it. I hoped and prayed that no semis would come through because I would have surely been crushed if they by chance did not see me during a turn. This was one time I wanted to be like Jackie Chan and squeeze myself through the smallest possible areas as I have seen him do in some movies. I had forgotten about plantar fasciitis, patellar tendonitis, blisters and hip pain; I just prayed and moved fast till I could find the end of construction. After I reached Exit 248 I found my support van. I was less than pleasant in my exchanges when I saw the driver. Anna chided me for my behavior.

The truckers must have made a pact to honk their horn when they saw me on the road just to greet me. This sometimes brought tears in my eyes because I felt so loved. I waved and smiled back.

Sagebrush and Saxifrage danced as the wind swayed them. This was no fox trot; it was more like a fast samba. I sometimes tried to emulate Al Pacino as I saw him in the movie *Scent of a Woman*. It was easier to imagine what the pioneers felt like walking through these brushes hitting against their shin and the cuts they must have had to deal with. I saw a few jackrabbits scurry through the bushes. I am sure they knew where the rattlesnakes were sleeping. The wind blew through the brushes and made a sound much like the sound we hear when the wind passes through a crack in a wooden door. The wind made steam on the surface of the water at times and at other times it seemed as though the wind made the river flow faster. I watched bubbles and sprays of water that gurgled several feet towards the sky with every gust of wind as though the river had to release its pressure valve to remain contained in its borders. The reflections of the sun made little rainbows through the sprays for me to enjoy as I marched merrily through the dust and the wind that enveloped me almost all day. My lips were parched and eyes were dry despite all the protection that lip balm and sunglasses could provide. I was the commander of my ship and my feet were the rudders and my pack was my sail and I moved fast into the wind.

I had stepped on a nail that was lying on the side of the road about four days back; it went through my socks and made my foot bleed. I had applied some iodine and bathed it in Epsom salt that evening. It was better but still a little sore. I had fifty-two pairs of socks with me when I started my walk so throwing away this one pair didn't upset me too much. I had decided to change my socks at least four times daily to avoid wet feet and fungal and bacterial infections, particularly since I had so many open wounds in my feet.

I knew now why the pioneers named this one city La Grande. It is a spectacular valley that one sees after heavy climbs and descents and I entered it after walking a circular path that had been cut through the mountains to build the interstate. I spoke with the newspaper department and the gentleman was most gracious and kind. He told me that the folks from *Hermiston Herald* would be calling me to do a story about SPAVA.

The battery in my phone had died and so I could not communicate further and my driver did not rent a phone from Canada because he was afraid that the phone may not work in the States! I of course was never able to communicate with my present driver except when I saw him. Well, we almost communicated. He said to me that every time he talks to me he has to "suffer in silence" later. I did not respond. My spirituality was being tested and I wanted to be the best pilgrim possible in my journey to peacedom!

Anna and I talked about the scientists who claim to know how man was made. One scientist had allegedly said that one day they could make man from dirt. So God told him to go ahead and make what he could but he was not allowed to use God's dirt. Professor James Cline of McGill University has written on the subject as to the origin of matter and why we are surrounded by "something" rather than "nothing." The Big Bang theory explains the origin of the universe well but it is believed that in the earliest moments of the big bang, matter and antimatter balanced each other perfectly but since then matter has taken over and thus we exist.

Russian scientist Andrei Sakharov in 1967 stated that matter is made up of protons and neutrons which make the atomic nucleus. Particle physicists call them baryons or heavy particles and as a matter of fact (no pun intended) they are 2,000 times heavier than electrons. Experiments have shown that these are formed by the combination of smaller particles called quarks. There can be ten billion microwave photons in the same space as a Baryon and the average density of a baryon is about 0.2 per cubic meter. Professor Cline explains in the *American Scientist* volume 92 that Baryonic universe requires an asymmetry (6 X 10 to the power minus 10) to exist. Light elements such as helium and lithium as well as the hydrogen isotope deuterium were formed within a few minutes after the big bang. Subsequent cooling allowed the protons and neutrons to stick and form the atomic nuclei. Collision with high-energy photons blasted these nuclei till they lost energy through the cooling when the universe expanded. To find an explanation for Baryogenesis another theory called Inflation has been suggested; more particles such as leptons, neutrinos and tau particles and a process called Sphaleron has also been described to find explanation for the creation of life. Now it is believed that we are not particles anymore but strings of energy as has been postulated by the string theory. So Anna asked, "Can we make a man without using God's dust?"

I said, "No, not yet. However, there is enough proof to not dispute evolution."

Anna said, "Don't forget that twenty percent of your genetic makeup is from the insects and that tells us that we have evolved."

By the time I reached Hermiston I had to go through significant heat and exhaustion. On average days I drank more that six liters of fluid. Between Exit 216 and Exit 210 I had to go over Deadmans Pass and then six miles downhill at a six percent grade. This was grueling in the heat. She was behind me and so she couldn't fall and I supported her so her knees didn't hurt. This was hard but possibly not as difficult as the walk from Thorang La Pass to Muktinath on gravel. My feet hurt really badly so I had to slow down but I walked till later in the evening to make up for the lost time. I thought even if my support van driver quits because I caused delay in his drinking scotch I could still make it on my own from here.

I met Chief Roberts at Pendleton and told him about the program and that we could start it for free if he wanted. I met Ms. Sarah at Hermiston. I went to her office. She told me that she was going to Louisville soon for a 4H project at the state fair in August. I told Anna that I was an older man and every dad should have an opportunity to have a daughter like her. She was polite, confident, and eloquent and she was barely a high school graduate. She published a wonderful story about SPAVA in the *Hermiston Herald*.

I passed a sign on the road that said "Dust Storms for next forty miles." I knew what to expect for the next two days and after that of course it would be walking along the Columbia Gorge, the windiest part of the entire interstate. I received a phone call from Dean Baker from the *Columbian* a bit before I reached The Dalles. He wanted to do an interview when I came a bit closer to Portland and so I told him that I was flattered and I would meet him about twenty miles outside Portland. I could let him know a day before my projected arrival date. I recall making a longer than usual stop at Exit 155 because the heat and the wind made it very exhausting for me. I was telling Anna that walking straight through is a lot more difficult than taking it easy and walking the distance in six months or a year. This is a little more distance than the Appalachian Trail or the Pacific Ocean Crest trail. I might take on one of those challenges after a year or two. I had been to Harper's Ferry, the midpoint of the Appalachian Trail, and I thought that I could do that straight through by starting in April in Maine and finish up by Thanksgiving.

The temperature in the shade was ninety-seven degrees Fahrenheit today. People exhibited kindness to me continuously. The owner of the Oregon Trail Restaurant had bought my lunch and Pam took our pictures. Today when I took Exit 137 for lunch it was John Day Park on the Columbia River. A wonderful couple from Baker City bought our lunch. I did not even get to know their names. I drank two milkshakes and four lemonades for lunch. When I got on the road the radio said the heat index was 108 degrees. After a bit of a walk I had to water the mountain and as I did I noticed fumes rose from the rock. I received a phone call from Ms. Shefali, a reporter from the Hood River newspaper. She did a detailed story about our organization.

I told Anna that I was destined to be a walker. "How so?"

"Once when I was ten years old I had a tiff with my dad and I walked fifteen miles on the main road carrying my little suitcase to my grandpa's house to get away from my dad. Grandpa was never surprised at my accomplishments. He never said to me 'I am surprised that you did so well,' whenever I did anything. I asked him about the way he complimented me. I could ask Grandpa anything. He said that to say it that way implies that I was not expected to achieve whatever I did. He always said that whatever I did was what I was expected to do! His statements always made me feel great. The value of positive emotions has been known for centuries but the fact that it is more than the tautology that 'it makes us feel good' is being studied carefully.

"The negative emotions produce autonomic changes, e.g. anger, fear, hatred cause changes in heart rate, increased sweating etc. whereas positive emotions do not produce any such changes.

"Professor B.L. Fredrickson ('The role of positive emotions in positive psychology: The broaden-and-build theory of positive emotions,' *American Psychologist* 56:218-226) postulated that positive emotions were needed for living in society and for building cohesion and well being of self and others. Moreover, positive emotions undid the cardiovascular ill-effects of negative emotion. He continued, people who give help for instance, can feel proud of their good deeds, and so experience continued good feelings. Plus people who receive help feel grateful and those who even merely witness good deeds can feel elevated. Each of these positive emotions—pride, gratitude and elevation—can in turn broaden people's mindsets and inspire further compassionate acts. He said that we can infuse ordinary events with meaning by expressing appreciation, love and gratitude, even for simple things."

The day was bright and I was walking fast. I received a phone call from M, our daughter, in the morning as had been usual every day since I started walking. But this phone call was most interesting because she wanted to know every detail of my walking including where I thought I would be in the next three hours etc. I told her that by 11:30 in the morning I would be at the 120 mile marker. We said goodbye after a bit of small talk. It was later on that I found that I knew the two persons who were sitting on the shoulder of Interstate 80. I could see the backs of their heads as I approached them. It was most joyful for me to see our son and his friend Ms. J to be the persons that came to give me a surprise visit. I couldn't have been more surprised than to see two persons wearing SPAVA shirts sitting on the shoulder of the expressway with their backs towards the oncoming traffic. They had flown from Dayton and New York respectively to Portland, Oregon, and our daughter helped to coordinate their connection with me while I was on the road. They were ready in their walking shoes and so after some hugging and greeting we walked together for a while. We walked towards Hood River and stopped for lunch. They went wind surfing after that and I on the other hand hit the interstate to finish my journey.

I was always sleeping well throughout my trip. I know the value of sleep and its ability to rejuvenate body function to be able to perform at full capacity. I have stayed up many nights during medical school and also during my practice days either for studying or because of sick patients in ICU or in the operating room. Mr. David McArthur, anchor for Channel 3 TV from Louisville, wanted me to call him at 2 a.m. so that he could do a live interview at 5 a.m. (East Coast). At first it sounded like an imposition but then I realized what a favor he was doing to our organization. So I was willing to give up twenty minutes of sleep knowing well that I might feel a bit tired the next day. When I was a little boy Grandmother always told me to go to bed early, particularly if there was a test scheduled the next day. Later on I did not follow her rules. New research suggests that sleep is critical to cognitive functions, particularly memory. These days surgical residents work only forty to eighty hours per week, I think, whereas during my training days it was not unusual for us to work 120 hours per week. I was always tired and walked about with a short fuse, i.e. the slightest provocation led to an aggressive reply. I know that I could operate well but did I reason correctly or at my best?

Well, Dr. Matthew Walker of Sleep Laboratory of Beth Israel Deaconess Medical Center shed some light on this subject.

REM sleep alternates with non-REM (slow wave) sleep every ninety minutes in humans and we dream most vividly during REM sleep. The hippocampus is the area for "declarative" memory in the medial part of the temporal lobe just behind our eyes whereas "non-declarative" memory is manifest as an action or behavior. It is divided into procedural and implicit memory and is controlled by the striatum (ability to hold and release a knife with agility), motor cortex (ability to remove a brain abscess or walk for that matter), and cerebellum (not to be shaky). For emotional learning the amygdala and for priming it is the neocortex and reflex pathways require the spinal cord to complete the connection. After we meet someone the brain stores the name and the face by the process of encoding and consolidation. Sleep is important for stabilization and enhancement of memory. Memories can be reorganized and moved to new sites by translocation and the brain keeps on learning even when we are not using that memory. Dr. Walker found that short daytime naps helped with memory enhancement and a nap helps also with a bit of improvement in learning visual skill.

Munna had told me that Ashoke had died while working at Nepal. He was a victim of violence. Phoebe came in my life and Munna did not know that. I knew Ashoke and I thought he might have had written a bit about me in his story as I could relate to some of it. But I didn't know how he knew so much about my grandfather and the rest of the story was his because I knew that he was writing a book.

I crossed the bridge at Hood River at Highway 14 and walked towards Washougal and Camas and translated the distance next day on my log to Interstate 84 as I walked towards Portland. This was easier for my driver and both roads ran parallel one across from the other divided by the Columbia River.

I had taken my brother to see Herman, the great sturgeon at Hood River, and we took a walk in the park and enjoyed the flowers. I lay down to rest on the grass and fell asleep while Brother viewed how the salmon grows in the hatchery. I think my memory was perhaps enhanced with the nap but my body was truly stronger after the rest. Since I have fished near Astoria and Long Beach I informed him of the rules about fishing salmon in the Pacific Northwest and the fact that we can only keep the hatchery fish, known by a cut dorsal fin, and the Fish and Wildlife checks for the BB that is planted near the head and so he cuts the head and takes it for keeping a proper count. Salmon population has declined significantly possibly because of acid rain and other environmental factors.

So next day I started from the 27 mile marker and Glen met me at the 20th mile marker with Dean, who interviewed me and wrote a story in the

Columbian on August 5. I attended the Rotary Clubs at Camas for breakfast as well as the Portland club during lunchtime. This allowed me two makeups for my club and I was able to bring awareness for our program. This was one of the days that I rested a full day and visited friends and planned for the end of the walk on August 5 at noon. It was less than ten miles from where we had left off and we walked across the Interstate 5 bridge to end the walk ceremonially at Ft. Vancouver where friends, well-wishers and Mr. Garcia, a blind gentleman who had heard about the walk, had come to congratulate me.

I put my backpack down and Glen and I hugged each other as we finished our walk together just like we had promised to do a year ago. Phoebe joined us as she was driving the support van after having taken my brother to the airport on the previous day when I rested. She told me that I should walk to Philadelphia from Louisville and then I would be able to say that I have walked from one side to the other. I said that before I walk anywhere again while I was on the West Coast my intention was to attend one of the classes of Father Rick Ganz at Gonzaga University at Spokane, Washington; the classes that are held in the campus bar called Theology on Tap. Here he gets the students involved in discussing spirituality and theology while enjoying a bit of beer. This is my kind of priest. If God could share wine with his friends and bless them, why not the priest?

I had reached my destination. I was exhilarated beyond comprehension. I sat in a quiet spot and tried to digest in my mind the fact that I actually finished the job I had undertaken. It was like another residency in neurosurgery but all compressed like in the handle of a broom representing the brainstem through which passed all the emotions and impulses from the wide part of the broom, the cortex. Anna sat by my side and said, "Good-bye. I have a new assignment. You can rest but I can't." I smiled. There was a cloud of joy above that protected me from the heat of the midday and Anna could not be seen anymore.

Final Chapter

I am an older man now than when I started my journey. But not a day went by that I didn't think about my grandfather. The lessons he gave me and the example that he set before me have been written in my brain with indelible ink. He practiced medicine with rather minimal tools and with not too much help from the pharmacist. However, he did remarkably well under those trying circumstances. I believe he had the faith and courage of Daniel and the smile and sincere resolve of Lord Krishna. At a time in his life when he couldn't explain as to why he should be doused with sorrow of a loss of a child he picked what he could from that morass of the overwhelming sadness. Lily, his daughter and my mother, had withered but he was given a tear of hope to hold. He whimpered and took the challenge. He bathed this little hope with love and joy and never let his tear of sadness touch this child of hope as long as he lived. I still believe that one of the reasons that he died without any suffering is that he had Ananda (supreme joy) in his heart. Although I could not be like him but I still remember his manners and his respect for fellow men. His sense of responsibility, caring and civic mindedness were of the highest order. He was a man of a different time when Caritas was important and wealth didn't matter much. His patients loved him. Everyone in the family adored him. Secretly, I knew he loved me the most.

I finished my journey across the country after I reached Ft. Vancouver, Washington. I sat in a quiet corner to contain myself. My friends had supported me; my well-wishers went with me in their thoughts and prayers and my God had walked with me. I was not as excited about my accomplishment as I was of being able to finish the journey which is no different possibly than the journey of my life.

Here I was able to see the laughter and the giggle of children in the sparkling waters of the rivers I had crossed and I was also able to imagine the resolve of the people who had walked before me across the big mountains of Idaho and Oregon.

Lord, I am grateful for the good fortune to be able to see and hear your touch in all my life. As I walked across the country I was neither alone nor lonely. In the past I had not understood my role in life. I had wept in the past when I couldn't buy all the chewing gum the little eight-year-old girl was selling at the roadside in Addis Ababa. I had agonized over not buying all the elephant and giraffe figurines from the vendor in Harare and I felt guilty for not having my shoes shined by the child outside the Katmandu Guest House, but Lord, I am content. The peace and ecstasy you have given me in my heart is the true state of Mahamudra because I have neither any needs nor any wants and I am fulfilled!

I am like Arjuna sitting in the chariot with my arrow drawn on a stretched bow but I know that you alone know the direction and force of the arrow when it needs to travel to its predestined spot. I end my journey with gratitude and I pray that I could be the donkey that took my Lord on its back and it never boasted because it didn't know its load! I want to live in the joy of innocence that envelops me and a balm of ecstasy that rejuvenates me. This is my prayer. I closed my eyes to see the Maya and to meld in the eternal dance of Nataraja.

> The Grizzly bear is huge and wild;
> He has devoured the infant child.
> The infant child is not aware
> It has been eaten by the bear.
> —A. E. Housman, "Infant Innocence"

I like to read Ezra Pound when I am happy and today I end my journey with Ananda.

> A son of God was the Goodly Fere *companion (Jesus)*
> That bade us his brothers be.
> I ha' seen him cow a thousand men,
> I have seen him upon the tree. *cross*
> He cried no cry when they drave the nails,
> And the blood gushed hot and free,
> The hounds of the crimson sky gave tongue
> But never a cry cried he.
> A master of men was the Goodly Fere,
> A mate of the wind and sea,
> If they think they ha' slain our Goodly Fere *Jesus*
> They are fools eternally.
> —"Ballad of the Godly Fere"

The End